GitLab Guidebook

From Basics to Expert Proficiency

Contents

Introduction

In the continuously evolving landscape of software development, GitLab has emerged as a cornerstone for managing code repositories, continuous integration and delivery (CI/CD), and DevOps practices. GitLab provides a comprehensive platform that integrates various facets of software development into a single interface, facilitating enhanced collaboration and efficiency for development teams of all sizes. This guidebook, "GitLab Guidebook: From Basics to Expert Proficiency," has been meticulously crafted to serve as a detailed resource for both novice and experienced users of GitLab.

Understanding the intricacies of GitLab begins with a solid foundation in its core concepts. This guidebook introduces you to the fundamental principles and progresses to advanced features, ensuring a well-rounded mastery of the platform. The initial chapters provide an introduction to GitLab's interface, helping you to understand its structure and essential terminology. These basics are crucial as they form the groundwork upon which advanced knowledge will be built.

Following the introduction, the book delves into the essentials of Git, the distributed version control system underlying GitLab's functionality. Mastery of Git is essential for effectively utilizing GitLab, as it enables efficient tracking and merging of changes in code repositories. This section covers the installation, configuration, and basic commands of Git, all of which are pivotal for a seamless GitLab experience.

Repository management is an integral aspect of GitLab, and this guidebook provides an exhaustive exploration of creating, managing, and customizing repositories. Issues and project management capabilities of GitLab allow for efficient task tracking and collaboration, elements crucial for any successful software project. By thoroughly understanding these features, users can leverage GitLab to streamline workflows and enhance productivity.

One of the most compelling facets of GitLab is its CI/CD capabilities. This guidebook offers a robust introduction to CI/CD within GitLab, detailing the setup, configuration, and optimization of pipelines. Advanced CI/CD techniques are also explored, providing insights into sophisticated configurations and best practices for achieving efficient and secure deployment processes.

In the context of DevOps, GitLab's comprehensive suite of tools and integrations makes it a powerful ally. This guidebook covers essential DevOps practices, illuminating how GitLab can be utilized to foster a culture of continuous improvement and automation. Detailed sections on GitLab Runner and custom executors provide practical guidance on optimizing build and deployment environments.
Security and compliance are paramount in software development, and GitLab offers features that support these critical requirements. This book includes a focused examination of GitLab's security capabilities, covering topics such as vulnerability management, code scanning, and audit logs. Ensuring compliance with industry standards and organizational policies is made manageable through GitLab's integrated tools.

Finally, the scalability of GitLab in cloud environments is discussed comprehensively. This includes setting up GitLab on various cloud platforms, leveraging Kubernetes for container orchestration, and implementing high availability and disaster recovery strategies. Performance tuning and cost management strategies are also examined to enable efficient and effective scaling of GitLab deployments.

The structure of this guidebook is deliberate and methodical, ensuring a logical progression of knowledge. Readers will find each chapter building upon previous ones, facilitating a cohesive and comprehensive understanding of GitLab. Whether you are new to GitLab or seeking to deepen your expertise, this guidebook is designed to be an authoritative resource, equipping you with the knowledge and skills to excel.

In conclusion, "GitLab Guidebook: From Basics to Expert Proficiency" is an essential companion for anyone looking to master GitLab. With a focus on detailed explanations, practical examples, and best practices, this guidebook provides a thorough exploration of GitLab's capabilities, ensuring users can harness its full potential to achieve their software development and DevOps goals.

Chapter 1

Introduction to GitLab

GitLab is a comprehensive DevOps platform that provides tools for source code management, continuous integration and delivery (CI/CD), and project management. This chapter lays the foundation for understanding GitLab by exploring its history, key features, editions, and pricing models. It also covers the initial steps for installing GitLab, navigating its interface, and creating your first project. You will become familiar with essential GitLab terminology and gain insights into migration strategies and best practices for new users.

1.1 What is GitLab?

GitLab is an end-to-end software development and DevOps lifecycle tool. It integrates various stages of the DevOps lifecycle, including source code management, continuous integration and continuous delivery (CI/CD), project planning, and more, into a single application. This unified approach facilitates seamless collaboration among developers, operations teams, product managers, and other stakeholders.

At its core, GitLab serves as a version control system based on Git. Git is a widely-used distributed version control system that allows multiple developers to work on the same codebase concurrently, branching and merging changes efficiently. GitLab enhances Git's capabilities by providing a web-based interface, project management tools, and powerful CI/CD pipelines.

One of GitLab's key distinguishing features is its comprehensive DevOps platform, which is divided into multiple stages and categories:

- **Source Code Management (SCM)**: GitLab provides repositories for storing and managing code, with features such as branching, merging, conflict resolution, and history tracking. It supports Git protocols like HTTP(S), SSH, and more, enabling flexible and secure access to repositories.
- **Continuous Integration (CI)**: GitLab CI allows automated testing of code on various environments. Using the .gitlab-ci.yml file, developers can define pipelines that automatically run tests and other scripts upon every code commit, ensuring code quality and consistency.
- **Continuous Deployment (CD)**: Building upon CI, GitLab CD automates the deployment of applications to different environments, including staging, production, and more. This reduces the risk of manual errors and accelerates the release process.
- **Project Management**: GitLab offers a suite of tools to manage projects efficiently. Features include issue tracking, task boards, milestones, and roadmaps, which help teams plan, track, and execute project activities.
- **Security and Compliance**: GitLab incorporates security scanning and monitoring tools, such as Static Application Security Testing (SAST), Dependency Scanning, and Container Scanning, thereby embedding security into the development process. It also provides audit logs and compliance-related features to meet regulatory requirements.
- **Collaboration and Code Review**: GitLab facilitates code review and collaboration through merge requests (MRs), where team members can discuss, review, and suggest changes to the code. This process enhances code quality and fosters collective code ownership.
- **Monitoring and Optimization**: GitLab includes monitoring tools that integrate with applications to track performance, identify bottlenecks, and optimize resource usage. It supports integration with Prometheus, Grafana, and other monitoring solutions.

In terms of deployment, GitLab offers flexibility through various deployment options:

- **GitLab.com (SaaS)**: A hosted service where GitLab manages the infrastructure, offering convenience and eliminating the need for self-managed hardware and maintenance.
- **Self-Managed (On-premises)**: Users can install GitLab on their own servers, providing more control over data, customization, and integration with other on-premises tools and services. Installation can be done using packages for different Linux distributions, Docker containers, and Kubernetes.
- **Hybrid Cloud Deployment**: GitLab supports deployment in hybrid environments, allowing organizations to leverage both on-premises and cloud infrastructure. This can aid in balancing workload distribution and enhancing resilience.

GitLab's architecture is modular, comprising several components that work together to deliver its wide array of functionalities. Key components include:

- **GitLab Rails Application**: The main web application, responsible for handling HTTP requests, rendering web pages, and serving the user interface.
- **GitLab Shell**: Extends Git functionality by providing SSH access to repositories, managing Git hooks and integrating with the GitLab Rails application.
- **Gitaly**: A service that provides high-performance, Git-specific RPC (Remote Procedure Call) endpoints, optimizing Git operations and scaling GitLab deployments.
- **GitLab Workhorse**: A daemon that handles Git HTTP(S) transport requests, file uploads, and other long-running processes, balancing load and enhancing system performance.
- **GitLab Runner**: A build agent that executes the tasks defined in .gitlab-ci.yml files. Runners can be installed on various platforms, including Docker, Kubernetes, and virtual machines.
- **PostgreSQL**: The primary database used by GitLab for storing metadata and other structured information.
- **Redis**: An in-memory data structure store used by GitLab for caching, session storage, and job queuing.

- **Sidekiq**: A background job processor for asynchronous tasks, such as sending emails, processing webhooks, and other background operations.

To enhance its extensibility and integration capabilities, GitLab supports a wide range of APIs and webhooks. These allow external applications and services to interact with GitLab, automate processes, and extend functionalities. GitLab APIs cover most aspects of the platform, including repository management, user administration, and CI/CD pipeline manipulation.

GitLab's commitment to open source fosters a vibrant community of contributors and users. The core GitLab application is released under the MIT license, enabling users to access, modify, and distribute the source code. This open-source foundation promotes innovation, transparency, and collective problem-solving.

Several editions of GitLab are available to cater to different organizational needs:

- **GitLab Community Edition (CE)**: The free and open-source version, which includes most core functionalities essential for managing and deploying code.

- **GitLab Enterprise Edition (EE)**: A subscription-based offering that provides additional features for large enterprises, such as advanced security, scalability, and support options.

By providing an all-in-one DevOps platform, GitLab streamlines the software development lifecycle, fosters collaborative workflows, and accelerates the delivery of high-quality software. Through continuous improvements and a commitment to user feedback, GitLab remains a critical tool for modern software development practices.

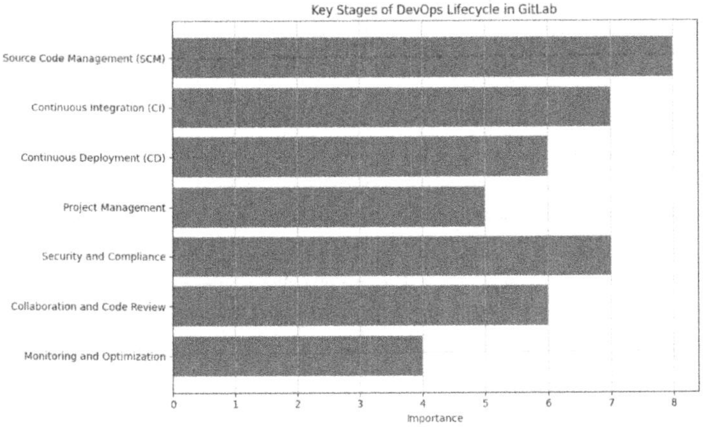

1.2 History and Evolution of GitLab

GitLab began as an open-source project in 2011, created by Dmitriy Zaporozhets and Valery Sizov. The primary goal was to provide a single application for the entire DevOps lifecycle, enabling developers and teams to collaborate more effectively. Initially, GitLab was designed as a source code management (SCM) tool, leveraging the Git version control system. However, it soon expanded its scope to include a wide range of functionalities that facilitate continuous integration, delivery, and deployment (CI/CD).

The first release of GitLab, version 1.0, was made available in October 2011 under an open-source license, allowing users to install and use it freely. Zaporozhets and Sizov continued to develop the product, adding features and resolving issues reported by the growing user community. The project's popularity surged, driven by its accessibility and the strong engagement of a dedicated open-source community.

2013 marked a significant milestone with the incorporation of GitLab Inc., co-founded by Zaporozhets and Sytse Sijbrandij. This transition enabled formal business operations and paved the way for structured development and support services. GitLab Inc. also introduced GitLab EE (Enterprise Edition), a paid version offering additional features tailored for enterprise environments. The open-source variant was rebranded as GitLab CE (Community Edition).

For a more efficient development process, GitLab implemented a monthly release cycle, ensuring consistent updates and feature improvements. The versioning followed a straightforward pattern, with major, minor, and patch updates systematically introduced.

```
# Example of GitLab's versioning
$ gitlab --version
GitLab Community Edition 11.4.0
```

As the platform matured, key integrations and services were added to enhance its functionality. Notably, GitLab CI, initially offered as a standalone project in 2012, was fully integrated into GitLab by 2015. This integration allowed users to configure and automate their build, test, and deploy processes directly within the GitLab interface, promoting more seamless CI/CD workflows.

```
stages:
  - build
  - test
  - deploy

build-job:
  stage: build
  script:
    - echo "Building the project..."
    - make build

test-job:
  stage: test
  script:
    - echo "Running tests..."
    - make test

deploy-job:
  stage: deploy
  script:
    - echo "Deploying the project..."
    - make deploy
```

Between 2016 and 2018, GitLab accelerated its feature set with the introduction of several seismic capabilities including GitLab Pages for static site hosting, Kubernetes integration for managing containerized workloads, and Auto DevOps for automated delivery workflows. These additions firmly established GitLab as a robust, end-to-end DevOps platform.

```
Output of a successful CI/CD pipeline:
$ echo "Building the project..."
Building the project...
$ make build
Build successful
$ echo "Running tests..."
Running tests...
$ make test
All tests passed!
$ echo "Deploying the project..."
Deploying the project...
$ make deploy
Deployment successful!
```

GitLab's commitment to fostering an inclusive community was underscored in 2018 when they transitioned to a dual license (MIT and GitLab EE License) model, clarifying the distinction between community contributions and proprietary code. This shift also facilitated better management of intellectual property and development resources.

The evolution of GitLab continued with the introduction of GitLab Ultimate in 2018, offering an extensive suite of features aimed at streamlining and securing the DevOps lifecycle for large-scale enterprises. GitLab's dedication to innovation was evident with the launch of features like the Web IDE, SAST (Static Application Security Testing), DAST (Dynamic Application Security Testing), and dependency scanning. These tools provided developers with the means to ensure code quality and security early in the development process.

By 2021, GitLab had grown exponentially, both in terms of its user base and its feature set. It stood as a leading example of a comprehensive DevOps platform, capable of supporting diverse development workflows and integrating seamlessly with various tools in the software development ecosystem. The year also marked GitLab's Initial Public Offering (IPO), signifying its maturity and stability as a key player in the DevOps space.

GitLab's history is marked by a vision of integrating all stages of the DevOps lifecycle into a single, cohesive application. This vision drove numerous innovative features and strategic decisions, enabling it to adapt to the evolving demands of software development. As the platform continues to evolve, GitLab remains committed to its roots in the open-source community while expanding its capabilities to serve the needs of enterprises around the globe.

1.3 Installing GitLab

Installing GitLab involves a series of steps to ensure that the platform is set up correctly and functions optimally. This section covers the prerequisites, installation methods, and post-installation configuration to help you get started with GitLab.

Prerequisites

Before installing GitLab, ensure that your system meets the following prerequisites:

- **Operating System:** GitLab supports various Linux distributions, including Ubuntu, Debian, CentOS, and RHEL. Ensure you are using a compatible version.
- **Hardware Requirements:** For optimal performance, a minimum of 4GB of RAM is recommended. Larger GitLab instances or instances running continuous integration jobs may require more resources.
- **Dependencies:** Certain packages and software dependencies are required. These include curl, openssh-server, ca-certificates, and Postfix (for sending email notifications).

Installation Methods

GitLab provides multiple installation methods, including using an Omnibus package, Docker, or from source. This guide focuses on the Omnibus package method, which offers an easy and quick installation process.

Step 1: Add the GitLab Repository

First, you need to add the GitLab repository to your system. Use the following command:

```
curl https://packages.gitlab.com/install/repositories/gitlab/gitlab-ee/script.deb.sh |
    sudo bash
```

Step 2: Install GitLab

After adding the repository, install GitLab using the package manager. The example below demonstrates installation on an Ubuntu system:

```
sudo apt-get update
sudo apt-get install gitlab-ee
```

Replace ‘gitlab-ee‘ with ‘gitlab-ce‘ if you are installing the Community Edition.

Step 3: Configure and Start GitLab

The Omnibus package simplifies the configuration process. You need to specify the external URL, which will be used to access GitLab:

```
sudo EXTERNAL_URL="http://yourdomain.com" gitlab-ctl reconfigure
```

This command automates the configuration and setup based on the external URL provided.

Step 4: Access GitLab

After the configuration process completes, GitLab will be running and accessible via the URL you specified. Open a web browser and navigate to ‘http://yourdomain.com‘ to access the GitLab login page.

Post-Installation Configuration

Once GitLab is installed, some configurations are recommended to enhance security and usability.

- **Set Up DNS Records:** Ensure that your domain's DNS records point to the server where GitLab is installed.
- **Configure Email Settings:** GitLab uses email to send notifications. Edit the configuration file located at ‘/etc/gitlab/gitlab.rb‘ to set up SMTP settings for email notifications:

```
gitlab_rails['smtp_enable'] = true
gitlab_rails['smtp_address'] = "smtp.server.com"
gitlab_rails['smtp_port'] = 587
gitlab_rails['smtp_user_name'] = "your_email@domain.com"
gitlab_rails['smtp_password'] = "your_password"
gitlab_rails['smtp_domain'] = "smtp.server.com"
gitlab_rails['smtp_authentication'] = "login"
gitlab_rails['smtp_enable_starttls_auto'] = true
```

  After setting up the SMTP settings, apply the changes:

```
sudo gitlab-ctl reconfigure
```

- **Enable HTTPS:** For secure communications, configure GitLab to use HTTPS. This involves obtaining an SSL certificate and modifying the external URL in the configuration file:

```
external_url "https://yourdomain.com"
nginx['redirect_http_to_https'] = true
nginx['ssl_certificate'] = "/etc/gitlab/ssl/yourdomain.com.crt"
nginx['ssl_certificate_key'] = "/etc/gitlab/ssl/yourdomain.com.key"
```

Apply the changes with the following command:

```
sudo gitlab-ctl reconfigure
```

Verification

After completing the installation and post-installation steps, it is crucial to verify that GitLab is functioning correctly.

- **Check Services:** Verify the status of GitLab services:

  ```
  sudo gitlab-ctl status
  ```

  This command lists all the services and their statuses. Ensure all services are running.
- **Access User Interface:** Log in to the GitLab web interface using the root account. GitLab prompts you to set a new password for the admin user during the first login.

Successful installation and configuration of GitLab ensure that you have a robust platform for source code management, CI/CD, and project management.

1.4 Navigating the GitLab Interface

GitLab's interface is designed to be intuitive for users at varying levels of proficiency, from beginners to advanced developers. A well-structured layout ensures efficient accessibility to the platform's diverse functionalities. This section delves into the core components of the GitLab interface, providing an in-depth understanding of each element to optimize user experience and productivity.

The primary components of the GitLab interface include the Dashboard, the Project Overview, the Navigation Bar, and various project-specific views.

Dashboard

The Dashboard serves as the central hub, offering a comprehensive overview of activities, projects, and assigned tasks. Upon logging in, users are presented with a customized Dashboard tailored to their contributions and engagements within different projects.

The Dashboard is divided into several key sections:

- **Recent Projects:** Displays a list of projects that the user has recently interacted with, allowing quick access.
- **Todos:** A task management feature that aggregates issues, merge requests, and other actionable items assigned to the user.
- **Activity:** Shows recent activities and updates within projects the user is involved in, including commits, comments, and changes.

Project Overview

The Project Overview page provides a detailed summary of a specific project, showcasing critical information and metrics:

- **Repository:** Access the project's source code, including branches, tags, and commits.
- **Issues:** A list of bugs, enhancements, or tasks related to the project. Users can create, view, and manage issues from this section.
- **Merge Requests:** Facilitates code review and collaboration by allowing users to propose changes to the project. This area lists all open, closed, and merged requests.
- **CI/CD:** Configuration and results of the project's continuous integration and continuous deployment pipelines.
- **Security & Compliance:** Tools and reports related to the security aspects of the project, including vulnerabilities and dependency scanning.
- **Analytics:** Provides insights and metrics on project performance, code contributions, and other key indicators.

Navigation Bar

The Navigation Bar, typically located to the left of the screen, is a persistent menu that allows users to quickly switch between different parts of GitLab. Key elements include:

- **Dashboard:** Takes the user back to the main dashboard.
- **Projects:** Lists all projects the user has access to, segmented by personal and group projects.

- **Groups:** Displays groups and subgroups the user is a member of, aiding in team collaboration and resource sharing.
- **Snippets:** Personal and project-level code snippets that can be shared and reused.
- **Profile:** User-specific settings including preferences, SSH keys, and activity logs.
- **Admin Area:** Available for users with administrative privileges, this section manages GitLab instance-wide settings and configurations.

Project-specific Views

When working within a specific project, additional views and controls become accessible. These include:

- **Files:** Explore the repository's file structure and content. Users can navigate through directories, view file contents, and make inline edits.
- **Commits:** A chronological list of commits made to the project, with detailed diffs and commit messages.
- **Branches:** Manage different branches of the project. Users can create, delete, and review branch-specific settings.
- **Tags:** Semantically version or mark specific points in the repository's history.
- **Pipelines:** Overview of CI/CD pipelines with detailed job statuses and logs.
- **Environments:** Visual representation of deployment environments and their statuses.
- **Packages and Registries:** Interfaces for managing packages and container images associated with the project.

```
# Example GitLab Pipeline status command using GitLab API
curl --header "PRIVATE-TOKEN: <your_access_token>" \
"https://gitlab.example.com/api/v4/projects/<project_id>/pipelines/<pipeline_id>/
    statuses"
```

```
{
  "id": 123,
  "sha": "abc123...",
  "ref": "master",
  "status": "success",
  "created_at": "2023-01-01T00:00:00Z",
  "updated_at": "2023-01-01T01:00:00Z",
  "web_url": "https://gitlab.example.com/project_slug/-/pipelines/123"
}
```


A thorough understanding of the GitLab interface enables users to leverage the platform's comprehensive features efficiently. Mastery of these components ensures optimized workflow, seamless project navigation, and successful project management.

1.5 Creating Your First Project

Creating your first project in GitLab is a foundational step towards leveraging its comprehensive DevOps platform capabilities. This section will guide you through the systematic process to initialize a project, ensuring clarity on the essential features and configurations necessary for efficient project setup.

To start, navigate to your GitLab instance and log in using your credentials. Upon successful login, you will be redirected to the GitLab dashboard. Locate the **New Project** button, typically situated on the top navigation bar or in the projects overview section. Clicking this button will usher you into the project creation interface.

- **Project Name:** Enter a descriptive and concise project name. This name should reflect the project's purpose or content. For instance, if you are setting up a new web application, a name like *WebApp* might be appropriate.
- **Project Slug:** This field is automatically generated from the project name. It is a URL-friendly version of the project name, used in the repository path.
- **Project Description:** Provide a brief but informative description of the project. This description will assist team members in understanding the project's objectives at a glance.
- **Visibility Level:** GitLab offers three visibility levels:
  - **Private:** Only project members can access the project.
  - **Internal:** Any authenticated user can access the project.

  - **Public:** The project is accessible by anyone, regardless of authentication.

- **Initialize Repository with a README:** It is advisable to initialize your repository with a README file. This file serves as the introductory part of your project, where you can outline essential information and instructions.
- **Add .gitignore:** Select an appropriate .gitignore template based on the technologies used in your project. A .gitignore file specifies intentionally untracked files to ignore, helping keep the repository clean.
- **Add a License:** Choosing the appropriate license for your project is crucial if you plan to share your code. GitLab provides several common licenses you can choose from.

After configuring these options, click the **Create Project** button. GitLab will set up the repository, and you will be redirected to the project's overview page.

The project overview page is the control center for your new project. Several tabs and controls enable you to manage the project's lifecycle efficiently. The **Files** tab displays the project files and directories, allowing you to navigate and manage the file structure.

```
git clone https://gitlab.com/username/WebApp.git
cd WebApp
```

To begin working on your newly created project, clone the repository to your local development environment using the instructions provided in the **Clone** button dropdown. The above command clones the repository and navigates into the project directory.

Adding new files and making your first commit can be done as follows:

```
echo "# WebApp" > README.md
git add README.md
git commit -m "Initial commit with README"
git push origin main
```

Here, a README file is created, staged using git add, committed with a descriptive message, and pushed to the remote repository.

The **CI/CD** tab in GitLab allows you to set up continuous integration and delivery pipelines. Using the .gitlab-ci.yml file, you can define the pipelines that will run automated jobs for building, testing, and deploying your code.

```
stages:
  - build
  - test
  - deploy

build_job:
  stage: build
  script:
    - echo "Compiling the code..."
    - make compile

test_job:
  stage: test
  script:
    - echo "Running tests..."
    - make test

deploy_job:
  stage: deploy
  script:
    - echo "Deploying application..."
    - make deploy
```

The above .gitlab-ci.yml file defines a simple pipeline with three stages: build, test, and deploy. Each job echoes a statement and runs a make command appropriate for each stage.

Within the **Members** section, you can add collaborators to your project by their GitLab username or email. Assign appropriate roles such as **Maintainer**, **Developer**, **Reporter**, or **Guest** based on the level of access required.

Issues and **Merge Requests** functionalities streamline project management and collaboration. Issues allow you to track tasks, bugs, and feature requests, while Merge Requests provide a mechanism for code review and integration.

Webhooks can be configured to notify external services when certain events happen in your project, such as code pushes or issue creations. Navigate to **Settings** → **Integrations** to add new webhooks.

Adhering to these guidelines ensures an effective and well-structured project setup, setting a solid foundation for collaborative development and deployment using GitLab's robust platform.

1.6 Understanding GitLab Terminology

The ability to navigate and effectively utilize GitLab requires a strong grasp of its fundamental terminologies. This section delves into key terms within GitLab, providing definitions and context to enhance comprehension and proficiency.

Repository (Repo): A repository is a storage space where your project's files and their revision history are stored. In GitLab, repositories are created to manage the entire lifecycle of source code development, enabling developers to store, manage, track, and collaborate on code.

Branch: A branch is a parallel version of a repository. It allows you to work on a feature or a bug fix independently of the main codebase (also known as the master or main branch). New branches are often created from the main branch and can be merged back into it once the work is complete. Here is an example command to create a branch:

```
git branch feature-branch
```

Merge Request (MR): Also known as pull requests in other platforms, a merge request allows you to merge code changes from one branch to another. It provides a collaborative space for code reviews and generates a record of the changes being proposed.

Pipeline: A pipeline is an automated process that consists of a series of steps to build, test, and deploy code. Pipelines in GitLab are defined using the .gitlab-ci.yml file and can include multiple stages such as build, test, and deploy. Below is a simplistic pipeline definition example:

```
stages:
  - build
  - test
  - deploy

build_job:
  stage: build
  script:
    - echo "Building the project"

test_job:
  stage: test
  script:
    - echo "Running tests"

deploy_job:
  stage: deploy
  script:
    - echo "Deploying the project"
```

CI/CD: Continuous Integration (CI) and Continuous Deployment (CD) are practices within DevOps to automate the integration and deployment of code changes. In GitLab, CI/CD is achieved through pipelines that run automated tests and deployments, ensuring fast and reliable delivery of code.

Runner: A runner is an agent that executes the jobs defined in GitLab CI/CD pipelines. Runners can be specific to a project, group, or be shared across many projects. Below is an example of registering a GitLab Runner:

```
gitlab-runner register
```

Issue: An issue is a single unit of work that needs to be completed. Issues are used for tracking bugs, tasks, or enhancements within a project. They can be assigned to team members, labeled, and commented on for better project management.

Board: Boards are Kanban-style boards that provide a visual overview of work in progress. They are used to organize the workflow and track the status of issues. Boards facilitate agile methodologies by representing the stages of work visually.

Milestone: A milestone is a collection of issues and merge requests that represent work to be completed by a specific deadline. Milestones help in tracking progress against project goals and are crucial for time-bound project management.

Tag: Tags are used to mark specific points in the history of a repository (such as releases). They are similar to branches but are immutable, meaning once a tag is created, it points to the same commit forever. Example:

```
git tag -a v1.0 -m "Initial release"
```

Group: A group in GitLab is a collection of projects. Groups simplify user management and provide a way to share repositories among team members with controlled permissions. Groups can contain subgroups, creating a hierarchy of projects.

Fork: Forking is making a copy of an existing repository under your own GitLab account. Forks allow developers to experiment with changes independently of the main repository. This process is often used when contributing to open source projects.

Commit: A commit is a snapshot of changes made to the repository files. Each commit includes a unique identifier (SHA), the changes made, and metadata such as the author, date, and commit message. Example:

```
git commit -m "Added new feature"
```

Wiki: The wiki in GitLab is a built-in extension feature for hosting documentation. Each project in GitLab can have its own wiki where documentation can be stored and versioned similarly to regular code repositories.

Snippet: A snippet is a small block of reusable code or text. Snippets can be public or private and can be shared across projects or with specific users. They are a useful way to manage reusable components or configurations.

Access Levels: GitLab offers various access levels that control what users can do within a project or group. These levels include Guest, Reporter, Developer, Maintainer, and Owner, each with distinct permissions.

Webhook: Webhooks are used to send real-time data to external services. They are HTTP callbacks that are triggered by specific events in a GitLab project, such as commits or issues. Webhooks enable integration with other applications.

These terminologies form the lexicon of GitLab usage and provide a foundational understanding critical for efficient navigation and utilization of the platform.

1.7 Introduction to GitLab Features

GitLab is rich with features that cater to various aspects of software development, from source code management to continuous integration/-continuous delivery (CI/CD), and from project management to security. This section delves into some of the critical features that make GitLab a preferred choice for many developers and teams around the globe. These features are broadly categorized into Source Code Management, Continuous Integration/Continuous Deployment (CI/CD), Project Management, Security, and Integration.

Source Code Management

One of GitLab's core functionalities is its robust source code management (SCM) tools. GitLab provides a Git repository, which is a distributed version control system that allows multiple developers to work on a project simultaneously without interfering with each other's work. Each change to the code is documented, providing a detailed history that facilitates easier code tracking and management. Key components of GitLab's SCM features include:

- **Repository Management:** GitLab repositories support features like branching, forking, and tagging, which are critical for managing code versions and releases efficiently.
- **Merge Requests:** GitLab's merge requests facilitate code review and collaboration by allowing team members to review and discuss code changes prior to merging them into the main branch.
- **Web IDE:** An integrated web-based Integrated Development Environment (IDE) enables developers to edit files, commit changes, and review code within the GitLab interface.
- **Snippets:** GitLab snippets allow users to share code or text across projects and teams, facilitating reuse and collaborative editing.

Here is a sample of creating a new branch and managing merge requests using GitLab CLI:

```
# Clone the repository
git clone https://gitlab.com/username/projectname.git
cd projectname

# Create and switch to a new branch
git checkout -b new-feature

# Add changes to the staging area
git add .

# Commit the changes
git commit -m "Add new feature"

# Push the branch to the remote repository
git push origin new-feature

# Create a new merge request from the web interface or using GitLab API
```

Continuous Integration/Continuous Deployment (CI/CD)

A standout feature of GitLab is its integrated CI/CD pipelines, which automate the process of running tests, building code, and deploying applications. The CI/CD functionality is built into the platform and can be customized to fit various deployment workflows. Components of GitLab's CI/CD features include:

- **.gitlab-ci.yml:** This configuration file, placed in the root directory of your repository, defines the pipeline's stages, jobs, and actions.
- **Runners:** GitLab Runners are lightweight, agent-based processes that execute jobs defined in the .gitlab-ci.yml file. Run-

ners can be hosted on the same server as GitLab or on external servers.

- **Job Artifacts:** Intermediate and final outputs of the CI/CD jobs can be stored and retrieved as job artifacts.
- **Environment Management:** Define and manage multiple deployment environments such as staging, production, and testing within the GitLab interface.
- **Auto DevOps:** A predefined CI/CD configuration that enables automatic build, test, and deployment with minimal configuration requirements.

A sample .gitlab-ci.yml file for a simple Node.js application might look like this:

```
stages:
  - build
  - test
  - deploy

build:
  stage: build
  script:
    - npm install

test:
  stage: test
  script:
    - npm run test

deploy:
  stage: deploy
  script:
    - npm run deploy
  only:
    - master
```

Project Management

GitLab's project management tools provide a cohesive way to plan, track, and manage projects. From issues and milestones to boards and roadmaps, GitLab integrates essential project management functionalities to keep teams organized:

- **Issues:** Track bugs, feature requests, and other work items with GitLab issues. Issues can be assigned labels, milestones, and users to streamline project management.
- **Milestones:** Group issues together within a specific timeframe to track progress more effectively.

- **Boards:** Kanban-style boards provide a visual representation of issues, facilitating task tracking across different states (e.g., to do, in progress, done).
- **Roadmaps:** Visualize the timeline and scope of work with roadmaps, which aggregate milestones and provide an overview of project progress.

Security

GitLab emphasizes security by integrating several security features directly into the development lifecycle. Key security features include:

- **Static Application Security Testing (SAST):** Analyzes source code to detect vulnerabilities early in the development process.
- **Dynamic Application Security Testing (DAST):** Scans deployed applications to find runtime vulnerabilities.
- **Dependency Scanning:** Checks project dependencies for known security issues.
- **Container Scanning:** Analyzes container images for vulnerabilities before they are deployed.
- **Security Dashboards:** Provides a centralized view of all security vulnerabilities, allowing teams to prioritize and address them promptly.

Integration

GitLab supports extensive integrations with various third-party services and tools, expanding its functionality and providing a seamless experience. These integrations include:

- **Webhook and API:** Integrate with various services using webhooks and GitLab's robust REST API.
- **Third-Party Services:** Integrate with popular tools like Jira, Jenkins, Slack, and many others to streamline workflows.
- **Custom Hooks:** Execute custom scripts on specific Git events (e.g., pre-commit, post-receive) through GitLab's custom hook functionality.

By incorporating these key features, GitLab aims to create a unified platform for all DevOps needs, enabling teams to collaborate more efficiently and effectively. The integration of source code management, CI/CD, project management, security, and extensive third-party integrations under one roof not only simplifies the development process but ensures that all aspects of a project are tightly coupled, resulting in higher quality software delivered in a more predictable and streamlined manner.

1.8 GitLab Editions and Pricing

GitLab offers several editions that cater to different needs and organizational scales, providing a range of features and pricing models. Understanding these editions and their associated cost structures is critical for selecting the most appropriate plan for your development and operational requirements.

The primary editions of GitLab are:

- GitLab Free
- GitLab Premium
- GitLab Ultimate

GitLab Free is the community edition, ideal for individuals and small teams looking to leverage GitLab's core capabilities without incurring costs. It provides essential features, including:

- Source Code Management (SCM)
- Continuous Integration (CI)
- Continuous Delivery (CD)
- Issue Tracking
- Basic project management tools

These features enable developers to collaborate, manage source code, automate the build process, and deploy applications efficiently.

GitLab Premium is designed for growing teams and organizations that require enhanced capabilities for more robust project management, performance, and security. GitLab Premium features include everything in GitLab Free plus:

- Advanced project management tools
- Priority support
- Faster code review and merge processes
- Enhanced security features like vulnerability management
- More CI/CD minutes for public projects

The pricing model for GitLab Premium is subscription-based with a per-user, per-month fee, making it scalable according to the team's size.

GitLab Ultimate is the most comprehensive package, suited for large enterprises that require the most robust security, compliance, and planning features. It includes all features from the Free and Premium editions plus:

- Advanced security and compliance features (e.g., SAST, Dependency Scanning, Container Scanning)
- Portfolio management tools
- Epics and roadmaps for complex project planning
- Value stream management
- 24/7 support with faster response times

GitLab Ultimate is priced at a premium per-user, per-month rate, reflecting the extensive suite of features and dedicated support.

Pricing details as of this writing can be found directly from GitLab's pricing page or requesting a quote from GitLab sales for the most accurate and up-to-date information.

GitLab also offers options for self-managed installations or GitLab SaaS (Software-as-a-Service). With the self-managed installation, organizations can deploy GitLab on their own servers, affording greater control over the environment, data residency, and compliance. The GitLab SaaS option allows organizations to leverage GitLab's infrastructure to avoid the overhead of server maintenance and management. Both self-managed and SaaS versions follow the same pricing tiers but may offer different levels of customization and support.

```
# Here is an example command line to retrieve pricing information
curl -H "Private-Token: <your_access_token>" https://gitlab.example.com/api/v4/
    plans
```


```
{
  "free": {
    "name": "GitLab Free",
    "price_per_user_per_month": 0,
    "features": ["SCM", "CI/CD", "Issue Tracking",...]
  },
  "premium": {
    "name": "GitLab Premium",
    "price_per_user_per_month": 19,
    "features": ["Advanced Project Management", "Priority Support", ...]
  },
  "ultimate": {
    "name": "GitLab Ultimate",
    "price_per_user_per_month": 99,
    "features": ["Advanced Security", "Compliance", "Value Stream Management", ...]
  }
}
```


Education and non-profit organizations may qualify for discounts or free access to GitLab's higher-tier features. GitLab regularly updates its pricing and features, so it is crucial to review the current offerings directly through their official site or by contacting GitLab representatives.

By selecting the appropriate edition, teams can scale their usage and features in alignment with their growth and project complexity, ensuring they get the most value from the platform. Each edition is designed to cater to specific needs, from small teams seeking core SCM features to large enterprises requiring comprehensive compliance and security controls.

1.9 Migrating to GitLab

Effective migration to GitLab from existing source code repositories and DevOps tools is a critical process that requires meticulous planning and execution. This section elucidates the step-by-step process of migrating to GitLab, covering essential aspects such as pre-migration preparation, data transfer techniques, and post-migration verification. Detailed guidance is provided to ensure a smooth transition while maintaining the integrity of your project data.

Pre-Migration Preparation

Before initiating the migration process, it is important to conduct a thorough assessment of your current environment. This includes understanding the current infrastructure, identifying all source code repositories, CI/CD pipelines, and connected third-party tools. Documenting the dependencies and configurations is essential to avoid unforeseen issues during migration. Consider the following preparatory steps:

- **Inventory Current Setup:** List all repositories, branches, tags, issues, and CI/CD configurations that need to be migrated.
- **Backup Existing Data:** Ensure that a complete backup of your existing repositories and configuration files is created.
- **Assess Team Readiness:** Communicate with your team regarding the migration timeline and provide necessary training on GitLab functionalities.
- **Allocate Resources:** Ensure that adequate computational resources and permissions are in place to facilitate the migration.

Data Transfer Techniques

Migrating to GitLab can involve moving data from various source control systems such as GitHub, Bitbucket, or SVN. GitLab provides a variety of tools and strategies to facilitate this process.

1. Migrating from GitHub

GitLab's import feature allows seamless migration from GitHub. You can utilize the GitLab UI to import repositories directly. The steps include:

1. **Create a New Project in GitLab:** Navigate to the GitLab instance and create a new project.
2. **Import Project from GitHub:** Select the "Import project" option and choose GitHub as the source.
3. **Authenticate GitHub Account:** Authorize GitLab to access your GitHub repositories using OAuth or Personal Access Token.
4. **Select Repositories:** Choose the repositories you wish to import and initiate the import process.

The following code snippet demonstrates how this can be managed programmatically using GitLab's API:

```
import requests

headers = {'Private-Token': 'your_access_token'}
data = {'target_namespace': 'your_namespace', 'github_username': '
    your_github_username', 'personal_access_token': 'your_github_token'}

response = requests.post('https://gitlab.example.com/api/v4/import/github', headers=
    headers, data=data)
print(response.json())
```

2. Migrating from Bitbucket

Similar to GitHub, GitLab facilitates the import of repositories from Bitbucket. The procedure is as follows:

1. **Create a New Project in GitLab:** Initiate a new project in GitLab.
2. **Import Project from Bitbucket:** Select Bitbucket as the import source in the "Import Project" section.
3. **Authenticate Bitbucket Account:** Allow GitLab to access your Bitbucket repositories using OAuth or Personal Access Token.
4. **Select Repositories:** Choose the repositories for migration and begin the transfer.

Again, the import can be managed programmatically:

```
import requests

headers = {'Private-Token': 'your_access_token'}
data = {'target_namespace': 'your_namespace', 'bitbucket_username': '
    your_bitbucket_username', 'personal_access_token': 'your_bitbucket_token'}

response = requests.post('https://gitlab.example.com/api/v4/import/bitbucket',
    headers=headers, data=data)
print(response.json())
```

3. Migrating from SVN

Migration from SVN to GitLab involves converting the SVN repository to Git format first. This can be achieved using the 'git svn' command. The steps are:

1. **Install Git SVN:** Ensure that 'git svn' is installed in your environment.
2. **Clone SVN Repository:** Use the 'git svn clone' command to convert the SVN repository to Git.

3. **Push to GitLab:** Create a new repository in GitLab and push the converted repository to GitLab.

Commands to perform the migration:

```
# Clone the SVN repository to a Git repository
git svn clone https://svn.example.com/repo --authors-file=authors.txt new-repo

# Navigate to the cloned directory
cd new-repo

# Add GitLab as a remote repository
git remote add origin https://gitlab.example.com/namespace/new-repo.git

# Push the repository to GitLab
git push -u origin master
```

Post-Migration Verification

Upon successful data transfer, it is necessary to verify the integrity and completeness of the migrated data. The following steps should be undertaken:

- **Repository Verification:** Ensure all branches, commits, tags, and files have been correctly imported.
- **CI/CD Pipeline Check:** Test and validate all CI/CD pipelines to ensure that they function as expected.
- **Permission Settings:** Validate user permissions and ensure that access controls are correctly configured.
- **Issue Tracking:** Verify the import of issues, labels, and milestones, ensuring that they reflect accurately in GitLab.
- **Third-Party Integrations:** Reconfigure and test any integrations with external tools such as Jenkins, JIRA, or Slack.

```
Verification Output:

Repository check: Successful
Branches: 10/10 verified
Commits: 1000/1000 verified
CI/CD Pipelines: Functional
Permissions: Configured
Issue tracking: 200/200 issues verified
Third-Party Integrations: Functional
```

Through careful preparation, methodical data transfer, and diligent post-migration verification, the transition to GitLab can be executed efficiently while maintaining the structural and operational integrity of your projects.

1.10 Best Practices for New GitLab Users

Effective utilization of GitLab entails more than familiarity with its interface and functionality. Appropriating best practices can enhance productivity, collaboration, and project quality. This section aims to provide a set of guiding principles and actionable practices for new GitLab users.

Commit Often, but Thoughtfully: Version control systems like GitLab thrive on tracking incremental changes. Small, frequent commits make it easier to identify and revert specific changes when necessary. Employ descriptive commit messages to summarize the changes made. Examples of proper commit messages include "Fixed issue with user login validation" or "Updated README with installation instructions".

```
$ git add .
$ git commit -m "Fixed issue with user login validation"
$ git push origin main
```

Branch Strategically: Utilize branching to isolate new features, bug fixes, or experimental code from the main codebase. This minimizes the risk of introducing bugs into the stable version of your project. Common branching strategies include feature branching, where each new feature is developed in its distinct branch, and release branching, where branches are created for each release version.

```
$ git checkout -b feature/new-login-module
# Work on feature
$ git add .
$ git commit -m "Implemented new login module"
$ git push origin feature/new-login-module
```

Merge with Care: To maintain codebase integrity, always merge branches using merge requests (or pull requests). This approach facilitates peer review, ensuring that code is reviewed, discussed, and approved before being integrated into the main branch. To create a merge request:

- Navigate to *Merge Requests* in your GitLab project.
- Click *New Merge Request*.
- Select the source and target branches, then click *Compare branches and continue*.
- Add a title and description, then click *Submit Merge Request*.

Code Reviews and CI Pipelines: Perform code reviews vigilantly. They are crucial for maintaining code quality and fostering knowledge sharing among team members. Incorporate Continuous Integration/-Continuous Deployment (CI/CD) pipelines to automate testing and deployment processes, ensuring that new changes do not break the existing codebase. Example of a simple CI/CD pipeline in .gitlab-ci.yml:

```
stages:
  - build
  - test

build_job:
  stage: build
  script:
    - echo "Compiling the code..."
    - gcc main.c -o main.out

test_job:
  stage: test
  script:
    - echo "Running unit tests..."
    - ./main.out
```

Documentation is Key: Maintain current and comprehensive documentation within your projects. Documentation should include, but not be limited to, installation instructions, usage guidelines, API documentation (if applicable), and a changelog. Keeping the README file updated provides new contributors with a clear understanding of the project's purpose and usage.

Security Protocols: Ensure that security best practices are integrated into your GitLab workflow. These include managing user permissions meticulously, regularly updating dependencies to patch known vulnerabilities, and utilizing GitLab's security features, such as Secret Detection and Dependency Scanning.

Effective Issue Tracking: Leverage GitLab's issue tracker to manage and prioritize tasks, bugs, and feature requests. Use labels, milestones, and issue boards to organize and monitor progress efficiently. Writing clear, concise issue descriptions with acceptance criteria can streamline the development process.

Regular Backups: Regularly back up your GitLab instance, including repositories, databases, and configuration files. This safeguard ensures that data loss due to hardware failures or other unforeseen events can be mitigated.

Consistent Naming Conventions: Establish and adhere to consistent naming conventions for branches, commits, tags, and other GitLab entities. This practice promotes clarity and predictability within your project's workflow. For branch names, consider using prefixes like feature/, fix/, release/, as illustrated below:

```
$ git checkout -b feature/module-refactor
$ git checkout -b fix/issue-456
$ git checkout -b release/v1.2.0
```

Metrics and Analytics: Use GitLab's built-in analytics tools to monitor project metrics, including code quality, deployment frequency, and issue resolution times. These insights can guide future improvements and strategic planning.

Implementing these best practices can significantly enhance your experience and productivity with GitLab. Always remember that continuous improvement and adaptation of workflows to your team's needs is critical for mastering GitLab.

Chapter 2

Getting Started with Git

This chapter provides an essential introduction to Git, a distributed version control system crucial for modern software development. It covers the installation and initial configuration of Git, introduces fundamental concepts like repositories, and explains basic commands. You will learn how to manage branches, merge changes, handle conflicts, and utilize tags and releases. The chapter also addresses different Git workflows and collaboration methods, concluding with how to integrate Git with GitLab for streamlined project management.

2.1 What is Version Control?

Version control is a system that records changes to a file or set of files over time so that you can recall specific versions later. It is a critical component in the context of software development, as it provides a systematic method of managing and tracking code changes. This becomes particularly essential in collaborative environments where multiple developers may be working on the same codebase simultaneously.

The primary objectives of version control are maintaining a detailed history of every file, facilitating collaboration among developers, and ensuring the integrity and consistency of files across different versions. Version control systems (VCS) achieve these objectives by monitoring changes, saving snapshots, and enabling users to revert to previous versions when necessary.

When we talk about version control, we commonly refer to two main types: centralized version control systems (CVCS) and distributed version control systems (DVCS).

Centralized Version Control Systems (CVCS)

In a CVCS, there is a single central repository where all the versioned files are stored. Users commit their changes to this central repository and can also update their working copies from it. This model simplifies certain aspects of version control by ensuring that all users always work with the latest version. However, it has some limitations, such as a single point of failure. If the central server becomes unavailable, developers cannot commit their changes or retrieve updates from the repository.

Distributed Version Control Systems (DVCS)

In a DVCS, each developer's working copy of the codebase is also a repository containing the complete history of all changes. Popular DVCS examples include Git and Mercurial. This approach offers several significant advantages:

- **No Single Point of Failure**: Since every working copy contains the entire repository history, any copy can restore the repository if needed.
- **Enhanced Collaboration**: Developers can work independently on their local repositories and sync changes with others as necessary. This facilitates a workflow where code changes are integrated more smoothly.
- **Offline Capabilities**: Developers can commit changes, review history, and perform many other operations without needing a network connection.

Basic Version Control Concepts and Terminology

Understanding version control systems also involves familiarizing oneself with various terms and concepts:

- **Repository (Repo)**: A storage location for software packages, often used to refer to a central place where data is stored and managed.
- **Commit**: A record of changes made to the repository. Each commit serves as a snapshot of the project's files at a given point in time, along with a log message describing the changes.

- **Branch**: A parallel version of the repository. Branches allow developers to work on features, bug fixes, or experiments in isolation from the main codebase.
- **Merge**: The process of integrating changes from one branch into another. A merge can sometimes result in conflicts when changes overlap or contradict each other.
- **Conflict**: A situation where changes from two different branches cannot be automatically reconciled and require manual resolution.
- **Tag**: A named reference to a specific commit, often used to mark release points (e.g., v1.0, v2.0).

Benefits of Using Version Control Systems

The use of version control systems provides numerous benefits:

- **History and Flexible Recovery**: Every change is stored, allowing teams to understand the evolution of the project and recover older versions if needed.
- **Collaboration and Synchronization**: Multiple developers can contribute to a project simultaneously, with mechanisms to merge changes and resolve conflicts.
- **Backup and Safety**: The entire history of the project acts as a backup. If any files are accidentally deleted, they can be restored from the repository.
- **Branching and Experimentation**: Developers can create branches to experiment with new features or fixes without risking the stability of the main codebase.
- **Traceability**: Each commit message can include detailed descriptions of what was changed and why, providing context and facilitating accountability.

Since version control is foundational for modern software development practices, understanding its principles is crucial. As we progress through this chapter, we will focus on Git, one of the most widely used distributed version control systems, to explore how these concepts are implemented and exemplified in real-world scenarios.

2.2 Introduction to Git

Git is a distributed version control system designed to handle everything from small to very large projects with speed and efficiency. It was created by Linus Torvalds in 2005 for the development of the Linux kernel, and since then it has evolved to become the most widely adopted version control system in the industry. This section aims to provide an understanding of the fundamental concepts and architecture that make Git a robust tool for version control.

Git emphasizes non-linear development through its branching and merging capabilities. Unlike centralized version control systems that store the entire project history on a central server, Git allows each contributor to maintain their own copy of the repository. This decentralized approach brings several advantages:

- **Resilience and Backup:** Each copy of the repository is a complete backup, meaning that the repository's history is preserved even if any single node on a network fails.
- **Speed:** By having a local copy, operations such as commits, diffs, and merging are performed locally, resulting in faster performance.
- **Flexibility:** Users can work independently on different branches and merge code changes as necessary, encouraging parallel development workflows.

At its core, Git works by tracking changes to a project in a repository. A repository, or repo, contains all of the project's files and the entire revision history. A user can clone a repository to their local machine, making a copy of it that they can modify independently.

The lifecycle of a change in Git typically flows through the following stages:

- **Working Directory:** This is the directory where the user makes changes to the project's files. Every file in the working directory can be in one of three states: modified, unmodified, or staged.
- **Staging Area:** Also known as the index, this is a file that contains information about what changes will go into your next commit. Changes must be added to the staging area before they can be committed.

- **Repository:** This is where the committed changes are stored. Commits in the repository are immutable records of the changes made to the project's files.

To illustrate these stages, consider the following sequence of commands:

```
# Initialize a new Git repository
git init

# Create a new file
echo "Hello, World!" > hello.txt

# Check the status of the repository
git status
```

The output of the git status command:

```
On branch master

No commits yet

Untracked files:
  (use "git add <file>..." to include in what will be committed)

    hello.txt

nothing added to commit but untracked files present (use "git add" to track)
```

At this point, the 'hello.txt' file is in the working directory and is untracked. To start tracking this file, it needs to be added to the staging area using the git add command:

```
git add hello.txt

# Check the status again
git status
```

The output of the git status command now:

```
On branch master

No commits yet

Changes to be committed:
  (use "git rm --cached <file>..." to unstage)

    new file:   hello.txt
```

With the file staged, it can now be committed to the repository:

```
git commit -m "Add hello.txt with initial content"

# Check the status once more
git status
```

And the output:

```
On branch master
nothing to commit, working tree clean
```

This simple example introduces several important Git concepts: the working directory, staging area, and repository. By staging and committing changes, Git ensures that every modification is recorded with a timestamp, a commit message, and author information, forming a detailed history of the project.

One of the key features of Git is its branching model. Branches allow users to diverge from the main line of development and continue to work separately without affecting the main codebase. This is extremely useful for developing new features, fixing bugs, or experimenting with new ideas. Users can create branches using the git branch command and switch between them using the git checkout command.

Consider the following example, which demonstrates creating and switching to a new branch:

```
# Create a new branch named 'feature'
git branch feature

# Switch to the 'feature' branch
git checkout feature

# Verify the current branch
git branch
```

This results in the following output:

```
* feature
  master
```

This indicates that the user is currently working on the 'feature' branch. Once the user has completed their work on this branch, it can be merged back into the main line (typically the 'master' or 'main' branch):

```
# Switch back to the master branch
git checkout master

# Merge the 'feature' branch into 'master'
git merge feature
```

Branching and merging are fundamental to Git's workflow, allowing multiple developers to work concurrently without interfering with each other's changes. Merging integrates the changes from one branch into another. When conflicts arise (changes that cannot be automatically reconciled), Git provides tools to help resolve them and ensure that the codebase remains consistent.

Understanding Git's architecture and basic commands provides the foundation for leveraging its more advanced features. As you advance, you will explore additional commands and workflows that further enhance collaboration and efficiency in software development. With a solid grasp of these core principles, you are well-equipped to manage a repository's evolution and collaborate effectively with others.

2.3 Installing Git

To begin utilizing Git for version control, it is essential to first install the software on your system. This section outlines the steps required to install Git on various operating systems including Windows, macOS, and Linux. Follow the appropriate instructions for your operating system to ensure a proper installation.

Windows

For Windows users, downloading and installing Git can be done using the Git for Windows installer:

1. Navigate to the official Git for Windows website: https://gitforwindows.org/ 2. Download the latest version of the Git setup executable file. 3. Once the download is complete, run the installer. You will be greeted by the Git Setup wizard. 4. Follow the Setup wizard steps:

- **Select Destination Location**: Choose the directory to install Git.
- **Select Components**: Options might include additional components such as Git Bash, Git GUI, and system-level tools. Select the components based on your preference.
- **Adjusting the PATH Environment**: Choose an option to adjust your PATH environment variable. It's recommended to select "Use Git from the command line and also from 3rd-party software."
- **Choosing a SSH executable**: Decide whether to use the built-in OpenSSH or your existing SSH installation.
- **Configuring the line ending conversions**: Opt for "Checkout Windows-style, commit Unix-style line endings" to handle cross-platform line endings.
- **Configuring the terminal emulator to use with Git Bash**: Default is MinTTY; continue with it unless there is a preference for Windows' ConHost.

5. Continue through the remaining prompts to complete the installation. 6. Once installed, verify the installation by opening the command prompt and executing:

```
git --version
```

7. The output should display the installed Git version:

```
git version X.X.X
```

macOS

macOS provides multiple ways to install Git. Below are the steps for using Homebrew, a popular package manager for macOS:

1. Ensure Homebrew is installed. Open Terminal and enter:

```
/bin/bash -c "$(curl -fsSL https://raw.githubusercontent.com/Homebrew/install/
    HEAD/install.sh)"
```

2. Once Homebrew is installed, update it:

```
brew update
```

3. Install Git using Homebrew:

```
brew install git
```

4. Verify the installation by checking the Git version:

```
git --version
```

```
git version X.X.X
```

Alternatively, Git can be installed via Xcode Command Line Tools:

1. Open Terminal. 2. Execute the command to install Xcode Command Line Tools:

```
xcode-select --install
```

3. Follow the prompts to complete the installation. 4. Verify Git installation:

```
git --version
```

```
git version X.X.X
```

Linux

Debian-based and Red Hat-based distributions have their own package managers for installing Git. Instructions for installing Git on Ubuntu (a Debian-based system) and Fedora (a Red Hat-based system) are provided below:

Ubuntu

1. Update the package list:

```
sudo apt-get update
```

2. Install Git:

```
sudo apt-get install git
```

3. Verify the installation:

```
git --version
```

```
git version X.X.X
```

Fedora

1. Update the package list:

```
sudo dnf update
```

2. Install Git:

```
sudo dnf install git
```

3. Verify the installation:

```
git --version
```

```
git version X.X.X
```

These steps ensure that Git is installed correctly on your operating system, enabling you to configure, use basic commands, and integrate Git with GitLab as detailed in subsequent sections of this chapter.

2.4 Configuring Git for the First Time

Upon successful installation of Git, the next step is to configure it. Git requires a few essential configuration settings to be defined before using it effectively. This setup involves specifying user information that is associated with your Git commits and setting default behaviors.

Firstly, you must set your user name and email address. These identifiers are stored in each commit you create and are crucial for tracking changes and collaboration. Open your command line interface and execute the following commands:

```
git config --global user.name "Your Name"
git config --global user.email "your.email@example.com"
```

These commands utilize the git config mechanism, which is a core utility for setting and querying Git configuration variables that control all aspects of Git's operation and look. The –global option ensures that these settings apply to all repositories on your system. If you want different configurations for specific projects, you may omit the –global option and run the commands separately within each repository.

Verification of these settings can be performed using:

```
git config --global --list
```

The output should display the configured user name and email:

```
user.name=Your Name
user.email=your.email@example.com
```

Next, it is recommended to configure the default text editor that Git will use for commit messages. The default editor is typically Vim, but this can be changed to any editor of your choice. For example, to set Nano as the default editor, use:

```
git config --global core.editor "nano"
```

If you prefer Visual Studio Code, the configuration would be:

```
git config --global core.editor "code --wait"
```

Another vital configuration parameter is the handling of line endings. Different operating systems use different conventions for line endings (LF for Linux/Mac and CRLF for Windows). Configuring Git to properly handle line endings between these environments ensures that the version history remains consistent and free of undesirable changes. The following command configures Git to automatically handle line endings for cross-platform projects:

```
git config --global core.autocrlf true
```

For Linux and macOS users working with Windows collaborators, you might prefer to configure:

```
git config --global core.autocrlf input
```

This setting ensures that Git will convert CRLF to LF on commit but leave LF endings untouched when checking out. This way, Unix-style line endings are maintained in repositories.

You might also configure Git to use a credential helper. This is particularly useful if you work with repositories over HTTPS, preventing constant password prompts. To cache your credentials for future uses, use:

```
git config --global credential.helper cache
```

Alternatively, to store your credentials securely using the Git credential store, use:

```
git config --global credential.helper store
```

Depending on your operating system, additional credential helpers can be configured. For Windows, you can leverage the Git Credential Manager with:

```
git config --global credential.helper manager-core
```

Lastly, setting up aliases can greatly simplify frequent Git commands. For instance, creating an alias for git status:

```
git config --global alias.st status
```

This configuration allows the use of git st as a shorthand for git status, enhancing productivity.

To summarize, the initial Git configuration includes setting up user identity, selecting a default text editor, managing line endings, configuring credential management, and optionally creating command aliases. Each of these settings ensures that Git is tailored to your workflow and operational environment, forming a strong foundation for effective version control.

By diligently following these configuration steps, you ensure that your Git setup is personalized and optimized, ready to support your development activities seamlessly.

2.5 Understanding Repositories in Git

A repository, often shortened to "repo," is a critical concept in Git that serves as the central directory where Git stores all the project files and the history of changes made to them. Repositories can be either local, residing on your personal machine, or remote, hosted on platforms such as GitLab. Effectively managing repositories is fundamental for maintaining a well-organized, version-controlled project. This section delves into the structure, creation, and utilization of repositories in Git.

To create a new Git repository, navigate to the desired directory on your local machine and execute the following command:

```
git init
```

Executing git init initializes a new Git repository in the current directory. This command creates a hidden subdirectory named .git that contains all the necessary metadata and objects for version control. The directory structure within .git includes several important subdirectories and files, such as:

- objects/: Stores all data content, including commits, trees, and blob objects.
- refs/: Contains pointers to commit objects that establish the branches and tags.
- HEAD: Points to the current branch reference.
- config: Stores configuration settings specific to the repository.
- index: Serves as a staging area for changes to be committed.

Understanding the differentiation between a working directory, the staging area, and the Git repository is crucial:

- **Working Directory**: Consists of files and directories you are currently working on. These are ordinary files that can be modified, added, or deleted.
- **Staging Area (Index)**: An intermediary area where changes can be listed in preparation for a commit. Before committing changes, they need to be added to the staging area using the command:

```
git add <file-name>
```

- **Repository**: Contains the history of all changes and metadata. Committing a change transfers it from the staging area to the repository, thus permanently recording it in the version history. This operation is executed using:

```
git commit -m "Commit message"
```

A commit in Git represents a snapshot of the project at a given point in time. Each commit has a unique SHA-1 hash identifier, which ensures its integrity and aids in tracking changes over time. The command

```
git log
```

displays the commit history, providing detailed information about each commit, including the commit ID, author, date, and commit message.

Connecting your local repository to a remote repository, such as one hosted on GitLab, allows you to push changes and collaborate with others. Use the following command to set up a remote repository:

```
git remote add origin <remote-repository-URL>
```

This command establishes a link between your local repository and the remote repository named origin, which is the default name for remote repositories in Git.

To synchronize changes between the local and remote repositories, the following commands are used:

- **Push Changes**:

  ```
  git push origin <branch-name>
  ```

  This uploads your commits from a local branch to the corresponding branch on the remote repository.

- **Pull Changes**:

  ```
  git pull origin <branch-name>
  ```

  This fetches updates from the remote repository and merges them into your local branch.

The concept of cloning a repository is also essential for collaborative work. Cloning creates a copy of a remote repository on your local machine, enabling you to work with the entire project. This can be achieved with:

```
git clone <remote-repository-URL>
```

This command not only copies the content of the remote repository but also configures the necessary references to simplify future synchronization.

Repositories in Git are powerful tools for organizing and tracking the development progress of your projects, providing a robust framework for both individual and collaborative work. By mastering the handling of repositories, one can leverage Git's full potential to maintain an efficient, transparent, and reliable development lifecycle.

2.6 Basic Git Commands

Understanding and mastering basic Git commands is fundamental for efficient version control and collaboration. This section covers essential commands needed for daily Git activities, including creating repositories, adding and committing changes, and inspecting the status and history of the project.

Creating a New Repository

To create a new Git repository, navigate to your project's directory and initialize the repository using the following command:

```
git init
```

This command initializes a new Git repository by creating a .git directory that contains all the necessary files and subdirectories used by Git to track project history and configuration.

Staging and Committing Changes

To start tracking files, they need to be staged and then committed to the repository. Use the git add command to stage files. For example, to stage a specific file:

```
git add filename
```

To stage all changes in the current directory, utilize:

```
git add .
```

After staging, commit the changes to the repository with a message describing the changes:

```
git commit -m "Commit message"
```

Each commit creates a snapshot of the project's files at that point in time, allowing for precise version control.

Checking the Status

To view the current status of the working directory and the staging area, use:

```
git status
```

This command shows which changes have been staged, which files are not being tracked by Git, and which changes in tracked files have not yet been staged.

Viewing the Commit Log

To see the history of commits in the repository, the following command is used:

```
git log
```

The `git log` command provides a detailed list of commits, including commit hashes, author information, and commit messages.

Cloning an Existing Repository

To create a copy of an existing repository, use the `git clone` command followed by the repository's URL:

```
git clone https://github.com/username/repository.git
```

This command copies the repository to your local machine, allowing you to contribute to the project or use it as a base for your own work.

Pulling Updates from a Remote Repository

To update the local repository with the latest changes from a remote repository:

```
git pull
```

The `git pull` command fetches new data from a specified remote repository and integrates it into the current branch.

Pushing Changes to a Remote Repository

After committing changes locally, push the commits to a remote repository using:

```
git push
```

This command uploads local repository content changes to a remote repository, facilitating collaboration by sharing updates with team members.

Removing Files

To remove a file from the working directory and the repository, apply the following command:

```
git rm filename
```

Similarly, to remove a file only from the staging area, preventing it from being included in the next commit:

```
git reset HEAD filename
```

Undoing Changes

If you need to discard changes in the working directory, execute the following command:

```
git checkout -- filename
```

Moreover, to unstage a file while preserving changes in the working directory:

```
git reset HEAD filename
```

Restoring previous commit states can be achieved using:

```
git reset --hard commit_SHA
```

This command resets the repository to the specified commit and discards any changes in the working directory and the staging area.

By proficiently using these basic Git commands, managing versions of a project becomes systematic and precise, assuring an organized workflow for software development and collaboration.

2.7 Branching and Merging

Branching and merging are fundamental aspects of Git that enable concurrent development, feature isolation, and efficient collaboration among team members. This section will provide a comprehensive understanding of how to create, manage, and merge branches in Git, emphasizing practical examples and common scenarios encountered in everyday development.

A branch in Git represents an independent line of development, allowing multiple tasks or features to be worked on simultaneously without interfering with the main codebase. The default branch in a new Git repository is called main or master, depending on the version of Git being used.

To create a new branch, use the git branch command followed by the name of the desired branch:

```
git branch feature-branch
```

This command creates a branch named feature-branch, which initially points to the same commit as the current branch. To switch to this newly created branch, use the git checkout command or the more modern git switch command:

```
git checkout feature-branch
\textit{or}
git switch feature-branch
```

Now, any changes made to the working directory will be recorded in feature-branch, keeping the main development line unaffected.

To view all the branches in the repository, execute:

```
git branch
```

This command lists all local branches, highlighting the current active branch with an asterisk (*). If you need to delete a branch after merging its changes into another branch, the git branch -d command can be used:

```
git branch -d feature-branch
```

The -d flag deletes the specified branch, but only if it has been fully merged. If it has not, Git will prevent the deletion unless the -D flag is used to force the deletion.

A crucial part of working with branches is merging them back into the main branch or another branch. Merging in Git can be either fast-forward or three-way merge, depending on the state of the branches involved.

A fast-forward merge occurs when the branch being merged is ahead of the current branch, and the pointer can simply be moved forward to the latest commit. This can be achieved with:

```
git checkout main
git merge feature-branch
```

If there have been diverging changes, a three-way merge is required. In this case, Git creates a new merge commit that incorporates changes from both branches. In such scenarios, conflicts may arise if the same lines of code have been altered in both branches. For example, after making changes to both main and feature-branch:

```
git checkout main
git merge feature-branch
```

If conflicts occur, Git will highlight the conflicts within the affected files, requiring manual intervention. Conflict markers within the file will appear as follows:

```
<<<<<<< HEAD
current change in main
=======
incompatible change in feature-branch
>>>>>>> feature-branch
```

The section between the ««« and ====== is the current change in the main branch, while the section between ====== and »»» represents changes from the feature-branch. The developer must manually resolve these conflicts by editing the file to contain the desired changes from both branches.

After resolving conflicts and staging the changes:

```
git add <filename>
```

Complete the merge by committing:

```
git commit
```

During interactive rebasing, developers can reorder, squash, or edit commits to produce a cleaner commit history. Use the following command to start an interactive rebase of the last n commits:

```
git rebase -i HEAD~n
```

A text editor will appear with a list of commits and instructions for modification. Adjust the commits as needed and save the file to proceed.

To abort a merge or rebase operation at any point, the following commands can be used, respectively:

```
git merge --abort
```

```
git rebase --abort
```

These commands revert the repository to its state before the merge or rebase operation began, preserving the current branch and commit history integrity.

By effectively utilizing branching and merging, developers can maintain an organized and efficient workflow, allowing for isolated feature development, quick integration of changes, and seamless collaboration among team members.

2.8 Handling Conflicts in Git

When working collaboratively on a project, conflicts are inevitable. A conflict arises in Git when changes to the same part of the same file are made in different branches or commits. These conflicting changes cannot be automatically merged by Git and require manual resolution. Understanding how to handle these conflicts is crucial to maintaining a smooth workflow.

A conflict usually occurs during the merging process. When you attempt to merge one branch into another, Git automatically tries to reconcile the differences. If it encounters changes that cannot be merged automatically, it flags these as conflicts, which must be resolved by the user.

Consider the following scenario: two developers, Alice and Bob, work on the same file, 'example.txt', in different branches. Alice creates a branch 'feature-alice' and makes some changes:

```
# Alice's workflow
git checkout -b feature-alice
echo "Alice's changes" >> example.txt
git add example.txt
git commit -m "Alice's changes"
```

Meanwhile, Bob creates his branch 'feature-bob' and modifies the same lines in 'example.txt':

```
# Bob's workflow
git checkout -b feature-bob
echo "Bob's changes" >> example.txt
git add example.txt
git commit -m "Bob's changes"
```

At some point, these changes need to be merged back into the 'main' branch. Alice merges her 'feature-alice' branch without any conflicts as she is the first to merge:

```
# Alice merges her branch
git checkout main
git merge feature-alice
```

Now, Bob attempts to merge his changes into the 'main' branch:

```
# Bob merges his branch
git checkout main
git merge feature-bob
```

Since both Alice and Bob have modified the same lines in 'example.txt', Git cannot automatically merge these changes, resulting in a conflict. Git will output a message similar to the following:

```
Auto-merging example.txt
CONFLICT (content): Merge conflict in example.txt
Automatic merge failed; fix conflicts and then commit the result.
```

To resolve the conflict, Bob needs to open 'example.txt' and see the changes marked by Git:

```
<<<<<<< HEAD
Alice's changes
=======
Bob's changes
>>>>>>> feature-bob
```

Git uses these markers to indicate where the conflicts are:

- '«««< HEAD': This marks the beginning of the conflicting changes from the current branch ('main' in this case). - '=======': This separates the conflicting changes. - '»»»> feature-bob': This marks the end of the conflicting changes from the branch being merged ('feature-bob').

Bob can now manually edit the file to combine the changes appropriately:

```
Alice's changes
Bob's changes
```

After resolving the conflict, Bob needs to add the file and complete the merge by committing:

```
# Staging the resolved file
git add example.txt

# Completing the merge
git commit -m "Resolved merge conflict between main and feature-bob"
```

Git now considers the conflict resolved, and the merge is complete. The project's history will reflect the changes made by both developers.

In more complex scenarios, where multiple files or more intricate changes are involved, resolving conflicts may require additional strategies and tools. Git provides several utilities to detect, analyze, and manage conflicts:

- **'git diff'**: This command can be used to inspect the conflicting changes more closely. It provides a detailed comparison of the difference between branches, helping to understand the nature of the conflict.

```
git diff main..feature-bob
```

- **'git mergetool'**: Git supports integration with various merge tools that provide graphical interfaces for resolving conflicts. This can be especially useful when dealing with complex files. To launch an external merge tool, use:

```
git mergetool
```

Configuring a preferred merge tool can be done by setting up Git's configuration:

```
git config --global merge.tool <tool-name>
```

Commonly used tools include 'kdiff3', 'meld', 'vimdiff', and others. Each tool provides unique features to facilitate the resolution process.

- **'git rerere'**: Stands for "reuse recorded resolution." This tool remembers how you have resolved a conflict and can automatically apply the same resolution the next time the same conflict occurs.

```
git config --global rerere.enabled true
```

Finally, preventing conflicts is another effective strategy. Regularly pulling updates from the main branch, communicating with team members, and making small, frequent commits can reduce the likelihood and complexity of conflicts. When conflicts do occur, a structured and systematic approach ensures that they are resolved efficiently and accurately, maintaining the integrity and consistency of the project.

2.9 Git Tags and Releases

In software development, managing different versions of your codebase is essential, particularly when you release software to users. Git provides powerful tools for handling versions, among which tags and releases stand prominently. Tags act as immutable markers in your repository's history, whereas releases offer a user-friendly way to distribute code.

A Git tag is a reference to a specific point in your Git history. Unlike branches, which move as you commit changes, tags are static and meant to capture a particular state. They are commonly used to mark important versions of your software, such as v1.0, v2.0, and so on. In Git, there are two main types of tags: annotated and lightweight tags.

Annotated tags are stored in the Git database as full objects and contain additional information, such as the tagger's name, email, date, and a tagging message. Lightweight tags, on the other hand, are simple references, much like branches, and do not carry any additional metadata.

To create a lightweight tag, you can use the following command:

```
git tag v1.0
```

Conversely, to create an annotated tag, you use:

```
git tag -a v1.0 -m "Release version 1.0"
```

Here, the -a flag tells Git to create an annotated tag, and -m allows you to include a message, which is important for documentation and future reference. Annotated tags are generally recommended for release purposes because they contain additional information, making them more helpful for tracking and auditing.

To see all the tags in your repository, use:

```
git tag
```

For detailed information about a specific tag, especially an annotated tag, you can use:

```
git show v1.0
```

This not only shows the commit associated with the tag but also includes tag metadata.

When tags mark significant points in the history of a project, releases make these points accessible and usable to the end-users. Git tags are often used by release systems within Git hosting services like GitLab to create releases.

In GitLab, a release is a set of release notes that are attached to a Git tag. This formalizes and contextualizes significant milestones in your repository. To create a release in GitLab, you can use the GitLab web interface or the GitLab Release API. Here is a step-by-step guide for creating a release through the web interface:

1. Navigate to your project in GitLab. 2. Go to the "Repository" menu and select "Tags". 3. Click "New release". 4. In the "Tag" field, specify the tag to which this release is attached. If the tag does not yet exist, you can create it directly here. 5. Fill in the "Release title" and "Description". The description often includes notable features, bug fixes, and other relevant changes. 6. If relevant, attach files, such as binaries or assets associated with the release, typically used for compiled programs or documentation. 7. Click "Create release".

The created release will now be visible in the project's releases section, providing users with a convenient download option that includes all the assets.

Another important use-case for tags and releases is Continuous Integration/Continuous Deployment (CI/CD). Using tags, you can trigger automated processes that package and deploy your software. For example, creating a tag could trigger a pipeline that builds the software and pushes it to a production server.

Consider the following GitLab CI/CD configuration example for building and releasing a tagged version:

```
stages:
  - build
  - release

build:
  stage: build
  script:
    - make build
  only:
    - tags

release:
  stage: release
  script:
    - make release
  only:
    - tags
```

In this example, the pipeline consists of two stages: build and release. Both stages are restricted to run only when a Git tag is pushed, ensuring that only specific tagged commits trigger the build and release procedures.

By understanding and leveraging Git tags and releases, effectively managing and distributing versions of software becomes more streamlined. Through these tools, developers and teams can maintain a historical record of significant points in the project, automate deployments, and provide clear, accessible versions of software to users.

2.10 Git Workflows

A Git workflow is a prescribed way of using Git to manage and collaborate on a software project. Workflows define conventions for when and how branches are created, merged, and deleted, ensuring that all team members follow consistent practices. Several established workflows can be tailored to the needs of different teams and projects. Understanding these workflows is critical for efficiently managing and contributing to a project. This section will detail some commonly used Git workflows, along with their purposes and key commands needed to execute them.

Centralized Workflow

The Centralized Workflow is a straightforward pattern for integrating Git in a manner similar to the centralized version control systems. This workflow operates around a central repository where every participant pushes their changes. It is suitable for smaller teams or less complex projects.

Below are the essential steps and commands for the Centralized Workflow:

- **Clone the Central Repository**

```
git clone <central-repo-url>
```

- **Make Changes and Commit**

```
git add <file>
git commit -m "Describe changes"
```

- **Push to Central Repository**

```
git push origin main
```

If someone else has pushed to the central repository since you last pulled, you need to pull their changes first:

```
git pull origin main
```

Resolve any conflicts if necessary and then push your changes again.

Feature Branch Workflow

The Feature Branch Workflow introduces the concept of "feature branches." Instead of committing directly to the main branch, developers create separate branches for each new feature or bug fix. This practice keeps the main branch free of direct modifications, which can be crucial for larger projects.

Key commands and processes for the Feature Branch Workflow:

- **Create a Feature Branch**

```
git checkout -b feature-branch-name
```

- **Make Changes and Commit on the Feature Branch**

```
git add <file>
git commit -m "Describe feature changes"
```

- **Merge Feature Branch into Main Branch**

```
git checkout main
git pull origin main
git merge feature-branch-name
```

  Resolve any conflicts that arise during the merge and commit the resolved changes.

- **Push the Main Branch**

```
git push origin main
```

  Optionally, delete the feature branch from the local and remote repositories:

```
git branch -d feature-branch-name
git push origin --delete feature-branch-name
```

Gitflow Workflow

The Gitflow Workflow is a more sophisticated branching model, introduced by Vincent Driessen, which serves as a guide for working with multiple versioned releases and continuous integration. It involves two long-lived branches, main and develop, along with supporting branches such as feature, release, hotfix, and support. This workflow is particularly useful for projects with a continuous release cycle.

Main steps and commands for the Gitflow Workflow:

- **Develop Branch**

```
git checkout -b develop origin/main
```

- **Feature Branch**

```
git checkout -b feature-branch-name develop
git add <file>
git commit -m "Describe feature"
```

When complete, merge the feature branch back into develop:

```
git checkout develop
git merge feature-branch-name
```

Delete the feature branch as needed:

```
git branch -d feature-branch-name
```

- **Release Branch**

```
git checkout -b release-branch-name develop
```

Optionally update release-specific changes and merge into main and develop:

```
git checkout main
git merge release-branch-name
git tag -a v1.0 -m "Release 1.0"
git checkout develop
git merge release-branch-name
```

Delete the release branch:

```
git branch -d release-branch-name
```

- **Hotfix Branch**

```
git checkout -b hotfix-branch-name main
```

Apply the changes, commit, and merge back into both main and develop:

```
git add <file>
git commit -m "Fix critical issue"
git checkout main
git merge hotfix-branch-name
git tag -a v1.0.1 -m "Hotfix 1.0.1"
git checkout develop
git merge hotfix-branch-name
```

Delete the hotfix branch once merged:

```
git branch -d hotfix-branch-name
```

Forking Workflow

The Forking Workflow is commonly used in open source projects. Instead of a central repository, each contributor has their copy of the repository – called a fork – in which they perform their work before proposing changes to the main repository. This workflow is described by the following key steps:

- **Fork the Repository** on the platform like GitHub or GitLab.
- **Clone the Forked Repository**

```
git clone <forked-repo-url>
```

- **Add the Main Repository as a Remote**

```
git remote add upstream <central-repo-url>
```

- **Fetch Updates from Main Repository**

```
git fetch upstream
```

- **Create a Branch for a New Feature or Bug Fix**

```
git checkout -b feature-branch-name
```

- **Commit Changes** to the feature branch:

```
git add <file>
git commit -m "Describe changes"
```

- **Push the Branch to Your Fork**

```
git push origin feature-branch-name
```

- **Open a Pull Request** on the platform for merging your changes into the main repository.

Each workflow has its own strengths and can be selected based on the project's requirements and team preferences. Awareness and correct implementation of these workflows enable streamlined code management and enhanced collaboration.

2.11 Collaborating with Others Using Git

Collaboration in Git involves sharing and synchronizing changes with other developers. This process ensures that each team member can work on different parts of a project simultaneously without interfering with one another's work. Understanding the core concepts such as cloning, pushing, pulling, and managing pull requests is essential for efficient teamwork.

Cloning a Repository

One of the first steps in collaborating with others is to create a copy of the project repository. This is achieved using the git clone command, which creates a local copy of the remote repository.

```
git clone https://github.com/username/repository.git
```

The above command downloads the repository from the given URL and creates a directory named *repository* containing all its files and history.

Fetching and Pulling Changes

Once a repository has been cloned, staying updated with the changes made by others is crucial. This can be done using git fetch and git pull commands.

Fetching retrieves new data from the remote repository but does not merge it with the local repository:

```
git fetch origin
```

git fetch updates the remote-tracking branches, allowing one to review changes independently before merging.

Pulling retrieves data and immediately merges it into the current branch:

```
git pull origin main
```

This command fetches changes from the main branch of the remote repository named origin and updates the local branch simultaneously.

Pushing Changes

After making changes locally, sharing these updates with other team members involves pushing them to the remote repository. This keeps everyone aligned with the latest codebase.

```
git push origin main
```

The above command pushes local commits from the main branch to the main branch of the remote repository origin.

Branching for Collaboration

Creating branches is fundamental in collaborative workflows. A branch allows developers to work in isolation on specific features or fixes without disturbing the main codebase. For instance, to create and switch to a new branch:

```
git checkout -b feature-branch
```

This command creates a new branch named feature-branch and switches to it.

After making necessary changes, push the branch to the remote repository:

```
git push origin feature-branch
```

Handling Pull Requests

Pull requests (PRs) are a pivotal element in collaboration. They enable code review processes and allow team members to discuss changes before merging them into the main codebase.

To create a PR, push the branch to the remote repository as shown earlier, then use the web interface of platforms like GitLab or GitHub to open a pull request. The review process helps maintain code quality and catch potential issues early.

Code Review and Merging Pull Requests

Once a pull request is created, other team members can review the changes. Code review includes examining code for bugs, ensuring consistency with the project's code style, and suggesting improvements. When the review is completed and the changes are approved, the pull request can be merged.

Reviewers might provide feedback or request changes. Addressing this feedback is crucial for maintaining a healthy and effective collaboration workflow.

Resolving Merge Conflicts

Merge conflicts arise when changes in different branches intersect in incompatible ways. These conflicts must be resolved manually. Git provides the tools to address these conflicts efficiently. When a merge conflict happens, Git will mark the conflicting areas within the files:

```
<<<<<<< HEAD
content from the current branch
=======
content from the branch being merged
>>>>>>> branch-being-merged
```

Edit the file to resolve the conflicts, then add and commit the resolved files:

```
git add conflicted-file
git commit -m "Resolved merge conflict in conflicted-file"
```

Understanding these processes and adapting to a workflow that suits the team's needs is key to efficient collaboration using Git.

2.12 Using Git with GitLab

Integrating Git with GitLab provides a feature-rich platform for software development, facilitating collaboration and streamlining project management. The seamless interaction between Git and GitLab empowers developers to maintain code quality, engage in continuous integration and continuous deployment (CI/CD), track issues, and utilize a suite of robust development tools. This section offers comprehensive guidance on effectively using Git with GitLab, extending from basic setup to more sophisticated operations.

Creating a Repository in GitLab

To begin working with GitLab, first create a repository within the GitLab interface. Navigate to the GitLab dashboard and follow these steps:

- Click on the **New Project** button.
- Choose between creating a **blank project**, importing a project, or selecting a template.
- Provide the project **name** and **path**.
- Set the **visibility level** (public, internal, or private).
- Click on **Create project**.

Cloning a Repository

Once the repository is created, clone it to your local machine to begin working on it. Use the HTTPS or SSH URL provided by GitLab. The command for cloning a repository is as follows:

```
git clone <repository_url>
```

For example, to clone a repository named example-repo:

```
git clone https://gitlab.com/username/example-repo.git
```

After cloning, navigate into the project directory:

```
cd example-repo
```

Configuring Remote Repositories

In some cases, you may need to interact with multiple remote repositories. Use the git remote commands to manage such connections.

To list existing remotes:

```
git remote -v
```

To add a new remote named upstream:

```
git remote add upstream <another\_repository\_url>
```

Pushing Changes to GitLab

Once changes are committed to the local repository, push them to GitLab using:

```
git push origin <branch\_name>
```

Replace <branch_name> with the appropriate branch, typically main or master.

Setting Up CI/CD with GitLab

GitLab's built-in CI/CD tools enable automatic testing, building, and deploying code changes. Set up CI/CD by creating a .gitlab-ci.yml file at the root of your repository.

A basic .gitlab-ci.yml file might look like this:

```
stages:
  - build
  - test

build\_job:
  stage: build
  script:
    - echo "Compiling the code..."
    - make

test\_job:
  stage: test
```

```
script:
  - echo "Testing the code..."
  - make test
```

Managing Merge Requests

Merge Requests (MRs) are pivotal in GitLab for code review and collaboration. To create an MR:

- Push a feature branch to the repository.
- Navigate to the GitLab project.
- Click on the **Merge Requests** tab.
- Click on **New Merge Request**.
- Select the source and target branches.
- Provide a title and description.
- Click **Submit**.

Handling Issues and Boards

GitLab also offers comprehensive issue tracking and project management. To create an issue:

- Navigate to the **Issues** tab within your project.
- Click **New Issue**.
- Provide a title and detailed description.
- Assign it to a team member, if necessary.
- Click **Submit issue**.

Issues can be organized and tracked using boards, which are accessible under the **Boards** tab.

Integration with Additional Tools

GitLab integrates well with external tools and services, enhancing productivity. Some of these integrations include:

- **Slack and Microsoft Teams** for notifications.

- **JIRA** for advanced issue tracking.
- **Docker** for containerized builds and deployments.
- **Kubernetes** for managing containerized applications.

Using GitLab Runners

GitLab Runner is a build instance for running your CI/CD jobs. Register a runner with the following steps:

```
# Install GitLab Runner
sudo apt-get install gitlab-runner

# Register the runner
sudo gitlab-runner register
```

During registration, you will be prompted to provide the GitLab instance URL and an authentication token, which can be found under **Settings** > **CI/CD** in the GitLab project.

Monitoring and Analytics

GitLab provides monitoring and analytics to help track project performance. Utilize these features by navigating to the **Analytics** tab, which offers insights such as:

- **Code Quality** reports.
- **Pipeline** efficiency.
- **Deployment** statistics.
- **Issue tracking** metrics.

Learning to leverage Git with GitLab ensures a robust workflow, enhancing collaboration and maintaining high standards of code quality across development teams.

Chapter 3

Repository Management in GitLab

This chapter delves into the intricacies of managing repositories within GitLab. It covers the creation, cloning, and customization of repositories, including settings and access controls. The chapter provides a thorough understanding of branch management, merge requests, and code reviews. It also explores the use of GitLab's Web IDE, repository maintenance practices, and integration with webhooks. Additionally, you'll learn about importing/exporting projects and utilizing the graphical commit viewer, as well as the insights and analytics available for repository management.

3.1 Creating a Repository in GitLab

Creating a repository is a fundamental task in GitLab, serving as the foundational container where all your project files, version histories, and collaborative features reside. To initiate the creation process, navigate to your GitLab instance and ensure you have appropriate permissions to create new repositories within your namespace or group.

Step-by-Step Guide to Creating a Repository:

- **Navigate to the project's dashboard:** Begin by logging into your GitLab account. From the dashboard, click the "New Project" button, typically located near the top-right corner. This action directs you to the project creation wizard.

- **Repository Initialization:** GitLab offers various templates for initializing your repository. Select the "Create Blank Project" option for maximum customization, or choose from predefined templates if you need a specific setup.
- **Setting Project Details:** Specify the project details:
  - **Project Name:** Provide a concise and descriptive name for your repository.
  - **Project Slug:** This is auto-generated based on the project name and forms the URL for accessing the repository.
  - **Project Description:** Optionally, include a brief description of the project's purpose and goals. This is helpful for collaborators and stakeholders to understand the project at a glance.
  - **Visibility Level:** Choose an appropriate visibility setting ("Private", "Internal", or "Public") to control access to your repository. **Private** restricts access to project members, **Internal** grants access to any authenticated user within the GitLab instance, and **Public** allows unrestricted access.
- **Repository Configuration:** You can enable or disable specific repository features according to your project's needs:
  - **Initialize with a README:** Including a README at initialization provides a space to document the repository's primary information and guidelines.
  - **Add .gitignore:** This file specifies untracked files that Git should ignore. GitLab offers templates for various development environments.
  - **Choose a License:** Including a license determines what others can and cannot do with your code. GitLab provides several templates based on common licenses like MLGPL, MIT, Apache 2.0, etc.
- **Finalizing the Repository Creation:** Click the "Create Project" button to finalize your setup. Once created, GitLab redirects you to the new repository's main page, where you can start populating it with code and other resources.

Managing the Newly Created Repository:

Immediately after creation, the repository is empty (barring any optional initializations like a README). Here's how to proceed:

- **Cloning the Repository:** Clone the repository to your local development environment to begin working on it. The clone URL can be found on the repository's main page. Execute the following command using the HTTP(S) or SSH link provided by GitLab:

```
git clone <repository-url>
```

- **Adding Local Work to the Repository:** After cloning, you can add files and directories to the local repository. Stage these changes using:

```
git add <file1> <file2> ... <directory>
```

  Commit these changes with a relevant message:

```
git commit -m "Initial commit with project setup"
```

  Push the changes to the remote repository:

```
git push origin main
```

- **Configuring Important Repository Settings:** Beyond initial creation, refining settings ensures the repository operates inline with project protocols:
  - **Branch Protections:** Configure branch protections to prevent unauthorized changes to important branches (e.g., main or master). This involves defining rules to restrict direct pushes and enforce merge request approvals.
  - **Webhooks:** Set up webhooks to integrate with other tools and services. Webhooks allow GitLab to send real-time data to external services in response to events like pushes, issues, or merge requests.
  - **Repository Members and Permissions:** Add collaborators by navigating to the members section. Assign appropriate roles such as Guest, Reporter, Developer, Maintainer, or Owner to ensure proper access control.

Verification and Utilization:

Confirm proper repository setup by inspecting the repository page. Verify that the README (if initialized), branches, and initial commit reflect as expected. Utilize GitLab's interface for operations like:

- Viewing and managing files via the repository file browser.
- Monitoring project activity through the activity feed.
- Creating issues and milestones to track project progress.

Creating a repository in GitLab is a crucial step towards efficient project management in a collaborative environment, laying the groundwork for structured, version-controlled development. By setting the parameters correctly and understanding the subsequent actions, the repository becomes a central hub for ongoing project coordination and version control practices.

3.2 Cloning a Repository

Cloning a repository is a fundamental operation in Git and GitLab, enabling developers to create a local copy of a remote repository on their machines. This operation is essential for contributing to projects, whether through coding, testing, or documentation.

To clone a GitLab repository, follow these steps:

1. Navigate to the Repository: Open the GitLab instance in your web browser and go to the project page of the repository you wish to clone.

2. Copy the Repository URL: Locate the "Clone" button typically found at the top of the repository page. Click on it, and you will be presented with several options such as cloning via HTTPS and SSH. Choose the appropriate URL based on your authentication method:

- **HTTPS URL:** Suitable for users who prefer simplified authentication using usernames and passwords.
- **SSH URL:** Recommended for users who set up SSH keys for enhanced security.

Copy the URL to your clipboard.

3. Clone the Repository Locally: Open a terminal or command prompt on your local machine. Navigate to the directory where you want to clone the repository. Execute the git clone command followed by the copied URL. For example, using HTTPS,

```
git clone https://gitlab.com/username/projectname.git
```

or using SSH,

```
git clone git@gitlab.com:username/projectname.git
```

This command initializes a new Git repository in a directory named projectname, fetches all repository data, and creates a working copy of the latest version.

Verifying the Cloning Operation: Once the cloning process is complete, navigate into the repository directory:

```
cd projectname
```

Here, you can inspect the cloned repository by listing its files or checking the Git configuration:

```
ls
git config --list
```

Common Issues and Solutions: Several issues may arise during the cloning process:

- **Authentication Failures:** Ensure that your credentials (username/password for HTTPS or SSH key for SSH) are correctly configured. For HTTPS, Git will prompt for the username and password. For SSH, ensure your public key is added to your GitLab account.
- **Permission Denied (publickey):** This error is common in SSH cloning. Verify that your SSH key is properly added to the SSH-agent and uploaded to GitLab. Use the following command to add your key to the SSH-agent:

  ```
  ssh-add ~/.ssh/id_rsa
  ```

Advanced Cloning Options: Git provides additional options during the cloning process for specialized needs:

Shallow Clone: Cloning a repository with a large history can be time-consuming. To clone only the latest few commits, use the –depth parameter:

```
git clone --depth 10 https://gitlab.com/username/projectname.git
```

This command clones only the last 10 commits, significantly reducing cloning time and disk usage.

Single Branch Clone: By default, git clone fetches all branches. To clone only a specific branch, use the -b option:

```
git clone -b branchname --single-branch https://gitlab.com/username/projectname.git
```

Template Directory: To control the directory structure of the cloned repository, use the –template option followed by the path to your template directory:

```
git clone --template=<template-directory> https://gitlab.com/username/projectname.
    git
```

This option allows custom hooks, configurations, and other template files to be copied over to the cloned repository.

Cloning with Specific Authentication: In some scenarios, cloning may require specific credentials for access. Git offers ways to handle such cases:

- **Credential Cache:** Temporarily caches credentials in memory for subsequent Git operations:

```
git config --global credential.helper cache
```

- **Personal Access Tokens:** Used for HTTPS cloning when two-factor authentication (2FA) is enabled on your GitLab account. Generate a token in GitLab and use it instead of your password.

Post-Cloning Actions: After successfully cloning a repository, you might want to perform several routine actions, such as:

- **Setting Up Remote Tracking:** Ensure that your local branches track the corresponding remote branches:

```
git branch --set-upstream-to=origin/branchname
```

- **Fetching Remote Changes:** Regularly update your local repository with changes from the remote repository:

```
git fetch origin
```

- **Creating Local Branches:** Create local feature branches from the main branch to isolate your work:

```
git checkout -b new-feature-branch
```

Output from a successful cloning operation typically looks like the following:

```
Cloning into 'projectname'...
remote: Enumerating objects: 88, done.
remote: Counting objects: 100% (88/88), done.
remote: Compressing objects: 100% (63/63), done.
remote: Total 88 (delta 20), reused 0 (delta 0), pack-reused 0
Receiving objects: 100% (88/88), done.
Resolving deltas: 100% (20/20), done.
```

Proper repository cloning ensures that you have a reliable and up-to-date workspace aligned with the project's remote repository, enabling an efficient and collaborative development process.

3.3 Repository Settings and Customization

Customization of repository settings in GitLab is crucial for tailoring the repository to fit specific project requirements. The settings include visibility levels, project features, repository files, and integrations with external tools. Effective customization enhances the overall management and usability of the repository, aligning it with the project's workflow and security needs.

Visibility Levels: Each repository in GitLab can have one of three visibility levels: Private, Internal, and Public.

- *Private* repositories are accessible only to members explicitly granted access.
- *Internal* repositories are accessible to any authenticated user on the GitLab instance.
- *Public* repositories are visible to anyone with internet access.

Setting the visibility level is crucial for controlling who can view and clone the repository. It is often set during the repository creation process but can be modified later through the repository's settings page.

Project Features: GitLab allows customization of several project features such as issues, merge requests, and CI/CD pipelines. These features can be enabled or disabled based on the project requirements.

Navigate to the repository settings and select or deselect the relevant features.

Example:

- Enabling **Issues** allows the project to track bugs, enhancements, and other tasks.
- Enabling **Merge Requests** facilitates code review workflows.
- Enabling **CI/CD Pipelines** allows the automation of code testing and deployment processes.

Repository Files: GitLab supports the customization of repository-level files such as the README, LICENSE, and .gitignore.

- **README:** The README file is essential for documenting the repository's purpose, setup instructions, and usage guidelines. GitLab supports Markdown for styling README files.
- **LICENSE:** Adding a LICENSE file specifies the legal limitations and permissions for using, modifying, and distributing the code.
- **.gitignore:** This file lists the patterns for files and directories to be ignored by Git, preventing them from being tracked in the repository.

To add or modify these files, simply create or edit the corresponding file in the root of your repository. For example, to add a 'LICENSE' file, navigate to the root directory of the repository, and create a LICENSE file with the desired content.

```
echo "MIT License" > LICENSE
echo "Permission is hereby granted, free of charge..." >> LICENSE
```

Integrations: GitLab supports integration with various external tools to enhance repository functionality, such as continuous integration systems, deployment environments, and third-party APIs. Integrations can be configured through the settings page under the **Integrations** section.

For example, to integrate a Slack channel for notifications:

- Navigate to the repository settings.
- Select **Integrations**.

- Choose **Slack notifications**.
- Provide the necessary Slack webhook URL and configure your preferences.
- Save the changes.

```
Webhook URL: https://hooks.slack.com/services/T00000000/B00000000/
    XXXXXXXXXXXXXXXXXXXXXXXX
Notify Only Broken Pipelines: true
Channel: #project-updates
```

Custom Badges: Adding custom badges to the repository's README can provide visual indicators of build statuses, test coverage, and other metrics. GitLab provides an option to add badges directly through repository settings.

To add a badge for build status:

- Navigate to the repository settings.
- Select **CI / CD**.
- Click on **Badges**.
- Click on **New Badge**.
- Fill out the required fields, such as *Badge Image URL* and *Link URL*.
- Save the changes.

Example:

```
Badge Image URL: https://gitlab.example.com/namespace/project/badges/master/pipeline.svg
Link URL: https://gitlab.example.com/namespace/project/pipelines
```

Repository Protection: Protecting branches and tags is essential for maintaining the integrity of critical parts of the repository. GitLab allows for branch and tag protection under the **Repository** settings.

- **Protected Branches:** Limits who can push, force-push, and delete branches.
- **Protected Tags:** Limits who can create or delete tags.

To protect a branch:

- Navigate to the repository settings.

- Select **Repository**.
- Click on **Protected Branches**.
- Specify the branch name or pattern.
- Configure the allowed actions and roles.
- Save the changes.

```
Branch: master
Allowed to push: Maintainers
Allowed to merge: Developers + Maintainers
```

Webhooks: Webhooks enable real-time notifications and can trigger automated actions when specific events occur in the repository. To add a webhook:

- Navigate to the repository settings.
- Select **Webhooks**.
- Click on **Add webhook**.
- Enter the *URL* to which the payload will be sent.
- Select the events that will trigger the webhook.
- Save the changes.

Example:

```
URL: https://example.com/webhook
Trigger Events: Push events, Merge request events
```

Setting up and customizing these various aspects of a GitLab repository allows for fine-grained control and robust project management, adhering to the required governance, functionality, and security standards tailored for your specific needs.

3.4 Access Controls and Permissions

Access controls and permissions in GitLab are essential for managing and securing the collaborative environment of a repository. Proper configuration ensures that team members have the appropriate level of access to perform their tasks while safeguarding the repository from unauthorized changes. GitLab uses a combination of roles, permissions, and visibility settings to control access.

Roles and Permissions

GitLab defines several roles that can be assigned to users within a project or group. Each role comes with a specific set of permissions. Below is a list of the primary roles available in GitLab:

- **Guest:** Can view the repository and raise issues. Limited to read-only access.
- **Reporter:** In addition to guest permissions, can create and comment on issues, view pipelines, and view commit details.
- **Developer:** Has write access to the repository. Can push code, create merge requests, view pipeline logs, and create tags.
- **Maintainer:** Has extensive control over the repository. Can manage project settings, create and delete branches, enable or disable CI/CD, and more.
- **Owner:** Exclusive to groups, has full administrative access. Can manage all aspects of the group, including adding/removing members and changing visibility settings.

Roles can be assigned at the project level or the group level. When assigned at the group level, the permissions apply to all projects within the group unless explicitly overridden.

Visibility Settings

GitLab projects can have different visibility levels, determining who can access the repository without explicit membership:

- **Private:** Only members can view or interact with the project. This setting is used to restrict access to authorized users only.
- **Internal:** Only authenticated users within the GitLab instance can access the project, making it suitable for internal collaboration within an organization.
- **Public:** Anyone, including unauthenticated users, can access the project. Ideal for open-source projects where broad visibility is desired.

Setting Up Access Controls

Configuring access controls begins with navigating to the project's settings. To do this, follow these steps:

1. Go to the project page in GitLab.
2. Click on the *Settings* menu and select *Members*.
3. Add members by entering their username or email and selecting the appropriate role.
4. Click *Add to project* to apply the changes.

It's important to periodically review the list of project members and their roles to ensure that access levels remain appropriate as the project evolves.

Protected Branches

Protected branches are a critical feature for enforcing access controls on important branches, such as main or master. Protection can prevent direct pushes and force-pushes, ensuring changes undergo code review and approval. To protect a branch:

1. Navigate to the project page.
2. Go to *Settings* → *Repository*.
3. Scroll to the *Protected Branches* section.
4. Select the branch you wish to protect from the dropdown.
5. Choose the desired protection settings, such as *Maintainers can push* or *No one can push*, and click *Protect*.

Developers can still propose changes via merge requests, but direct modifications to protected branches require higher-level permissions.

Code Owners

In addition to protected branches, GitLab supports defining *Code Owners* within a repository. Code owners are responsible for specific files or directories and must approve merge requests that modify their areas of the codebase. This feature helps distribute code review responsibilities. To define code owners, create a CODEOWNERS file in the repository:

```
# Each line is a file pattern followed by one or more owners
# File patterns can be exact or wildcard-based
# Owners can be users or groups
docs/* @doc-maintainers # Group owner for all documentation files
*.js @frontend-devs # Group owner for all JavaScript files
lib/core @johnsmith # User owner for the core library
```

The CODEOWNERS file follows a straightforward syntax, where each line assigns owners to file patterns. Upon submitting a merge request affecting owned files, GitLab will require approval from the code owners before merging.

Managing Group-level Permissions

Groups in GitLab offer a way to manage multiple projects collectively, with permissions cascading from the group level to the project level. To manage group-level permissions:

1. Go to the group page.
2. Click on *Group settings* → *Members*.
3. Add or remove members and assign appropriate roles.

Members of a group automatically inherit permissions for all projects within the group, simplifying permissions management for large teams working across multiple repositories.

Implementing proper access controls and permissions is fundamental to maintaining the integrity, security, and efficiency of your projects in GitLab. Through the use of roles, protected branches, code owners, and group-level management, GitLab provides comprehensive tools to manage user access and responsibilities effectively.

3.5 Branch Management

In software development, branching serves as a powerful tool, enabling developers to diverge from the main codebase to work on features or fixes without disrupting the primary workflow. GitLab offers robust tools to manage these branches effectively.

To create a branch within an existing GitLab repository, use one of the following methods:

Creating a branch via Git command line:

```
git checkout -b new-feature-branch
git push origin new-feature-branch
```

GitLab's web interface also provides an intuitive way to create branches:

1. Navigate to the repository. 2. Click on the "Repository" menu. 3. Select "Branches". 4. Click the "New Branch" button. 5. Enter the branch name and choose the branch source. 6. Click "Create Branch".

Proper branch naming conventions improve readability and collaboration. Common conventions include:

- feature/*description* for new features.
- bugfix/*description* for bug fixes.
- hotfix/*description* for critical hotfixes.
- release/*version* for release branches.

After branch creation, merging, and ensuring synchronization with the main branch is imperative. GitLab supports various merge strategies, including Fast-Forward, Merge Commit, and Squash Merge. The choice of strategy should be aligned with the team's workflow and repository guidelines.

Using the Fast-Forward strategy:

```
git checkout main
git pull origin main
git merge --ff-only new-feature-branch
```

The Merge Commit strategy, which preserves history:

```
git checkout main
git pull origin main
git merge --no-ff new-feature-branch
```

The Squash Merge strategy, which condenses commit history:

```
git checkout main
git pull origin main
git merge --squash new-feature-branch
```

Visualizing branch history can be done using GitLab's graphical commit viewer. Accessible from the repository's "Network" tab, it provides a clear view of all branches, commits, and their relationships. This visualization aids in understanding the project's progression and identifying potential integration issues.

Setting branch protection rules is fundamental in enforcing workflow policies. Protected branches in GitLab prevent force pushes, deletions, and unauthorized merges. To configure branch protection:

1. Navigate to the repository settings. 2. Select "Repository" and then "Protected Branches". 3. Specify the branch name. 4. Define protection levels:

- *No one can push.*
- *Developers + Maintainers (roles with merge/push access).*
- *No one can merge.*

5. Click "Protect".

Implementing Continuous Integration (CI) practices in branch management improves code quality and deployment efficiency. GitLab CI/CD pipelines are configured using the .gitlab-ci.yml file. An example CI/CD pipeline for branch testing:

```
stages:
  - test
  - build
  - deploy

test_branch:
  stage: test
  script:
    - echo "Running tests"
    - npm test
  only:
    - branches

build_branch:
  stage: build
  script:
    - echo "Building application"
    - npm run build
  only:
    branches

deploy_branch:
  stage: deploy
  script:
    - echo "Deploying application"
    - npm run deploy
  only:
    - branches
```

This pipeline defines three stages: test, build, and deploy, which execute only on branches. The test_branch job runs tests, the build_branch job builds the application, and the deploy_branch job deploys the application.

Regular branch cleanup is crucial for maintaining repository hygiene. Stale branches should be reviewed and deleted when no longer needed. To list and delete merged branches via Git:

```
git branch --merged
git branch -d branch-name
```

For remote branch cleanup, the commands are:

```
git push origin --delete branch-name
```

Integrating these practices into your branch management workflow will enhance collaboration, reduce conflicts, and streamline the development process.

3.6 Merge Requests and Code Reviews

Merge requests (MRs) are fundamental components of collaborative development workflows in GitLab. They enable team members to merge their branches into a target branch, typically the main branch, after review and approval. MRs are instrumental in maintaining code quality, facilitating collaboration, and ensuring that changes do not introduce regressions or bugs. Here, we will examine the process of creating and managing merge requests and the best practices for code reviews within GitLab.

Creating a Merge Request

To create a merge request in GitLab, follow these steps: 1. Navigate to your project's repository. 2. Click on the "Merge Requests" tab on the left sidebar. 3. Click on the "New merge request" button. 4. Select the source branch that contains your changes and the target branch into which you want to merge the changes. 5. Preview the changes, add a suitable title, description, and any related issue numbers or labels. 6. Assign reviewers and set the desired merge options. 7. Click the "Submit merge request" button.

```
# Example of command line MR creation using GitLab CLI (GLab)
$ glab mr create --source my-feature-branch --target main --title "Add new feature" --
    description "This merge request adds a new feature to the project."
```

Reviewing a Merge Request

When a merge request is created, the assigned reviewers are notified. Reviewers should examine the proposed changes for correctness, style, efficiency, and adherence to project guidelines. They can provide feedback, request changes, or approve the MR. The review process can be managed using the following steps:

1. Open the merge request by clicking its title from the "Merge Requests" tab. 2. Review the changes by examining the diff view, which highlights additions and deletions. 3. Add comments directly on specific lines of code or in the general discussion section. 4. Use the "Request changes" button if modifications are needed, or approve the MR if everything looks good.

Resolving Merge Conflicts

Merge conflicts occur when changes in the source branch conflict with the target branch. GitLab provides tools to resolve these conflicts:

1. Upon detecting a merge conflict, GitLab informs the user. 2. Click on the "Resolve conflicts" button in the merge request. 3. Use the built-in conflict resolution editor to manually reconcile the differences between the conflicting files. 4. Mark the conflicts as resolved and commit the changes.

Best Practices for Merge Requests and Code Reviews

To ensure effective and efficient merge requests and code reviews, consider the following best practices:

1. **Small, Focused Changes:** Keep merge requests small and focused on a single feature or bug fix to simplify the review process. 2. **Descriptive Titles and Descriptions:** Use clear and descriptive titles and descriptions for merge requests to convey the purpose and scope of the changes. 3. **Automated Tests:** Ensure that automated tests are run for each merge request to catch errors and regressions early. 4. **Regular Reviews:** Encourage regular and timely reviews to maintain a smooth workflow and prevent bottlenecks. 5. **Constructive Feedback:** Provide constructive and respectful feedback to support collaborative improvement of the codebase. 6. **Use Labels and Milestones:** Organize merge requests using labels and milestones to signal their priority, type, and relevance to specific project goals.

Integrating CI/CD with Merge Requests

GitLab's continuous integration and continuous deployment (CI/CD) pipelines can be integrated with merge requests to automate testing and deployment processes. By defining a pipeline in a '.gitlab-ci.yml' file, you can automate building, testing, and deploying code whenever a merge request is created or updated.

Example '.gitlab-ci.yml' for running tests on MR creation:

```
stages:
  - test

test:
  stage: test
  script:
    - make test
  only:
    - merge_requests
```

```
# Output of a successful pipeline execution for a merge request
Job ID: 1234
Stage: test
Status: Passed
Duration: 2m 15s
```

Extending the power of merge requests with integrated CI/CD ensures that every change is vetted for quality and performance, aligning with DevOps practices for continuous improvement.

3.7 Using GitLab's Web IDE

The Web Integrated Development Environment (IDE) provided by GitLab offers a powerful tool for developers to write, review, and manage their code directly from the browser. This section describes the primary functionalities of the Web IDE, its advantages, and step-by-step instructions on utilizing this feature effectively.

GitLab's Web IDE is designed to streamline the development workflow by allowing users to:

- Edit files directly from the repository without cloning it locally.
- Review and resolve merge requests.
- Utilize syntax highlighting and linting.
- Execute code snippets and debug issues.
- Use extensions and tools integrated within GitLab.

Accessing the Web IDE

To start using the Web IDE, navigate to your GitLab repository. Locate the Repository menu and select Files. Once you are in the file list view, click on the Web IDE button, typically positioned at the upper right part of the screen. This action opens the Web IDE in a new tab or window, displaying the repository's directory structure on the left and the file editor in the central pane.

Editing Files

In the Web IDE, you can edit any file within the repository. Click on a file from the directory structure to load it in the editor. The Web IDE supports various programming languages and provides features like syntax highlighting, auto-completion, and code folding, which enhance the editing experience.

```
def hello_world():
    print("Hello, World!")

hello_world()
```

After making changes, save the file by clicking the disk icon beside the file name or using keyboard shortcuts (e.g., Ctrl + S or Cmd + S).

Committing Changes

Once edits are made, changes can be committed to the repository. Below the editor pane, there is a commit area where you can add a commit message, select the target branch, and even amend the previous commit. To commit your changes:

1. Enter a descriptive commit message in the Commit message field.
2. Choose the branch where the changes will be committed. The default branch is usually main or master, but you can specify any branch or create a new one.
3. Optionally, stage specific changes by selecting checkboxes next to modified files.
4. Click the Commit button to finalize your changes.

Working with Merge Requests

The Web IDE facilitates seamless creation and management of merge requests. After committing changes to a non-default branch, you are typically prompted to create a merge request. This prompt appears at the bottom of the IDE interface.

Reviewing merge requests within the Web IDE allows developers to view code diffs, add comments, suggest changes, and resolve conflicts. To streamline this process:

- Open a merge request in the Web IDE by navigating to the Merge Requests tab of your GitLab project.
- Select the merge request you want to work on and click Open in Web IDE.
- Review code changes, add inline comments, and make any necessary edits.

Exploring Built-in Terminal

The Web IDE includes a built-in terminal, providing a command-line interface for executing commands on the repository. This feature is particularly useful for running tests, building applications, or utilizing command-line tools integrated with your project. To access the terminal, click the Terminal tab located at the bottom of the IDE interface.

```
$ ls
README.md  app.py  requirements.txt  tests
$ python3 app.py
Hello, World!
```

Utilizing Extensions and Tools

GitLab's Web IDE supports extensions and additional tools to enhance the development experience. These extensions can range from linters, debuggers, to formatters, and they work out of the box or with minimal configuration. For instance, enabling ESLint for JavaScript code can significantly improve code quality by automatically identifying and fixing common issues.

```
const greeting = "Hello, World!";
console.log(greeting);
```

Advantages of Using the Web IDE

Utilizing GitLab's Web IDE offers several advantages, especially for distributed teams or developers who prefer a quick, browser-based coding environment:

- Immediate availability without the need for local setup.
- Consistent environment across different devices and locations.
- Simplified workflow for minor edits, making changes directly in the repository.
- Integrated features like merge requests and terminals, facilitating an all-in-one development experience.

Overall, the Web IDE is a robust tool within GitLab's ecosystem, empowering developers to efficiently manage and develop their codebases directly from the web.

3.8 Repository Maintenance

Proper maintenance of repositories is critical to ensure streamlined development workflows, security, and performance. GitLab offers multiple features and best practices to keep repositories well-maintained. This section covers the key aspects of repository maintenance, including performing regular clean-up operations, managing large files, and ensuring repository hygiene.

Regular Clean-Up Operations

Regular clean-up operations help in maintaining the repository size and structure. GitLab provides functionalities to remove unused branches, tags, and history. To delete a remote branch, use the following command:

```
git push origin --delete <branch_name>
```

Similarly, to delete a tag from the remote repository:

```
git push origin --delete <tag_name>
```

Make sure to also prune local references to deleted branches and tags using:

```
git fetch --prune
```

Managing Large Files

Large files can significantly slow down repository operations and affect performance. It is advisable to use .gitignore to prevent large files from being committed:

```
# .gitignore
*.log
*.tmp
large_file.zip
```

For projects that need to handle large files, consider using Git Large File Storage (LFS). First, install Git LFS:

```
git lfs install
```

Track specific file types:

```
git lfs track "*.psd"
```

Commit and push changes as usual:

```
git add .gitattributes
git commit -m "track PSD files via LFS"
git push origin main
```

Ensuring Repository Hygiene

Maintaining repository hygiene involves adhering to coding standards and ensuring consistency in the project. GitLab CI/CD pipelines can automate code linting and formatting checks. Create a .gitlab-ci.yml file:

```
stages:
  - lint

lint_job:
  stage: lint
  script:
    - npm install # install necessary tools
    - npm run lint
```

Additionally, use the CODEOWNERS file to specify which individuals are responsible for particular parts of the codebase:

```
# CODEOWNERS
* @project-owner
docs/* @documentation-team
src/* @dev-team
```

Repository Optimization

GitLab repositories can be optimized by periodically running git gc (garbage collection). This commands cleans up unnecessary files and optimizes the local repository:

```
git gc --prune=now
```

Running the above command once in a while ensures that the repository remains efficient and performs adequately. Consider automating this process through scheduled jobs in GitLab's CI/CD pipeline:

```
stages:
  - cleanup

cleanup_job:
  stage: cleanup
  script:
    - git gc --prune=now
  only:
```

```
  - schedules
```

Managing Repository Security

Regularly auditing the repository for security vulnerabilities and ensuring secure coding practices is crucial. GitLab's Dependency Scanning and Container Scanning features can be integrated into the CI/CD pipeline:

```
include:
  - template: Dependency-Scanning.gitlab-ci.yml
  - template: Container-Scanning.gitlab-ci.yml
```

Additionally, configure branch protection to prevent force pushes or changes to important branches:

```
# Protect branches via GitLab UI
Settings > Repository > Protected Branches > Add Rule
```

Set the desired branch protection rules, ensuring only authorized users can push or merge changes.

Regularly maintaining a repository involves strategic clean-up operations, managing file sizes, ensuring coding standards, optimizing repository operations, and securing the codebase. These practices contribute significantly to the overall health and performance of the repository, making collaboration and development more efficient.

3.9 Importing and Exporting Projects

Efficient handling of project data transfer is pivotal in collaborative and scalable software development. GitLab provides robust mechanisms for importing and exporting projects, facilitating seamless migration and backup processes. This section delves into these functionalities with a precise focus on practical implementations.

Importing projects into GitLab can be done using various methods, including direct import from other version control systems, transferring from another GitLab instance, or using a repository URL. The import functionality is designed to be user-friendly while preserving the integrity and history of the data.

Exporting projects serves two primary purposes: backup and migration. GitLab's export feature ensures that all repository contents, metadata, and associated resources are encapsulated in a manner conducive to restoration or transfer to another instance or version control system.

To illustrate, consider the following scenarios and the corresponding steps for importing and exporting projects:

- **Importing from GitHub:**
  Navigate to your GitLab instance and proceed to the import options. GitLab offers a well-integrated GitHub importer, allowing for the transfer of repositories, issues, pull requests, and other relevant data.

  1. Login to your GitLab instance.
  2. Navigate to New Project and select Import project.
  3. Choose GitHub as the source.
  4. Authenticate with your GitHub credentials and grant GitLab the necessary permissions.
  5. Select the repositories you wish to import and initiate the process.

- **Using a Repository URL:**
  Another method involves cloning an existing repository using its URL, which is particularly useful for repositories hosted outside GitHub.

  1. On the GitLab dashboard, navigate to New Project.
  2. Select Import project followed by Repo by URL.
  3. Enter the URL of the repository you wish to import and provide a suitable project name.
  4. Click on Create project to start the import process.

These import methods ensure the fidelity and integrity of the transferred data, maintaining the commit history and structure of the original repository.

Example: Importing with Command-Line Tools

```
# Clone the repository from an external source
git clone https://github.com/user/repository.git

# Change directory to the cloned repository
cd repository

# Add a new remote for the GitLab instance
git remote add gitlab https://gitlab.com/your-username/new-repository.git

# Push the repository to GitLab
git push -u gitlab master
```

In terms of exporting projects, GitLab facilitates the generation of an export archive containing essential elements of a project. This archive can be used for restoration or transfer to another instance.

- **Generating an Export:**
  1. Navigate to the project you wish to export.
  2. Go to Settings and select General.
  3. Scroll down to the Advanced section and click on Export project.
  4. Wait for the export process to complete and download the generated archive.

The export archive encompasses more than just the repository content. It includes:

- Repository data and Git history.
- Issues, merge requests, and associated discussions.
- Project settings and metadata.
- CI/CD pipelines and configurations.

```
Export File Structure:
- repository/
- issues/
- merge_requests/
- project.json
- ci_cd/
```

Example: Using the API for Export

```
# Initiate the export request
curl --request POST --header "PRIVATE-TOKEN: <your_access_token>" \
    "https://gitlab.example.com/api/v4/projects/:id/export"

# Fetch the status and download the export
curl --header "PRIVATE-TOKEN: <your_access_token>" \
    "https://gitlab.example.com/api/v4/projects/:id/export/download"
```

The import and export functionalities of GitLab are powerful tools for project mobility and integrity assurance, enabling efficient project management and continuity in various deployment scenarios.

3.10 Using GitLab's Graphical Commit Viewer

The Graphical Commit Viewer in GitLab provides developers and project managers with an intuitive way to navigate and analyze the commit history of a repository. This tool is essential for understanding the evolution of a project, identifying changes, and collaborating more effectively. Its graphical interface allows for a comparably straightforward inspection of the repository's commit sequence, including details such as commit messages, authors, and time stamps.

To access the Graphical Commit Viewer in a GitLab project repository, navigate to the repository's main page, click on the **Repository** tab in the left sidebar, and select **Commits**. This action displays a list of commits, but by clicking on the **Graph** option, you will transition to the graphical representation of the commit history.

The Graphical Commit Viewer consists of several components designed to facilitate comprehensive commit analysis. The main components include the graph structure, commit details, and branch indicators.

- **Graph Structure**: The graph structure visualizes the branching and merging of commits. Vertical lines represent branches, while dots on these lines represent individual commits. The connectivity between dots illustrates the commit history and how branches diverge and converge.

- **Commit Details**: Clicking on a commit dot reveals the commit details, such as the author's name, commit message, associated files, and diffs. These details are essential for understanding the nature of the changes introduced by the commit.

- **Branch Indicators**: Labels attached to branches indicate branch names and help differentiate between various branches. Tags and other references might also be displayed, providing additional context.

To illustrate the usages, suppose we have a repository with a complex branching structure. The graphical representation will immediately highlight points of divergence where new branches were created and points of convergence where branches were merged back into the mainline. For each commit node, the branching lines help trace the origin and path of code changes across different branches.

```
* 5321abc - Merge branch 'feature-x' into 'main' (1 hour ago) <John Doe>
|\
| * 31c8734 - Add feature X implementation (2 hours ago) <Jane Smith>
|/
* d3b8cd6 - Merge branch 'documentation' into 'main' (5 hours ago) <Alice Brown>
|\
| * 907bdf5 - Update README with usage instructions (6 hours ago) <Bob Stone>
|/
* 9a1c0ef - Initial commit (10 hours ago) <Alice Brown>
```

In the example above, the commit 5321abc represents a merge commit from the feature-x branch into the main branch. Similarly, d3b8cd6 represents a merge from the documentation branch. Each branch's progression and eventual merge points are clearly depicted, aiding in comprehension of how the codebase evolved.

When analyzing a commit, the Graph Viewer allows you to explore the diffs associated with the commit. Diffs are highlighted changes between the current commit and its parent. This visualization of changes makes it easier to review code and identify issues or unintended modifications. The following is an example of how GitLab presents diffs.

```
diff --git a/src/main.py b/src/main.py
index 5f3ef58..d81c6f7 100644
--- a/src/main.py
+++ b/src/main.py
@@ -1,5 +1,6 @@
 def main():
     print("Hello, World!")
+    print("Feature X added")
```

The diff output clearly shows the addition of a new line in src/main.py, where the message Feature X added was included. This granular detail assists in code reviews, ensuring that all changes are thoroughly examined before integration.

Utilizing the Graphical Commit Viewer effectively requires familiarity with its features and navigation options. Some navigational aids include:

- **Zooming and Scrolling**: Use zooming options to get a closer or broader view of the commit history. Scrolling allows movement through the timeline of commits.
- **Filtering Commits**: Filter commits by author, date, or commit message keywords to isolate specific changes or periods of interest.

- **Searching**: The search functionality helps locate specific commits based on various criteria such as commit hash, author, or message content.

By adeptly leveraging the Graphical Commit Viewer in GitLab, teams can enhance their repository management practices. It simplifies the complexity of branch management and clarifies the contributions over the codebase's history, contributing to more effective collaboration and code quality maintenance.

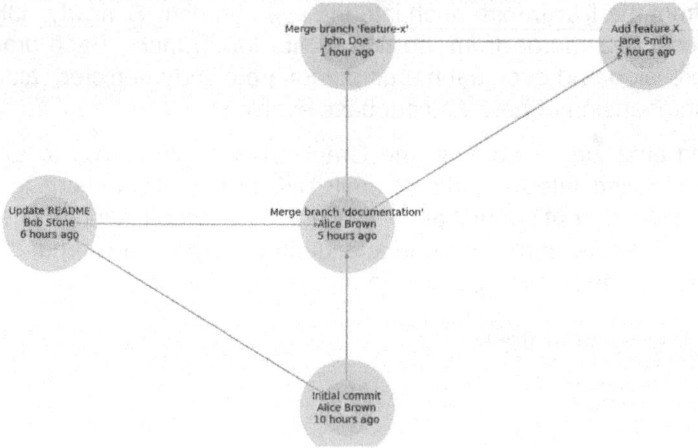

3.11 Webhook Integration

Webhooks in GitLab provide a mechanism for integrating your GitLab repository with other systems and services. They allow you to trigger predefined actions or notify external services when specific events occur within your repository. This section explores the process of setting up and managing webhooks in GitLab, detailing configuration steps, types of events supported, and best practices for using webhooks effectively.

To begin integrating webhooks, navigate to your repository in GitLab, then go to Settings and click on Webhooks. Here, you will find the interface for adding and managing webhooks.

Creating a Webhook: 1. **URL:** This is the endpoint to which GitLab will send payloads. This should be the URL of the service you intend to notify. 2. **Trigger Events:** Specify which events trigger the webhook. Options include push events, issues events, merge request events, tag push events, and more. You can select one or multiple events based on your requirements. 3. **Secret Token:** For added security, you can specify a secret token. This token will be included in the header of each webhook request so that the receiving service can verify the source of the request.

The following is an example of configuring a webhook to trigger on push events:

```
curl --request POST --header "PRIVATE-TOKEN: <your_access_token>" \
  --data "url=http://example.com/webhook&push_events=true&token=secret_token"
      \
  "https://gitlab.example.com/api/v4/projects/:id/hooks"
```

Upon receiving an event notification, the specified endpoint will receive a payload in JSON format, which includes detailed information about the event. For instance, a push event payload might contain the following structure:


```
{
  "object_kind": "push",
  "event_name": "push",
  "before": "95790bf891e76fee5e1747ab589903a6a1f80f22",
  "after": "d4b364dbacef96f47a4fae3ec1ba6a1f2b56a6b7",
  "ref": "refs/heads/main",
  ...
  "repository": {
    "name": "my_project",
    "url": "git@example.com:my_project.git",
    ...
  },
  ...
}
```


Processing Webhook Payloads: A critical aspect of using webhooks is ensuring that your receiving endpoint can handle the incoming payloads efficiently. Below is a Python example of a simple HTTP server that processes push event payloads using the Flask framework:

```
from flask import Flask, request, jsonify

app = Flask(__name__)

@app.route('/webhook', methods=['POST'])
def handle_webhook():
    if request.headers.get('X-Gitlab-Event') == 'Push Hook':
        payload = request.json
        # Extracting relevant data from the payload
        branch = payload['ref'].split('/')[-1]
        commits = payload['commits']
        for commit in commits:
            print(f"Commit {commit['id']} by {commit['author']['name']} on branch {
                branch}")
```

```
        return jsonify({'status': 'processed'}), 200
    return jsonify({'status': 'ignored'}), 200

if __name__ == '__main__':
    app.run(port=8080)
```

Securing Webhooks: Security of webhook data is paramount. Utilizing a Secret Token allows the server to verify that requests originate from GitLab:

```
import hmac
import hashlib

def verify_gitlab_signature(request, secret_token):
    header_signature = request.headers.get('X-Gitlab-Token')
    if not header_signature:
        return False
    return hmac.compare_digest(header_signature, secret_token)
```

Best Practices: 1. **Use Secret Tokens:** - Always configure a secret token for verifying incoming webhook requests. This prevents unauthorized systems from sending fake payloads.

2. **Limit Trigger Events:** - Choose trigger events carefully to avoid unnecessary processing. Only enable events that your application needs to respond to.

3. **Debounce Requests:** - Implement debouncing mechanisms to handle burst activity efficiently. This ensures your system remains responsive during high activity periods.

4. **Error Handling:** - Implement robust error handling in your webhook receiver to gracefully manage unexpected input or connection failures.

By leveraging webhooks, you can seamlessly integrate your GitLab repository with a multitude of external systems, facilitating enhanced automation, monitoring, and collaboration across your development workflows.

3.12 Repository Insights and Analytics

GitLab provides a comprehensive suite of tools to gain insights and perform analytics on repository data. Understanding how to effectively utilize these tools can greatly enhance your productivity and streamline project management.

GitLab's insights and analytics are indispensable for tracking the health, activity, and productivity of projects. They include various metrics and visualizations which allow project managers, developers, and stakeholders to understand better how the repository evolves over time. Important tools in this suite include repository statistics, commit histories, activity graphs, contributor analytics, and code frequency metrics.

The **Repository Statistics** tab can be found in the project's main dashboard. It offers an overview of the project, including the number of commits, branches, tags, and files. To access repository statistics, navigate to your project and click on *Repository > Graph*. Here you will see visualizations summarizing the overall structure and engagement within the repository.

GitLab offers detailed **Commit History** through which you can monitor the trajectory of development within the project. This is accessible under the *Repository* section by selecting the *Commits* link. Each commit entry displays the commit hash, author, date, and a commit message. This feature allows tracking of specific changes over time and understanding the incremental development steps.

The **Activity Graph** is another powerful tool for visual understanding of the repository's engagement level. This visualization aggregates data over several months and displays activities such as pushes, merge requests, and comments in a consolidated view. This can be accessed by navigating to *Analytics > Repository* within the project menu. Such graphs help identify peaks in development activity and can highlight productivity trends.

Contributor Analytics provide insights into the contributions of individual developers. GitLab enables you to visualize who the top contributors are, how many commits each person has made, the distribution of contributions over time, and the review comments by each contributor. To utilize this feature, navigate to *Analytics > Contributions*. This can aid in understanding the distribution of work among team members and identifying key contributors to the project.

In addition to these, **Code Frequency Analytics** illustrate the addition and deletion of code within the repository over a specified period. This feature highlights the growth and refactoring trends of your codebase. To access this, go to *Analytics > Repository* and select *Code frequency*.

```
# Command to display code frequency within a local git repository
git log --pretty=format: --numstat | awk '{ add += $1; subs += $2; loc += $1 - $2 }
    END { printf "added lines: %s, removed lines: %s, total lines: %s\n", add, subs,
    loc }'
```

The output from this command could be as follows:

```
added lines: 3486, removed lines: 1594, total lines: 1892
```

Commit Statistics also prove crucial to understanding repository dynamics. GitLab can track commits across multiple dimensions such as author, time period, and type of change. This can help to monitor developer activity and time-based trends in your project. Access this feature by going to *Analytics > Repository > Commits*.

Another potent feature is the **Cycle Analytics**, which help track the time taken to complete tasks from issue creation to code deployment. It segments the lifecycle into various phases such as issue, plan, code, review, and deploy, among others. Accessing Cycle Analytics involves navigating to *Analytics > Cycle Analytics*.

Visual representations in GitLab extend to **Merge Request Analytics** as well. This tool provides insights into the merge request lifecycle, including metrics such as the number of merge requests opened, closed, and merged over time. To utilize this feature, move to *Analytics > Merge Requests*.

GitLab's **CI/CD Analytics** dashboards offer insights into the performance and frequency of pipelines. This includes metrics such as build times, success and failure rates, and deployment frequency. Navigate to *Analytics > CI/CD* to access this feature.

Understanding these analytics tools enables comprehensive monitoring and strategic decisions, aiding in efficient repository management and robust project development. By leveraging these insights, teams can maintain high productivity, identify potential bottlenecks early, and ensure continuous improvement in their development processes.

Chapter 4

Issues and Project Management

This chapter covers the fundamental aspects of managing issues and projects within GitLab. It examines creating and managing issues, using labels, milestones, and assigning tasks for better collaboration. The chapter introduces GitLab's boards, lists, epics, and roadmaps for effective project organization. It also includes productivity tools like time tracking and issue templates, as well as automating issue tracking and integrating issues with CI/CD pipelines. The chapter concludes with reporting and analytics features and strategies for effective project management.

4.1 Introduction to Issues in GitLab

Issues in GitLab are central to project management, serving as the primary mechanism for tracking work items, bugs, feature requests, and other actionable tasks. Each issue acts as a single unit of work, encompassing a detailed description, assignees, labels, and a timeline. Understanding how to effectively utilize issues within GitLab is crucial for maintaining an organized and efficient workflow.

Creating Issues: To create an issue in GitLab, navigate to the Issues tab within your project and click on New issue. This opens a form where various details can be provided, including the title, description, and any relevant attachments. Providing a detailed description of the issue helps team members understand the context and the scope of the work needed.

```
# Command line interface example using GitLab API
curl --request POST --header "PRIVATE-TOKEN: <your_access_token>" \
  --data "title=New Issue Title&description=This is a new issue" \
  "https://gitlab.example.com/api/v4/projects/<project_id>/issues"
```

The above example demonstrates how to create a new issue using the GitLab API. Replace *<your_access_token>* and *<project_id>* with your actual GitLab access token and project ID, respectively.

Issue Details: Issues in GitLab can contain several elements, each contributing to better tracking and management:

- **Title:** A brief summary of the issue.
- **Description:** A detailed explanation including steps to reproduce, expected behavior, and any additional context.
- **Labels:** Categorize issues by type (e.g., bug, feature, enhancement).
- **Assignees:** Allocate the issue to one or multiple team members.
- **Milestones:** Associate the issue with specific project milestones.
- **Due Date:** Specify a deadline for the issue to be resolved.

```
# Example PATCH request to update an issue with labels
curl --request PATCH --header "PRIVATE-TOKEN: <your_access_token>" \
  --data "labels=bug,urgent" \
  "https://gitlab.example.com/api/v4/projects/<project_id>/issues/<issue_id>"
```

Issue Lifecycle: Once created, an issue goes through various states from inception to completion. The key stages in an issue lifecycle include:

- **Open:** When an issue is created, it is in the open state.
- **In Progress:** When work begins, the issue is moved to in progress.
- **Closed:** Once the work is complete or the issue is resolved, it is marked as closed.

```
+--------------------+   +---------------------+   +---------------+
|   Open             | -> |   In Progress       | -> |   Closed      |
+--------------------+   +---------------------+   +---------------+
```

Collaborative Aspects: GitLab issues support collaboration through comments and notifications. Team members can discuss the issue within its thread, mention specific users using @username, and reference other issues or merge requests by using #issue_id or !merge_request_id.

Example of Commenting on an Issue:

```
# POST request to add a comment to an issue
curl --request POST --header "PRIVATE-TOKEN: <your_access_token>" \
  --data "body=This is a comment" \
  "https://gitlab.example.com/api/v4/projects/<project_id>/issues/<issue_id>/
     notes"
```

Configuring Notifications: Users can configure their own notification settings to stay informed about updates related to specific issues. This can be done through the user's GitLab settings under Notifications where they can specify the level of detail for notifications they wish to receive (e.g., global, group, project).

Integrating issues into the broader workflow involves customizing the issue templates, automation through GitLab CI/CD pipelines, and generating detailed reports for analysis purposes. This foundational understanding of issues in GitLab sets the stage for more advanced management practices discussed later in this chapter.

4.2 Creating and Managing Issues

The management of issues in GitLab is a core aspect of the project management workflow. Creating and managing issues effectively ensures tasks are clearly defined, assigned, and tracked throughout the project lifecycle. This section details the processes for creating, viewing, and managing issues, enhancing team productivity and collaboration.

The process of creating an issue in GitLab starts with navigating to the specific project where the issue needs to be logged. Once in the project, users should access the **Issues** tab and select the **New issue** button. This action opens the issue creation form, which is essential for capturing the details of the task or problem to be addressed.

Mandatory fields in the issue creation form include:

- **Title**: A concise and descriptive title that summarizes the issue.

- **Description**: A detailed explanation that provides context, requirements, and any steps to reproduce a bug or clarify the task.

Additional elements that can be included to aid in issue management are:

- **Labels**: Tags that categorize the issue, aiding in filtering and sorting.
- **Milestone**: Assigning an issue to a milestone ties it to project progress and deadlines.
- **Assignees**: Designating responsible team members who will address the issue.
- **Due Date**: Setting a deadline to ensure timely completion.

The following is an example of a command to create an issue using the GitLab API:

```
curl --request POST --header "PRIVATE-TOKEN: <your_access_token>" \
  --data "title=Bug in the login feature" \
  --data "description=Login button fails to redirect" \
  --data "labels=bug" \
  --data "assignee_ids[]=23" \
  --data "milestone_id=1" \
  "https://gitlab.example.com/api/v4/projects/5/issues"
```

This command demonstrates using curl to send a POST request to create a new issue with a title, description, label, assignee, and milestone.

Once created, issues can be viewed and managed from the **Issues** tab of the project. The issue list provides a range of filtering and sorting options:

- Filter by labels, milestones, assignees, or status.
- Sort issues by creation date, updated date, or priority.

To edit an existing issue, including updating its status, modifying its description, or reassigning it to a different team member, you should open the issue and select the **Edit** button. The issue management capabilities of GitLab support the dynamic nature of development teams and projects, where tasks often evolve from their initial conception.

Issues in GitLab support comments, and editing through a rich text editor or Markdown, enabling detailed discussions and rich formatting.

Commenting allows team members to provide updates, request clarifications, and close the feedback loop within the context of the issue itself.

An example of adding a comment to an issue using the GitLab API is shown below:

```
curl --request POST --header "PRIVATE-TOKEN: <your_access_token>" \
  --data "body=We need to prioritize this issue" \
  "https://gitlab.example.com/api/v4/projects/5/issues/42/notes"
```

This command sends a POST request adding a comment to an existing issue identified by its ID (in this case, 42).

One key feature to effectively manage issues is the use of task lists within an issue description. These are checkboxes that help track progress on sub-tasks linked to the main issue. Task lists provide a granular level of detail and are particularly useful for large or complex issues that encompass multiple steps or components.

For example, a task list in Markdown format:

```
- [ ] Design login page
- [ ] Implement authentication logic
- [ ] Verify validation constraints
- [ ] Test and deploy feature
```

These checklists dynamically reflect the task's status, ensuring transparency and visibility across the team.

Creating versatile issue templates can standardize the format and information required, enhancing consistency and comprehensiveness. Templates can pre-fill common fields and guide users to include necessary information. Setting up issue templates in the repository involves creating markdown files in the .gitlab/issue_templates/ directory.

A sample bug report template might look like this:

```
# Summary
(Provide a detailed summary of the bug or issue)

# Steps to reproduce
(How one can reproduce the issue - this is very important)

# What is the current bug behavior?
(What actually happens)

# What is the expected correct behavior?
(What you should see instead)

# Relevant logs and/or screenshots
(Paste any relevant logs - please use code blocks (\`\`\`) to format console output, logs, and code as it's easy to read)

# Possible fixes
(If you can, link to the line of code that might be responsible for the problem)
```

By providing such predefined structure, issue templates ensure essential information is not overlooked, speeding up resolution times and promoting best practices in issue documentation.

Effectively creating and managing issues in GitLab requires attention to detail and consistent practices. By leveraging the various tools and features GitLab offers, such as labels, milestones, assignees, and task lists, and by utilizing API commands for automated workflows, teams can maintain a high level of productivity and collaboration, ensuring tasks are not just logged but actively managed to completion.

4.3 Using Labels and Milestones

Labels and milestones are essential tools in GitLab for organizing work, facilitating collaboration, and tracking progress. They allow teams to categorize issues and merge requests, making project management more efficient and streamlined.

Labels in GitLab are used to tag issues and merge requests with relevant metadata. These tags can represent various elements, such as stages of development, types of issues, priorities, or any other custom classification that suits the project's needs. Labels make it easier to filter and search for specific sets of issues, providing a high-level overview of the project's status and workload distribution.

To create a label in GitLab:

```
1. Navigate to the project in GitLab.
2. Go to 'Settings' > 'Labels'.
3. Click on 'New label'.
4. Enter the label name, select a color, and provide a description (optional).
5. Click 'Create label'.
```

After labels have been created, they can be applied to issues and merge requests. To apply a label:

```
1. Open the issue or merge request.
2. On the right sidebar, find the 'Labels' section.
3. Select the appropriate labels from the list of available labels.
4. The selected labels will be displayed on the issue or merge request.
```

Labels improve the issue tracking process and facilitate better communication within the team by providing context. For example, a label indicating 'bug' can quickly notify developers that an issue requires bug fixing, while a 'feature' label can denote new feature requests.

Milestones, on the other hand, are used to group issues and merge requests that are meant to be delivered together, typically by a specific due date. Milestones help in tracking the progress of larger goals or releases and can consist of one or many issues that need to be completed. To create a milestone in GitLab:

```
1. Navigate to the project in GitLab.
2. Go to 'Issues' > 'Milestones'.
3. Click on 'New milestone'.
4. Enter the title, description, start date, and due date for the milestone.
5. Click 'Create milestone'.
```

Issues or merge requests can then be assigned to milestones to effectively group work items. To assign an issue or merge request to a milestone:

```
1. Open the issue or merge request.
2. On the right sidebar, find the 'Milestone' section.
3. Select the appropriate milestone from the dropdown menu.
4. The selected milestone will be displayed on the issue or merge request.
```

Milestones enable better project planning and progress tracking. They provide an overview of what needs to be completed by certain deadlines and allow teams to focus on delivering specific functionalities or resolving particular sets of issues. Additionally, milestones can be used to create burndown charts, which provide visual representations of the team's progress towards completing the milestone.

Integrating labels and milestones within GitLab's boards further enhances their usability. Boards offer a visual way of managing issues and merge requests by placing them under columns that represent different stages of the workflow. Labels can be used to create board filters, making it easier to focus on specific categories of work. For example, you can create columns for 'To Do', 'In Progress', and 'Done', and use labels to filter issues by these stages. Each issue's progress can then be visualized and managed on the board.

To create a board in GitLab:

```
1. Navigate to the project in GitLab.
2. Go to 'Issues' > 'Boards'.
3. Click on 'New board'.
4. Enter a name for the board and add columns as needed.
5. Configure each column by dragging and dropping labels into the columns.
6. Click 'Create'.
```

With an established board, the integration of labels and milestones facilitates dynamic issue tracking and efficient workflow management. Issues can be dragged and dropped between columns to update their status, and filters can be applied to focus on specific labels or milestones. This approach encourages transparency, collaboration, and a shared understanding of project priorities.

In project management, combining labels and milestones ensures that issues are not only categorized effectively but also aligned with the project's timelines and goals. By focusing on the strategic importance and due dates provided by milestones, while leveraging the categorization and filtering capabilities of labels, teams can enhance their productivity and maintain a clear perspective on the progress and status of their projects. Through these tools, GitLab supports robust project management practices that adapt to various team needs and project requirements.

4.4 Assigning Issues and Collaborating

Assigning issues and collaborating within GitLab involves efficiently directing tasks to team members and fostering a collaborative environment to resolve issues effectively. This process leverages GitLab's user management, notification systems, and collaborative tools such as comments, mentions, and issue linking. Mastering these functionalities ensures that the workflow remains streamlined and that all team members are aligned with their responsibilities and project goals.

Assigning Issues: In GitLab, assigning issues to team members ensures that tasks are clearly designated and that accountability is established. To assign an issue, navigate to the issue's detail page. On the right sidebar, you will find the **Assignees** section. Follow these steps:

1. Click on the **Edit** button next to the **Assignees** label.
2. A dropdown menu will appear, showing a list of team members.
3. Select one or more team members to assign them the issue.
4. The selected members will be notified about their assignment, and their avatars will be displayed in the **Assignees** section.

Assigning issues to the right team member involves considering their expertise, current workload, and involvement in the project. GitLab allows for multiple assignees to support collaborative work on complex issues.

Collaborative Tools: GitLab fosters collaboration through a variety of tools integrated into the issue tracking system:

- **Comments:** Add comments to issues to discuss potential solutions, clarify requirements, share updates, and provide feedback. Comments can include text, images, code snippets, and references to other issues or merge requests.
- **Mentions:** Use the @ symbol followed by a username to mention specific team members in comments. This action notifies the mentioned users, drawing their attention to the comment and potentially prompting immediate review or action.
- **Issue Linking:** Issues can be interrelated, and linking them helps maintain context and track dependencies. You can link issues by including keywords such as closes #123, relates to #123, or duplicates #123 within the comments or description.
- **Attachments:** Include attachments such as screenshots, diagrams, and documents in comments or the issue description to provide additional context. This feature is particularly useful for visualizing problems and proposed solutions.

Real-Time Collaboration: Real-time collaboration in GitLab is achieved through automated notifications and integrations with communication tools. Notifications can be configured to alert users via email or through integrated tools like Slack and Microsoft Teams. These integrations ensure that team members are promptly informed as issues evolve.

Activity Logs: Each change within an issue, whether it's a comment, status change, or new assignee, is logged in the Activity section. This chronological log keeps a comprehensive record of all interactions and modifications, aiding in transparency and accountability.

```
Example Activity Log:
 - John Doe added a comment on 2023-10-04: "Investigating the cause of the error."
 - Jane Smith assigned to the issue.
 - Issue status changed from "Open" to "In Progress".
```

Best Practices for Collaboration: Successful collaboration in GitLab requires adhering to certain best practices:

- **Clear Communication:** Ensure that all comments and descriptions are clear and concise. Ambiguity can lead to misunderstandings and delays.
- **Timely Updates:** Regularly update issues with progress notes, even if there is no significant change. This keeps stakeholders informed and maintains project momentum.

- **Use of Labels and Milestones:** Leverage labels and milestones to categorize issues and align them with project phases or goals. This facilitates a higher level of organization and prioritization.
- **Review and Feedback:** Encourage the use of peer reviews and feedback on proposed solutions. Collaborative problem-solving often leads to more robust and innovative solutions.
- **Documentation:** Document resolutions and significant discussions within the issue. This serves as a valuable reference for future similar issues and for onboarding new team members.

Applying these collaborative strategies within GitLab not only improves efficiency and project tracking but also enhances team cohesion and communication, ultimately leading to more effective project management and successful outcomes.

4.5 Boards and Lists in GitLab

Boards and lists in GitLab are essential tools for organizing and managing issues effectively within a project. These features provide a visual method of tracking the progress of work items, facilitating better collaboration and prioritization. In this section, we will explore how to utilize boards and lists to enhance project management efficiency.

A GitLab board offers a kanban-style interface, presenting issues in columns that represent different stages of the workflow. Each column corresponds to a list, and issues move through these lists as they progress from one stage to another. The primary components of boards in GitLab include the backlog, to-do, in-progress, and done lists, among others. Custom lists can also be created to fit specific workflow needs.

To create a new board in GitLab, navigate to the project's sidebar, click on **Boards**, and select **New Board**. You will be prompted to give the board a name and configure its settings. Once the board is created, you can begin adding lists. Lists can be created based on labels, assignees, or milestones, allowing for flexible categorization of issues.

```
# Creating a new board
1. Go to your project.
2. In the left sidebar, click on 'Boards'.
3. Click 'New Board'.
4. Enter the name of the board and configure its settings.
```

```
# Adding a new list to the board
1. Open your board.
2. Click '+ Add list'.
3. Select the basis of the list: Label, Milestone, or Assignee.
4. Configure the chosen basis with specific details.
```

The board can be customized by creating lists that match the project's specific workflow. For example, if a project uses labels such as "backend", "frontend", "review", and "testing", lists can be created for each label. Issues tagged with these labels will automatically appear in their respective lists, ensuring easy tracking and management.

Managing issues on a board involves dragging and dropping them between lists as they progress through different stages. This feature not only provides a clear visual representation of the project's state but also allows team members to effortlessly update the status of their tasks. Lists can also be reordered to reflect changes in priority or workflow adjustments.

```
Board:
--------------------------------------------------------------------------------
| To Do          | In Progress     | Review          | Done            |
--------------------------------------------------------------------------------
| Issue #123     | Issue #125      | Issue #124      | Issue #126      |
| Issue #127     | Issue #128      |                 | Issue #129      |
--------------------------------------------------------------------------------
```

Additionally, GitLab boards support filtering and grouping issues for better visibility and focus. Filters can be applied based on labels, assignees, milestones, and other criteria, refining the view to only show relevant issues. Grouping helps in aggregating issues by common attributes, providing insights into workload distribution and task dependencies.

```
# Filtering issues by label
1. Open your board.
2. Click on the 'Filter' button.
3. Select the label to filter on (e.g., "bug", "enhancement").

# Grouping issues by milestone
1. Open your board.
2. Click on the 'Group by' dropdown.
3. Select the grouping criteria (e.g., Milestone, Assignee).
```

Moreover, GitLab boards are tightly integrated with other GitLab features such as epics and roadmaps. Issues linked to an epic will appear in the board and reflect the progress of broader project goals. The roadmap provides a high-level overview of milestones and their associated issues, complementing the detailed view of boards and lists.

Boards also support collaborative features such as comments and mentions directly within issues. Team members can discuss tasks, provide updates, and mention colleagues to bring them into the conversation, all from within the board interface. This fosters a centralized and transparent communication channel, reducing the risk of miscommunication and ensuring that all stakeholders are aligned.

```
# Adding a comment to an issue
1. Open the issue from the board.
2. Scroll down to the comment section.
3. Enter your comment and click 'Comment'.

# Mentioning a team member
1. Within your comment, type '@' followed by the username.
2. Select the username from the dropdown.
3. Finish your comment and click 'Comment'.
```

The use of boards and lists in GitLab emphasizes visibility and accountability. By clearly depicting the stages of issue progression and allowing real-time updates and interactions, they become integral tools for effective project management. Understanding how to utilize these features fully will significantly enhance the workflow and collaboration within any project team.

4.6 Epics and Roadmaps

GitLab's *Epics* and *Roadmaps* are crucial features that enable structured and hierarchical project management, providing a clear overview of complex, multifaceted projects and their progress. These tools help track work across multiple issues and projects, facilitating higher-level planning and ensuring alignment with broader business objectives.

An **Epic** is a significant body of work that comprises many smaller tasks, represented as issues. It provides a high-level overview of progress toward a substantial goal, encapsulating multiple related issues that collectively achieve the strategic objective. Epics can transcend individual projects, enhancing cross-functional collaboration and long-term planning.

To create an Epic in GitLab:

```
1. Navigate to the 'Epics' section within your Group.
2. Click on 'New Epic'.
3. Fill in the title, description, and labels as necessary.
4. Assign a start and due date if needed.
5. Click 'Create Epic'.
```

Here is an example of creating an Epic using GitLab's API:

```
import requests

url = "https://gitlab.example.com/api/v4/groups/:group_id/epics"

payload = {
    "title": "New Epic",
    "description": "Description of the epic",
    "start_date": "2023-01-01",
    "due_date": "2023-12-31"
}

headers = {
    "PRIVATE-TOKEN": "your_access_token"
}

response = requests.post(url, data=payload, headers=headers)

print(response.json())
```

When working with epics, it's beneficial to link related issues. This linkage establishes a clear relationship between smaller tasks and the overarching goal, promoting consistency and organization.

- **Linking Issues to an Epic**: To link existing issues to an epic, navigate to the epic's page and use the 'Add' section under 'Issues', specifying which issues to link.
- **Hierarchy**: Epics can contain other epics as sub-epics, allowing you to build a multi-level hierarchy that reflects the project's complexity.
- **Labels and Milestones**: Epics can be tagged with labels and associated with milestones for better filtering and tracking.

Roadmaps visualize epics over time, offering a timeline view of work. This feature is particularly useful for understanding project duration, identifying dependencies, and tracking progression towards deadlines.

To view a Roadmap:

```
1. Navigate to your group.
2. Click on 'Roadmap' in the left-hand navigation.
3. Adjust the timeline view to your preference (weeks, months, quarters).
4. Expand or collapse epics to see nested relationships and progress details.
```

The Roadmap displays:

- **Timeline Bars**: Represent the duration of each epic, indicating start and end dates.

- **Colored Segments**: Indicate the progress of the epic based on the completion of associated issues.
- **Filters**: Provide the ability to filter epics based on labels, milestones, assignees, and more.

Additionally, the Roadmap feature supports milestone overlays, allowing you to see how milestones align with epic timelines. This alignment aids in ensuring that your project stays on track against set deliverables.

```
+----------------+----------------+----------------+
|                 Roadmap Overview                    |
+----------------+----------------+----------------+
| Q1             | Q2             | Q3             |
|      |                                               |
|------|    ----------------------------------------|
| Epic 1|    |                                        |
|      |   |                                        |
|                                         |       |
|------|   |                                      |
| Epic 2|    |                                        |
|      |    ----------------------------------------|
+----------------+----------------+----------------+
```

Epics and Roadmaps also integrate seamlessly with GitLab's CI/CD pipelines for continuous updating of progress. For example, closing issues through merged commits reflects in the associated epics, offering real-time updates on the Roadmap.

Combining these strategic tools, GitLab enables a robust, hierarchical approach to managing large-scale projects. These functionalities support detailed planning, clear visualization, and effective tracking, ensuring that all aspects of a project are aligned and progressing as intended.

4.7 Time Tracking and Productivity

Time tracking in GitLab provides a systematic approach to monitor progress and estimate effort for tasks and projects. By utilizing time tracking effectively, teams can manage their work more efficiently and ensure that deadlines are met without overburdening team members. This section delves into the mechanisms of setting up and using time tracking within GitLab and explores its integration with productivity tools to maximize project efficiency.

Enabling Time Tracking

To use time tracking, it must be enabled in the project's settings. This allows team members to log the time they spend on issues and merge requests.

```
1. Navigate to the project.
2. Click on "Settings" (gear icon) > "General".
3. Expand the "Visibility, project features, permissions" section.
4. Toggle the "Issues" and "Merge requests" features to ensure time tracking is
      available.
5. Click "Save changes" to implement the settings.
```

Once enabled, time tracking can be used across issues and merge requests. It is essential to familiarize yourself with specific commands to set and track time.

Setting Time Estimates

Estimating time for issues helps in planning and resource allocation. Time estimates can be set via the GitLab interface or through comments in the issue.

```
/estimate 3h
/estimate 1d
```

The above commands set an estimate of 3 hours and 1 day respectively for an issue. These estimates provide valuable data for planning sprints and tracking project timelines. The times can be entered in different units such as 'm' (minutes), 'h' (hours), 'd' (days), and 'w' (weeks).

Logging Time Spent

Recording the actual time spent on tasks is integral for evaluating productivity and understanding the accuracy of initial estimates.

```
/spend 2h
/spend 30m
```

Here, the commands log 2 hours and 30 minutes respectively. Adding the actual time spent helps in tracking progress and reviewing workload distribution.

Benefits of Accurate Time Tracking

1. **Productivity Analysis:** By comparing estimated and actual times, teams can analyze productivity and identify areas for improvement. 2. **Resource Allocation:** Understanding the time requirements for tasks aids in efficient resource planning. 3. **Deadline Management:** Accurate time tracking ensures that deadlines are realistic and manageable. 4. **Historical Data:** Maintains a log of time spent on various tasks, which can be useful for future project planning.

Integrating with Productivity Tools

GitLab's time tracking can be integrated with several productivity tools to enhance workflow management. These tools provide advanced features and analytics that complement GitLab's native capabilities.

External Integrations

Integrating with external tools such as Jira, Trello, or Asana allows for synchronization of time tracking data. This ensures seamless transitions and unified reporting across different platforms.

```
1. Navigate to 'projects settings.
2. Click on "Integrations".
3. Select the integration tool (e.g., Jira).
4. Add required credentials and configuration.
5. Click "Save changes".
```

With integration, time logged within GitLab can be accessed and visualized in the external tool, providing a holistic view of the project timeline.

Time Tracking with CI/CD Pipelines

For tasks that involve automation or continuous integration/continuous deployment (CI/CD) pipelines, time tracking can also be mapped to pipeline jobs.

```
stages:
  - build

build_job:
  stage: build
  script:
    - echo "Starting build"
    - sleep 3600
    - echo "Build complete"
  tags:
    - build
  time_tracking:
    estimate: 1h
```

This configuration example showcases associating a time estimate with a CI/CD job. The estimate refers to the expected duration for the build job to complete. Tracking time for pipeline jobs helps in assessing their efficiency and detecting bottlenecks.

Visualization and Reporting

GitLab provides predefined reports and graphs to visualize time tracking data. These tools help in understanding the overall allocation of time across various issues and merge requests.

```
1. Navigate to the 'projects "Analytics" section.
2. Click on "Value Stream Analytics" or "Cycle Analytics".
```

```
3. Browse through "Time Tracking" reports to visualize data.
```

These reports depict how time is spent within a project, highlighting trends and potential areas for optimization.

Best Practices for Time Tracking

1. **Regular Updates:** Consistently log time to ensure data is up-to-date. 2. **Review Estimates:** Periodically compare estimated time versus time spent to refine estimation accuracy. 3. **Collaborative Logging:** Encourage team members to accurately log their time to gather comprehensive project insights. 4. **Integrate Automation:** Utilize CI/CD pipeline integration to automatically log time for automated tasks. 5. **Analyze Reports:** Regularly review time tracking reports to identify productivity trends and potential inefficiencies.

Effective time tracking within GitLab not only helps in managing individual tasks but also contributes to the broader scope of project management by providing critical data for planning, resource allocation, and productivity analysis.

4.8 Using Issue Templates

Issue templates in GitLab streamline the process of creating standardized issues, promoting consistency, and ensuring that all required information is captured. Templates are particularly crucial for larger teams or projects with recurring issue types, as they can predefine fields, provide guidance, and enforce structure.

To create an issue template in GitLab, navigate to the .gitlab/issue_templates/ directory in your repository. Here, you can create Markdown files that define the template content. For instance, to create a bug report template, follow the outlined steps:

```
# Navigate to project root directory
cd path/to/your/project

# Create necessary directory
mkdir -p .gitlab/issue_templates

# Create the bug report template
touch .gitlab/issue_templates/Bug_Report.md
```

Once the file is created, edit its content using your preferred text editor:

```
# Bug Report
```

```
**Summary:**

_Provide a concise description of the issue._

**Steps to Reproduce:**

1. Step one
2. Step two
3. Step three

**Expected Result:**

_Describe what you expected to happen._

**Actual Result:**

_Describe what actually happened._

**Screenshots:**

_If applicable, add screenshots to help explain the issue._

**Additional Information:**

_Any other information you believe is relevant to the bug report._
```

The above template ensures that users reporting bugs include all necessary details to reproduce and investigate the issue. This prevents the need for back-and-forth communication to gather additional information.

To utilize the created template when opening a new issue, click on the New issue button. GitLab will display the available templates, allowing you to select the one that matches your needs. Next, an issue form pre-populated with the template content will appear, and you can fill in the specific details.

GitLab also allows the creation of multiple templates tailored to different types of issues such as feature requests, tasks, and more. Here is an example structure illustrating how to organize different templates:

```
.gitlab/
 issue_templates/
     Bug_Report.md
     Feature_Request.md
     Task.md
```

Below is a possible content for a Feature Request template:

```
# Feature Request

**Description:**

_Provide a detailed description of the feature._

**Problem:**
```

```
_What problem does this feature aim to solve?_

**Proposed Solution:**

_Describe your proposed solution or implementation approach._

**Alternatives Considered:**

_Mention any alternative solutions you have considered._

**Additional Context:**

_Include any other information that might be useful._
```

Using such templates, teams can ensure that all necessary information is captured efficiently, improving collaboration and reducing the overhead of follow-up communications.

For advanced scenarios, you can specify default labels, assignees, or milestones directly within the Markdown template using special front-matter syntax. Here is an example modifying the bug report template to include default labels and assignees:

```
---
name: "Bug Report"
about: "Use this template for reporting bugs."
labels: ["bug", "triage"]
assignees: ["username1", "username2"]
milestone: "Next Release"
---

# Bug Report

**Summary:**

_Provide a concise description of the issue._

**Steps to Reproduce:**

1. Step one
2. Step two
3. Step three

**Expected Result:**

_Describe what you expected to happen._

**Actual Result:**

_Describe what actually happened._

**Screenshots:**

_If applicable, add screenshots to help explain the issue._

**Additional Information:**

_Any other information you believe is relevant to the bug report._
```

This approach leverages GitLab's capabilities to automate some of the manual processes involved in issue management, ensuring that pertinent labels and assignees are automatically applied when the template is used.

Employing issue templates thus enhances efficiency, ensures consistency in issue documentation, and facilitates effective project management by standardizing communication and expectations across the team.

4.9 Automating Issue Tracking

Automation in issue tracking within GitLab leverages various features to streamline the process of managing and resolving issues efficiently. Automation minimizes manual intervention, thereby reducing human error and conserving valuable time. Several aspects of GitLab facilitate this automation.

Automation with GitLab CI/CD Pipelines

GitLab CI/CD (Continuous Integration/Continuous Deployment) plays a pivotal role in automating issue tracking. By defining CI/CD pipelines, developers can automate the testing, deployment, and even resolution of issues. The following is an example of a basic GitLab CI/CD configuration that tests a project and updates the issue status based on the test outcomes.

```
stages:
  - test
  - update

test_job:
  stage: test
  script:
    - make test
  when: on_success

update_issue_status:
  stage: update
  script:
    - curl --request POST \
      --header "PRIVATE-TOKEN: <your_access_token>" \
      --data "state_event=close" \
      "https://gitlab.example.com/api/v4/projects/:id/issues/:issue_iid"
  when: on_success
  only:
    - master
```

This pipeline has two stages: test and update. Upon passing the tests (executed in the test_job), the pipeline proceeds to update the issue status using the GitLab API. This approach automates the process of marking an issue as resolved when corresponding tests pass in the master branch.

Using Issue Boards for Automation

GitLab Issue Boards provide a visual representation of issues based on labels and milestones, allowing users to create automated workflows. When an issue moves from one list to another on a board, the status or labels of the issue can be automatically updated. This is particularly useful for tracking the lifecycle of issues in various stages of development.

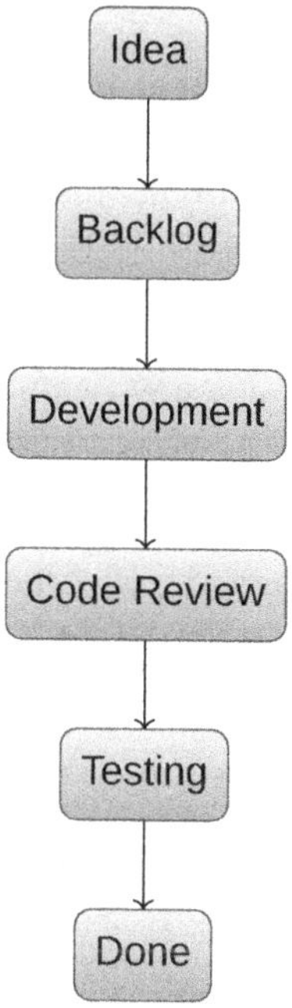

In this example, an issue starts from the "Idea" list and progresses through "Backlog", "Development", "Code Review", "Testing", and finally to "Done". Automation rules can be set up within the board to, for instance, automatically assign a reviewer when an issue moves to "Code Review".

Triggering Pipelines with Issue Events

GitLab supports webhooks that trigger specific actions when issue events occur. For example, a webhook can be configured to trigger a CI/CD pipeline whenever a new issue is created or updated. This ensures that relevant pipelines are executed automatically based on issue events.

```
# Webhook setup (example)
webhooks:
  - url: https://your-ci-cd-system.example.com/webhooks
    events:
      - issues
      - issue_comments
```

With this configuration, any change to issues or their comments will trigger the specified webhook URL, initiating an automated process in the CI/CD system integrated with GitLab.

Auto-closing Issues via Merge Requests

Another efficient automation feature is automatically closing issues through merge requests. By referencing specific issues in commit messages or merge request descriptions using keywords such as Closes #issue_number, GitLab can automatically close these issues once the merge request is accepted.

```
# Example commit message
Implement feature X

This commit includes the implementation of feature X.
Closes #42
```

Here, the issue numbered 42 will be automatically closed when the merge request containing this commit is merged into the target branch.

Automation with GitLab Runner Tags

GitLab Runners can be tagged to ensure that specific jobs run on designated runners. Tags provide a method to automate the allocation of jobs to appropriate runners, enhancing the efficiency and reliability of CI/CD processes.

```
test_job:
  stage: test
  script:
    - make test
  tags:
    - docker
  only:
    - develop
```

This configuration specifies that test_job should run on any runner tagged with docker, ensuring that jobs run in a suitable environment and automating the process of environment selection.

Exploring these automated mechanisms in GitLab's issue tracking system can profoundly enhance the workflow and project management efficiency, allowing development teams to focus more on resolving critical issues rather than managing the operations manually.

4.10 Integrating Issues with CI/CD

Integrating issues with Continuous Integration and Continuous Deployment (CI/CD) in GitLab enhances the project management process by automating workflows and providing real-time feedback on code changes. This integration streamlines the development pipeline, ensuring higher quality and faster delivery of features.

To begin the integration of issues with CI/CD, it is essential to configure GitLab CI/CD pipelines that are aware of the issues being worked on. When a developer references an issue in a commit message or merge request, the corresponding CI/CD pipeline can be triggered to perform necessary tasks such as building, testing, and deploying code. Here is a detailed look into the practical steps and configurations involved.

```
git commit -m "Fixes #123 issue fixed with new validation rule"
```

In this example, the commit message references issue #123. This linkage allows the CI/CD pipeline to take action based on this reference. Next, we configure a .gitlab-ci.yml file to define the pipeline stages and jobs.

```
stages:
  - build
  - test
  - deploy

build_job:
  stage: build
  script:
    - echo "Building the application..."
    - make build

test_job:
  stage: test
  script:
    - echo "Running tests..."
    - make test
  after_script: # Ensures issue updates after tests
    - echo "Update issue with test results"

deploy_job:
  stage: deploy
  script:
    - echo "Deploying to production..."
```

```
  - make deploy
only:
  - master
```

This configuration outlines three stages: build, test, and deploy. Each stage has corresponding jobs that execute specific commands. The after_script section under test_job illustrates updating the issue with the test results. Utilizing GitLab's API, this step can automate issue updates.

To update issues automatically, integrate the GitLab API within the CI/CD pipeline. This can be done by obtaining a private token and using it within the pipeline script.

First, generate a personal access token from GitLab:

- Navigate to your GitLab profile settings.
- Select "Access Tokens" under the "User Settings" menu.
- Name the token, select api scope, and create it.

Store this token securely as a CI/CD variable. Go to your project's "Settings" → "CI/CD" → "Variables" and add the token there.

Example of using the GitLab API to update an issue status:

```
update_issue_status() {
  curl --request PUT --header "PRIVATE-TOKEN: $CI_JOB_TOKEN" \
       --header "Content-Type: application/json" \
       --data '{"state_event": "close"}' \
       "https://gitlab.example.com/api/v4/projects/$CI_PROJECT_ID/issues/
            $CI_MERGE_REQUEST_IID"
}

after_script:
  - update_issue_status
```

Including the function update_issue_status within an after_script ensures that the status of the issue linked to the CI/CD job gets updated after completion. The role of the GitLab API here is crucial for maintaining accurate issue tracking, ensuring that issues move through their lifecycle states based on CI/CD process outcomes.

Moreover, it's possible to automate issue creation based on CI/CD events. For example, you can configure jobs within the pipeline to create issues when certain conditions fail, such as a failed test job, thus keeping a proactive check on potential problems.

Here is a sample script to create an issue post-test failure:

```
create_issue_on_failure() {
  if [ "$CI_JOB_STATUS" != "success" ]; then
    curl --request POST --header "PRIVATE-TOKEN: $CI_JOB_TOKEN" \
      --header "Content-Type: application/json" \
      --data '{
        "title": "Failed test job",
        "description": "Test job failed in pipeline $CI_PIPELINE_ID",
        "labels": "bug"
      }' \
      "https://gitlab.example.com/api/v4/projects/$CI_PROJECT_ID/issues"
  fi
}

after_script:
  - create_issue_on_failure
```

This approach ensures that new bugs or tasks are logged directly into the issue tracker for further investigation or resolution by the development team, increasing the project's overall health and visibility of issues.

Finally, the integration of issues with CI/CD pipelines enhances visibility and traceability. Developers, project managers, and stakeholders can observe the progress of code changes, issue resolutions, and deployments in a cohesive and integrated fashion. The issue-commit linkage, automated status updates, and issue creation based on CI/CD outcomes form a robust framework for effective project management within GitLab.

Integrating issues with CI/CD further aligns development practices with project goals, ensuring that each step in the development pipeline is traceable, automated, and systematically aligned with project objectives.

```
Pipeline #9876 (build, test)
----------------------------
1. Build: Successful
2. Test: Passed
3. Deploy: Completed

Linked Issue: #123 (Automatically closed)
```

4.11 Reporting and Analytics for Issues

Effective project management in GitLab involves not only creating and managing issues but also understanding the progress and performance through comprehensive reporting and analytics. This section delves into the tools and features GitLab provides to help visualize and analyze issue data, enabling better decision-making and enhanced project tracking.

GitLab provides various reporting and analytics functionalities aimed at offering insights into the state of issues within a project. These tools help teams identify trends, track progress, and detect bottlenecks.

Issue Burndown Charts: Burndown charts are a visual representation of work left to do versus time. They help teams monitor their progress toward completing a milestone or sprint.

To generate a burndown chart in GitLab:

- Navigate to the project.
- Go to the Milestones section.
- Select the Milestone for which you want to see the burndown chart.

The burndown chart displays the number of issues or story points remaining over the lifecycle of the milestone, allowing teams to track whether they are on pace to meet their deadlines. The horizontal axis represents time, while the vertical axis represents the remaining work (issues or story points).

Issue Board Analytics: Issue boards in GitLab provide a Kanban-style view of issues, grouped by lists based on their status. To analyze the state of issues directly from the board view, GitLab offers the Cycle Analytics feature.

Cycle Analytics measures the time taken for an issue to move through various stages in the workflow. It covers:

- Issue created
- Plan
- Code
- Test
- Review
- Staging
- Production

Cycle Analytics can be accessed by navigating to Analytics > CI/CD > Cycle Analytics in the project pane.

```
# Sample command line to navigate to Analytics
gitlab-project> ui/pages/analytics.py
```

Once on the Cycle Analytics page, users can view detailed metrics about the time spent in each stage. This helps in identifying stages where the flow might be slowing down, pointing to potential inefficiencies or bottlenecks.

Issue Weight Reporting: In GitLab, issues can be assigned relative weights to indicate their complexity or size.

- Assign weights when creating or editing an issue.
- Use the Weight parameter located in the issue description pane.

To generate reports based on issue weights, navigate to the Analytics > Issues section in the project pane. Here, reports can be generated to show the number of issues and total weight of issues for different labels, due dates, and milestones. This enables teams to assess the distribution of workload and prioritize effectively.

Time Tracking Reports: GitLab also offers time tracking capabilities for issues. Time tracking involves logging the time spent working on individual issues, making it an invaluable tool for resource management and project estimation.

```
# Example: Log 3h 45m of work on an issue
/issue #1234_time_spent 3h 45m
```

Reports on time tracking can be accessed by navigating to Analytics > Issues > Time Tracking. These reports can display:

- Total time spent on issues per user.
- Time spent on issues per milestone.
- Comparison of estimated vs actual time spent on issues.

Custom Reports with GitLab API: For more specific reporting needs, GitLab's API can be utilized. The API provides endpoints to fetch data about issues, projects, milestones, and more.

Example: Fetching all issues for a project using the API.

```
import requests

api_url = 'https://gitlab.example.com/api/v4/projects/PROJECT_ID/issues'
headers = {'PRIVATE-TOKEN': 'your_token'}

response = requests.get(api_url, headers=headers)

if response.status_code == 200:
    issues = response.json()
    for issue in issues:
        print(issue['title'])
else:
    print(f'Failed to retrieve issues: {response.status_code}')
```

This Python script fetches and prints the titles of all issues in a given project. Such basic API interactions can be extended to compile extensive reports tailored to specific organizational requirements.

: Leveraging GitLab's robust reporting and analytics features is crucial for monitoring the health and progress of projects. Whether through built-in tools like burndown charts and cycle analytics, or custom reports using the GitLab API, these insights are essential for making informed decisions and maintaining the efficiency of project workflows.

4.12 Effective Project Management Strategies

Efficient project management in GitLab requires a systematic approach to ensure clear communication, task delegation, progress monitoring, and timely delivery. Implementing effective strategies can help teams maximize productivity, reduce bottlenecks, and improve overall project outcomes.

1. Establish Clear Project Goals and Objectives

Defining precise goals and objectives at the project's inception is essential. Transparent expectations help teams align their efforts and focus resources on crucial tasks. Goals should be Specific, Measurable, Achievable, Relevant, and Time-bound (SMART). This ensures that deliverables are clear and progress is trackable.

2. Utilize Labels and Milestones

Leverage GitLab's labels to categorize and prioritize issues. Labels can indicate the type of issue (e.g., bug, feature, documentation), priority levels (e.g., high, medium, low), and other relevant categories.

Milestones help in grouping issues into significant phases, providing a structured timeline for achieving project segments. This promotes better planning and targeted tracking of progress for each phase.

3. Assign Tasks and Define Responsibilities

Clarify team members' roles and responsibilities by assigning tasks accordingly. Clearly designated ownership of issues ensures accountability and enables efficient workload distribution. Regularly review and adjust assignments to address any imbalances or changes in team capacity.

4. Implement Boards for Visual Project Tracking

GitLab boards offer a visual method for tracking issue progress. Configure boards with columns representing different stages of the workflow (e.g., To Do, In Progress, Review, Done). This visual representation helps teams quickly identify bottlenecks, manage workload, and streamline task transitions.

5. Effective Communication and Collaboration

Ensure seamless communication among team members via GitLab's built-in commenting features on issues and merge requests. Regular update meetings, such as daily stand-ups or weekly syncs, can reinforce communication. Document decisions and discussions within GitLab to maintain a written record accessible to all team members.

6. Utilize Epics and Roadmaps for High-Level Planning

Epics are useful for organizing and tracking large bodies of work that span multiple issues and milestones. Roadmaps provide a high-level overview of the project's timeline, showing how different epics and milestones align over time. This facilitates strategic planning and helps in communicating the project's progress to stakeholders.

7. Time Tracking for Productivity Monitoring

Integrating time tracking into your GitLab workflow allows for precise monitoring of time spent on tasks. Team members can log hours directly into issues, providing visibility into workload distribution and project pacing. Analyze time tracking data to identify efficiency trends and potential areas for process improvement.

8. Utilize Issue Templates for Consistency

Creating standardized issue templates can streamline the process of issue creation and ensure that all necessary information is captured consistently. Templates can include predefined fields for descriptions, steps to reproduce (for bugs), acceptance criteria (for features), and other relevant details.

9. Automate Processes with CI/CD Integration

Automating workflow processes using GitLab CI/CD pipelines minimizes manual effort and reduces the risk of human error. Integrate issue tracking with CI/CD to automate testing, deployments, and notifications related to issue status changes. Automation ensures that updates occur promptly and consistently.

10. Leverage Analytics and Reporting Tools

Utilize GitLab's built-in reporting features to track issue metrics, such as issue completion rates, average time to resolve, and workload distribution. Analyze these metrics to identify patterns, performance bottlenecks, and opportunities for process optimization. Regular reports can aid in maintaining transparency with stakeholders and guiding strategy adjustments.

11. Continuous Improvement and Feedback Loops

Establishing a culture of continuous improvement is vital. Solicit regular feedback from team members and stakeholders to understand pain points and areas for improvement. Incorporate this feedback into iterative updates of project management practices, ensuring that the team remains agile and adaptable to changes.

Employing these strategies within GitLab fosters an organized, transparent, and efficient project management environment. Utilizing the available tools and features effectively can drive improved team performance and successful project completions.

Chapter 5

Introduction to CI/CD with GitLab

This chapter introduces the principles and benefits of Continuous Integration and Continuous Delivery (CI/CD) within GitLab. It covers the initial setup and configuration of CI/CD pipelines, explaining key concepts such as jobs, stages, and the .gitlab-ci.yml file. You will learn about the role of Runners and Executors, and how to use them effectively. The chapter also delves into pipeline visualization, monitoring, artifacts, and caching, concluding with best practices for optimizing CI/CD pipelines.

5.1 What is CI/CD?

Continuous Integration (CI) and Continuous Delivery (CD) are two interconnected software development practices aimed at enhancing the productivity and quality of software projects. CI/CD streamlines and automates the software development process, enabling teams to deliver code changes more frequently and confidently.

Continuous Integration (CI) refers to the practice of integrating code changes from multiple contributors into a shared repository several times a day. Each integration is automatically verified by running tests to detect integration errors as quickly as possible. This practice is designed to detect problems early and improve the quality of the software.

In CI, developers frequently commit their code to the version control repository. A build server, often called a CI server, monitors the repository and initiates a new build and test process whenever changes are detected. The typical steps involved in a CI process include fetching the latest code, compiling the code, running unit tests, performing static code analysis, and deploying to a staging environment if necessary.

The benefits of CI include:

- **Early error detection:** Integration errors are detected early in the development cycle, reducing the cost and effort required to fix them.
- **Improved collaboration:** Developers are encouraged to commit their changes frequently, leading to better collaboration and fewer integration conflicts.
- **Faster delivery:** Automated builds and tests accelerate the development process, enabling teams to deliver features more quickly.

Continuous Delivery (CD) extends the principles of CI by ensuring that code changes can be automatically deployed to production at any time. CD focuses on automating the release process so that software can be released safely and predictably. It builds upon CI by automating additional steps such as integration testing, end-to-end testing, and deploying to production or other environments.

The key objectives of CD are to minimize manual intervention, reduce deployment risks, and enable faster feedback loops. By automating the deployment process, teams can achieve a higher level of confidence in their releases and thereby deliver value to their users more rapidly.

The benefits of CD include:

- **Reduced deployment risk:** Automated deployments reduce the risk of human error and make the deployment process more reliable.
- **Rapid feedback:** Continuous delivery provides rapid feedback on the impact of changes, allowing teams to respond quickly to issues.
- **Increased release frequency:** Automation enables teams to release features and fixes more frequently, delivering value to users faster.

CI/CD isn't just about automation—it's a cultural shift that involves adopting processes and tools that support continuous improvement and rapid iteration. It emphasizes the importance of maintaining a state where software is always ready to be released, which requires close collaboration between development, operations, and quality assurance teams.

The **CI/CD Pipeline** is a key component of this approach, comprising a series of automated steps that code changes go through to be released to production. A typical CI/CD pipeline includes stages such as:

- **Source stage:** Where the latest code is pulled from the version control system.
- **Build stage:** Where the code is compiled and built into deployable artifacts.
- **Test stage:** Where automated tests are executed to verify the integrity of the code.
- **Deploy stage:** Where the code is deployed to staging or production environments.

CI/CD is a cornerstone of modern software development practices, particularly in methodologies like Agile and DevOps. It not only fosters a faster and more reliable release process but also enhances collaboration and accountability within development teams. By integrating CI/CD into the development lifecycle, organizations can achieve higher software quality and expedite the delivery of new features and updates to their users.

5.2 Benefits of CI/CD

The implementation of Continuous Integration (CI) and Continuous Delivery (CD) within a software development lifecycle can yield significant advantages for both developers and stakeholders. These benefits are rooted in the automation, consistency, and streamlined workflows that CI/CD practices enforce. Below, we explore these benefits in detail.

1. Accelerated Development Cycle

CI/CD pipelines dramatically speed up the development process. By automating repetitive tasks such as building, testing, and deploying code, developers can focus more on coding and innovation. This automation reduces the need for manual intervention, which can be prone to errors and is time-consuming. Consequently, development cycles become shorter, enabling faster delivery of features and enhancements.

2. Improved Code Quality

CI/CD enforces a rigorous testing regimen, where code is consistently tested in an automated manner. Each commit made by a developer triggers a series of tests that validate the code against predefined criteria. This frequent and automated testing helps identify bugs and issues early in the development process, significantly improving code quality. Moreover, static code analysis and unit tests can be integrated into the CI/CD pipeline to ensure adherence to coding standards and practices.

3. Reduced Integration Risks

In a traditional development setup, code integration often happens at the end of the development cycle, leading to what is known as "integration hell." CI/CD mitigates this risk by ensuring frequent and incremental code integration. Developers integrate their changes into the main branch multiple times a day, allowing for continuous validation and immediate detection of integration issues. This approach reduces the complexity and risk associated with merging disparate codebases at the end of a project.

4. Enhanced Collaboration and Transparency

CI/CD systems foster better collaboration among team members. The automated nature of CI/CD means that the status of the build, test, and deployment phases is always up-to-date and visible to all team members. Tools such as GitLab provide detailed dashboards and reports, ensuring that everyone is aware of the current state of the project. This visibility promotes transparency and allows team members to address issues promptly, fostering a collaborative environment.

5. Consistent Deployment Process

With CI/CD, deployment processes become more consistent and reliable. The automation of build and deployment scripts ensures that the deployment process is uniformly applied across different environments, reducing variance and the potential for errors that are common in manual processes. Continuous Delivery takes this a step further by automating the deployment to production environments, ensuring that every deployed version is consistent with what has been tested and verified.

6. Faster Feedback Loops

One of the key principles of agile development is the ability to obtain and incorporate feedback quickly. CI/CD pipelines support this principle by providing immediate feedback on the code legitimacy and functionality upon each commit. Developers do not need to wait for a daily or weekly build to know if their changes have caused any issues. This immediate feedback loop enhances agility and reduces the turnaround time for bug fixes and feature adjustments.

7. Lower Costs and Higher Efficiency

By automating tedious and repetitive tasks, CI/CD reduces the overall man-hours required for such activities, leading to lower operational costs. Additionally, early bug detection means less time spent debugging late in the development cycle, which is typically more costly. The efficient use of resources and time ultimately translates to cost savings and higher operational efficiency.

8. Increased Customer Satisfaction

Frequent releases facilitated by CI/CD pipelines ensure that customers receive new features, improvements, and bug fixes regularly and more quickly. This continuous delivery of value keeps users engaged and satisfied with the software product. Furthermore, as bugs are detected and resolved more swiftly, software stability improves, boosting user confidence and satisfaction.

```
# A sample .gitlab-ci.yml configuration for a JavaScript project
stages:
  - test
  - build
  - deploy

test_job:
  stage: test
  script:
    - npm install
    - npm test

build_job:
  stage: build
  script:
    - npm run build

deploy_job:
  stage: deploy
  script:
    - echo "Deploying application..."
```

In a CI/CD pipeline, the above .gitlab-ci.yml configuration demonstrates how easily one can automate testing, building, and deploying processes, reinforcing the discussed benefits. The script not only accelerates development but ensures consistency and reliability across deployments, embodying the core advantages of CI/CD systems.

9. Easier Rollbacks

CI/CD practices include robust mechanisms for version control and deployment tracking. In the event of an unforeseen complication, these mechanisms facilitate quick and efficient rollbacks to previous stable versions of the software. The ability to swiftly revert changes minimizes downtime and mitigates the impact of any issues that occur post-deployment.

10. Continuous Improvement

The iterative nature of CI/CD fosters a culture of continuous improvement. With each cycle, feedback is incorporated, processes are refined, and the overall system is enhanced. CI/CD pipelines can be continuously optimized based on performance metrics and feedback, continually driving improvements in efficiency, quality, and deployment speed.

```
$ gitlab-ci-multi-runner register
Please enter the gitlab-ci coordinator URL (e.g. https://gitlab.com/):
https://gitlab.com/
Please enter the gitlab-ci token for this runner:
xxxxx
Please enter the gitlab-ci description for this runner:
[devops-runner]:
```

The benefits associated with CI/CD are substantial and far-reaching, significantly enhancing various facets of software development and deployment. These benefits, realized through rigorous adherence to CI/CD principles and practices, make CI/CD indispensable in the modern software engineering landscape.

5.3 Introduction to GitLab CI/CD

Continuous Integration (CI) and Continuous Delivery (CD) are cornerstones for modern software development, providing a systematic approach to code integration, testing, and deployment. GitLab CI/CD encompasses tools and methodologies that automate and streamline these processes. This section will elucidate the role of GitLab CI/CD in the software development lifecycle and introduce the foundational concepts integral to leveraging these capabilities within GitLab.

At its core, GitLab CI/CD is built upon a robust pipeline mechanism that allows developers to define and manage workflows through a series of stages and jobs. These workflows are delineated using the .gitlab-ci.yml file, which is placed in the root of the project repository. The file specifies the sequence of steps—termed jobs—that comprise the pipeline, and these jobs can be executed independently or in sequence, depending on the specified stages.

For context, each GitLab pipeline can be divided into multiple stages such as build, test, and deploy. Each stage consists of one or more jobs. For example, the build stage might have jobs for compiling code, while the test stage might include jobs for unit and integration testing. Upon successful completion of all jobs in the test stage, the pipeline progresses to the deploy stage, where the deployment job publishes the application to the production environment.

To illustrate, consider a straightforward .gitlab-ci.yml configuration:

```
stages:
  - build
  - test
  - deploy

build_job:
  stage: build
  script:
    - echo "Compiling the code..."
    - gcc -o myapp myapp.c

test_job:
  stage: test
  script:
    - echo "Running unit tests..."
    - ./run_tests.sh

deploy_job:
  stage: deploy
  script:
    - echo "Deploying application..."
    - scp myapp user@production:/path/to/deployment
```

In this configuration, there are three distinct stages: build, test, and deploy. Each stage contains a job that performs a specific task:

- build_job – compiles the application using gcc.
- test_job – runs unit tests by executing run_tests.sh.
- deploy_job – deploys the compiled application to a production server.

GitLab CI/CD utilizes runners to execute these jobs. A runner is an agent or server that processes pipeline instructions. Each job runs on a runner, and GitLab allows the use of shared runners (provided by GitLab) or specific runners (managed within your infrastructure). The configuration and management of runners will be detailed later in this chapter.

The detailed configuration of the pipeline resides in the .gitlab-ci.yml file, which supports various parameters to customize job execution. Some key parameters include:

- script: Specifies the commands to run for a job.
- before_script and after_script: Define tasks to be executed before and after the main script.
- only and except: Control the conditions under which a job is executed, based on branches or tags.
- artifacts: Configure files or directories to be preserved after job execution.
- cache: Defines paths to be cached to speed up builds.

A deeper understanding of these parameters allows for sophisticated pipelines capable of handling complex workflow requirements.

For example, the artifacts and cache keywords in the .gitlab-ci.yml file enable artifact preservation and caching of dependencies, greatly enhancing efficiency.

```
build_job:
  stage: build
  script:
    - echo "Building the code..."
    - gcc -o myapp myapp.c
  artifacts:
    paths:
      - myapp

test_job:
  stage: test
  script:
    - echo "Running tests..."
    - ./run_tests.sh
  cache:
    paths:
      - dependencies/
```

In this example, the build_job artifacts are the built application myapp, which can be subsequently used by the test_job. The test_job caches the dependencies directory to reuse it in future pipeline runs.

Monitoring and managing pipelines in GitLab is intuitive, with features like pipeline status visualization and job logs. Real-time feedback and detailed logging assist in identifying and resolving issues efficiently. The pipeline view in GitLab provides an overview of different stages and their statuses, while job logs offer insights into the execution details and errors encountered.

Ultimately, mastering GitLab CI/CD involves understanding these core components and effectively utilizing them to automate and optimize your development and deployment workflows. By leveraging the capabilities of GitLab CI/CD, teams can achieve higher productivity, reduced integration issues, and faster delivery cycles.

5.4 Setting Up CI/CD in GitLab

To set up Continuous Integration and Continuous Delivery (CI/CD) in GitLab, it's essential to understand the components and configurations required to optimize the workflow. This section breaks down the step-by-step process to get your CI/CD pipeline operational, ensuring a seamless integration with GitLab.

The initial step involves navigating to your project's settings to enable the CI/CD feature. Within the GitLab interface, locate and select your project. Next, go to the *Settings* tab located on the left sidebar, then expand the *CI/CD* settings.

GitLab requires a .gitlab-ci.yml file placed in the root directory of your repository to define your pipeline configuration. This file uses YAML syntax to specify the various stages, jobs, and scripts your pipeline will execute. Here is an example of a minimal .gitlab-ci.yml file:

```
stages:
  - build
  - test
  - deploy

build_job:
  stage: build
  script:
    - echo "Compiling the code..."
    - gcc -o myapp myapp.c

test_job:
  stage: test
  script:
    - echo "Running tests..."
    - ./test_script.sh

deploy_job:
```

```
  stage: deploy
  script:
    - echo "Deploying application..."
    - ./deploy_script.sh
```

The stages keyword defines the distinct phases of the pipeline: build, test, and deploy. Each job is assigned a stage and contains a series of script commands to be executed in sequence.

Ensure your GitLab Runner is configured correctly. Runners are the agents that execute the jobs specified in your .gitlab-ci.yml file. To set up a GitLab Runner, you must first register it. Navigate to the *Runners* section under the *CI/CD* settings of your project, and click on the *New project runner* button. Follow the provided instructions to install and register the runner. An example configuration for registering a GitLab Runner is shown below:

```
sudo gitlab-runner register
# Enter your GitLab instance URL:
URL https://gitlab.example.com
# Enter the registration token:
Token: <your-registration-token>
# Provide a description for the runner:
Description: "My Project Runner"
# Specify the runner executor (e.g., shell, docker, etc.):
Executor: shell
```

GitLab Runners can be shared across multiple projects or specific to a single project. Shared runners are managed by the GitLab instance admin and can be run on different machines, providing a pool of runners for all projects. Specific runners are dedicated to a single project, ensuring exclusive resource usage.

After setting up the runner, each commit pushed to the repository triggers the pipeline defined by your .gitlab-ci.yml file. You can monitor the pipeline's execution on the GitLab interface under the *CI/CD > Pipelines* section, which provides detailed insights into each stage and job's status.

Artifcats and caching are advanced features used for optimizing the pipeline execution. Artifacts allow you to store and pass data between different jobs or stages. For instance, compiling a project in the build stage produces binary artifacts used in subsequent stages, such as testing and deployment. Define artifacts in your .gitlab-ci.yml file as follows:

```
build_job:
  stage: build
  script:
    - gcc -o myapp myapp.c
```

```
  artifacts:
    paths:
      - myapp

test_job:
  stage: test
  script:
    - ./myapp --run-tests
  dependencies:
    - build_job
```

Caching helps in storing dependencies or computed results to speed up future runs. By caching directories like node_modules for Node.js projects or packages for other language environments, redundant computations are avoided. Here is an example configuration for caching:

```
build_job:
  stage: build
  script:
    - npm install
  cache:
    paths:
      - node_modules/
```

Proper configuration and usage of artifacts and caching lead to efficient and quicker pipelines. Optimize these settings based on your project's specific requirements.

The provided configurations and steps offer a foundational understanding to set up CI/CD in GitLab efficiently. The .gitlab-ci.yml file, Runner setup, pipeline monitoring, and advanced features like artifacts and caching are integral to achieving a robust CI/CD environment.

5.5 Understanding GitLab Pipelines

In GitLab, a pipeline is a collection of jobs that are executed sequentially and/or in parallel based on the defined stages. Each job represents a distinct unit of work, which can range from compiling code, running tests, deploying applications, and more. The pipeline configuration is specified in a file named .gitlab-ci.yml located at the root of the repository.

A pipeline typically consists of multiple stages, such as build, test, and deploy. Each job within a stage can be executed concurrently, but stages are generally executed sequentially. For instance, the deployment stage will only begin once all jobs in the test stage have completed successfully.

- **Stages:** Stages define high-level phases of the pipeline, ensuring that work is divided into meaningful steps. These steps are executed in a predefined order.
- **Jobs:** Jobs are tasks that define what should be done at each stage. A job may include script commands, file paths, or references to deployment environments.

To illustrate, consider the following .gitlab-ci.yml example:

```
stages:
  - build
  - test
  - deploy

build_job:
  stage: build
  script:
    - echo "Compiling the code..."
    - gcc -o myapp main.c

test_job:
  stage: test
  script:
    - echo "Running tests..."
    - ./myapp_test

deploy_job:
  stage: deploy
  script:
    - echo "Deploying the application..."
    - scp myapp user@server:/var/www/
```

In this configuration, the pipeline is divided into three stages: build, test, and deploy. Each stage contains one job. The build_job compiles the code, the test_job runs tests on the application, and the deploy_job handles deployment to a server.

```
$ git commit -m "Add .gitlab-ci.yml"
$ git push origin main
```

Upon pushing the changes to the repository, GitLab automatically detects the .gitlab-ci.yml file and initiates the pipeline. The pipeline's progress and results can be monitored on the GitLab web interface.

Each job runs on a Runner, which is a lightweight process designed to interpret and execute the commands specified in the script tags of each job. The Runner can run on different environments, such as Docker containers or virtual machines, providing flexibility and isolation for the tasks.

Pipeline Status: Once initiated, a pipeline can exist in several statuses:

- **Pending:** The pipeline is waiting for a Runner to pick up the job.
- **Running:** At least one job in the pipeline is currently being executed.
- **Passed:** All jobs have completed successfully.
- **Failed:** One or more jobs have failed.
- **Canceled:** The pipeline has been manually canceled.
- **Skipped:** The pipeline or parts of it have been skipped, likely due to conditions not being met.

Pipeline Visualization: GitLab provides an intuitive visual representation of pipeline progress. Each stage and job is displayed with real-time status indicators. This visualization assists in identifying bottlenecks and failed jobs quickly.

Pipeline Execution and Dependencies: Execution order is determined by the stages array. Jobs within the same stage can run in parallel unless explicitly instructed otherwise. Inter-job dependencies can be managed using the needs keyword, ensuring that certain jobs only run after others have completed successfully.

```
stages:
  - build
  - test
  - deploy

build_job:
  stage: build
  script:
    - echo "Compiling the code..."
    - gcc -o myapp main.c

test_job:
  stage: test
  needs: ["build_job"]
  script:
    - echo "Running tests..."
    - ./myapp_test

deploy_job:
  stage: deploy
  needs: ["test_job"]
  script:
    - echo "Deploying the application..."
    - scp myapp user@server:/var/www/
```

In this modified example, the test_job specifies a needs dependency on build_job, and the deploy_job depends on the test_job. This dependency management ensures the correct execution sequence.

Understanding these foundational concepts of GitLab pipelines allows users to create, manage, and optimize their CI/CD workflows efficiently within GitLab. Proper configuration and practice can lead to significant enhancements in code quality, deployment speed, and overall development cycle.

5.6 Creating a Basic .gitlab-ci.yml File

The .gitlab-ci.yml file is the cornerstone of GitLab CI/CD, defining the pipeline configuration, including the jobs to be executed, the stages, and the order in which they run. This configuration file resides in the root directory of your repository and is essential for automating your build, test, and deployment processes.

At its simplest, a .gitlab-ci.yml file is a YAML file, which is a data serialization standard that is easy to read and write. Each line in this file represents different aspects of your CI/CD pipeline, such as stages, jobs, and script to execute those jobs. A basic understanding of YAML syntax is advantageous for crafting this file.

An elementary .gitlab-ci.yml file might look like this:

```
stages:
  - build
  - test
  - deploy

build_job:
  stage: build
  script:
    - echo "Building the application..."
    - make build

test_job:
  stage: test
  script:
    - echo "Running tests..."
    - make test

deploy_job:
  stage: deploy
  script:
    - echo "Deploying the application..."
    - make deploy
```

To decode this configuration, a careful examination is necessary. Initially, we define the stages of the pipeline. In this example, there are three stages: **build**, **test**, and **deploy**. Each stage encompasses a logical phase in the CI/CD process.

```
stages:
  - build
  - test
  - deploy
```

Here, **build_job**, **test_job**, and **deploy_job** are designated as jobs. Each job specifies the stage it belongs to and the actual script to be executed within that stage.

The **build_job** is associated with the **build** stage and contains a series of commands under the script section.

```
build_job:
  stage: build
  script:
    - echo "Building the application..."
    - make build
```

In this job, the commands indicated by echo produce basic output to the pipeline logs, and make build is a placeholder for an actual build command, which would typically compile your application.

Next, **test_job** runs during the **test** stage.

```
test_job:
  stage: test
  script:
    - echo "Running tests..."
    - make test
```

The commands specified here would execute your test suite, validating the code generated in the build stage. echo "Running tests..." provides a textual representation of the step being performed, whereas make test would include the actual instructions to run tests in your project.

Finally, **deploy_job** runs in the **deploy** stage.

```
deploy_job:
  stage: deploy
  script:
    - echo "Deploying the application..."
    - make deploy
```

This job will handle deploying your application, with make deploy representing the commands necessary to push your code to a production environment.

A crucial feature of the .gitlab-ci.yml file is its ability to define dependencies and sequences. By specifying the stages in order, GitLab ensures that jobs in the **build** stage complete successfully before proceeding to those in the **test** stage, and similarly for the **deploy** stage.

Two additional fields, before_script and after_script, allow for commands to be run before and after every job.

```
before_script:
  - echo "Setting up..."

after_script:
  - echo "Cleaning up..."
```

before_script typically includes commands to set up the environment, such as installing dependencies or configuring settings, while after_script might be employed for cleanup activities.

Furthermore, job-level specifications can be refined using the only and except parameters to dictate when a job should be executed.

```
test_job:
  stage: test
  script:
    - echo "Running tests..."
    - make test
  only:
    - master
  except:
    - tags
```

In this enhanced **test_job**, the only keyword restricts the job to run only on the master branch, whereas the except keyword excludes it from running when tags are created.

This is a fundamental illustration of configuring a GitLab CI/CD pipeline using a .gitlab-ci.yml file. The flexibility and powerful features of GitLab CI/CD, combined with the nested structure of YAML, allow for extensive customization according to the needs of various projects, encompassing multiple pipelines, conditional execution, and more.

5.7 Jobs and Stages in GitLab CI/CD

In GitLab CI/CD, jobs and stages are fundamental constructs used to define the sequence and structure of the CI/CD pipeline. This section provides a comprehensive understanding of how jobs and stages work, how they are configured, and their interdependencies.

A **job** is the smallest unit of work that GitLab Runner executes. Jobs are defined in the .gitlab-ci.yml file and are executed on the GitLab Runner. Each job performs a specific task, such as running tests, building software, or deploying applications.

Here is a minimal example of a job definition in the .gitlab-ci.yml file:

```
job_name:
  script:
    - echo "This is a job"
```

In this example, job_name is the identifier for the job, and script lists the commands that the job will execute.

Stages are used to group jobs and control their execution order. A stage contains one or more jobs, and stages are executed sequentially. By default, all jobs belong to the test stage if no stages are explicitly specified. Here is an illustration of how stages are defined:

```
stages:
  - build
  - test
  - deploy
```

This definition specifies three stages: build, test, and deploy. Jobs within each stage will run concurrently, but the stages themselves are processed in order.

Consider the following example, which defines jobs across multiple stages:

```
stages:
  - build
  - test
  - deploy

build_job:
  stage: build
  script:
    - echo "Building the project"

test_job:
  stage: test
  script:
    - echo "Running tests"

deploy_job:
  stage: deploy
  script:
    - echo "Deploying the project"
```

In this example, build_job runs in the build stage, test_job runs in the test stage, and deploy_job runs in the deploy stage. Here, build_job is executed first, followed by test_job, and finally, deploy_job.

Jobs can be customized further using several configurations, such as specifying dependencies or conditions for execution. The dependencies keyword allows specifying job dependencies explicitly. For example:

```
build_job:
  stage: build
  script:
    - echo "Building the project"
  artifacts:
    paths:
      - build/

test_job:
  stage: test
  script:
    - echo "Running tests"
  dependencies:
    - build_job
```

In this example, test_job will only run after build_job has completed successfully. The output of build_job is specified as an artifact and used by test_job.

Another useful configuration is the only and except keywords, which control when a job should be executed. The example below illustrates this:

```
build_job:
  stage: build
  script:
    - echo "Building the project"
  only:
    - master

test_job:
  stage: test
  script:
    - echo "Running tests"
  except:
    - tags
```

In this configuration, build_job will only run on the master branch, while test_job will run on all branches except those tagged.

Additionally, jobs can be configured to run in parallel using the parallel keyword. This is useful for jobs that can be partitioned into smaller chunks and executed concurrently to save time. An example of parallel job configuration is as follows:

```
test_job:
  stage: test
  script:
    - echo "Running test \$CI_NODE_INDEX"
  parallel:
    number: 5
```

Here, test_job will be executed in parallel with five instances running concurrently, identified by $CI_NODE_INDEX.

The interplay between jobs and stages enables the creation of complex pipelines, allowing fine-grained control over the build, test, and deployment processes. Understanding and mastering these constructs is essential for optimizing CI/CD workflows in GitLab.

5.8 Runners and Executors

GitLab Runners are integral to the execution of CI/CD pipelines. They are the agents that execute jobs defined in the .gitlab-ci.yml file, thereby automating the entire build, test, and deployment process. Understanding the nuances of Runners and Executors is critical to optimizing the performance and efficiency of your CI/CD pipelines.

Runners can be broadly categorized into **shared** and **specific** Runners. Shared Runners are available to all projects within the GitLab instance, providing a scalable solution where multiple projects share the same Runner resources. Specific Runners, also known as project-specific Runners, are dedicated to particular projects or groups, offering more control over the Runner's environment and properties.

Executors are the specific environments in which your CI/CD jobs run. Executors enable Runners to execute jobs in different isolation mechanisms. Common types of Executors include Docker, Shell, Kubernetes, and VirtualBox.

Docker Executor is one of the most commonly used Executors due to its flexibility and isolation capabilities. Each job runs in a new Docker container, ensuring a clean and reproducible environment. Here is a basic example of setting up a GitLab Runner with a Docker Executor:

```
gitlab-runner register --non-interactive \
  --url "https://gitlab.com/" \
  --registration-token "YOUR_REGISTRATION_TOKEN" \
  --executor "docker" \
  --docker-image "alpine:latest" \
  --description "My Docker Runner" \
  --tag-list "docker,aws,linux" \
  --run-untagged="true" \
  --locked="false"
```

This command registers a new Runner with the GitLab instance at https://gitlab.com/, using the specified registration token. The Runner uses Docker as the Executor and the alpine:latest Docker image as the base for running jobs. The Runner is described as "My Docker Runner" and tagged with "docker", "aws", and "linux", allowing jobs tagged similarly to be executed by this Runner.

The Shell Executor runs jobs directly on the host machine's shell. While it is simpler and does not require a containerization setup, it lacks the isolation provided by Docker Executors. The Shell Executor is an appropriate choice for quick setups or for environments where Docker might not be available or necessary.

The Kubernetes Executor is beneficial for teams using Kubernetes for container orchestration. This Executor schedules CI/CD jobs as Kubernetes Pods. Below is an example configuration snippet for a Kubernetes Executor in the GitLab CI Runner configuration file (config.toml):

```
[[runners]]
  name = "Kubernetes Runner"
  url = "https://gitlab.com/"
  token = "YOUR_REGISTRATION_TOKEN"
  executor = "kubernetes"

  [runners.kubernetes]
    host = "https://kubernetes.default.svc"
    cert_file = "/path/to/cert.crt"
    key_file = "/path/to/cert.key"
    ca_file = "/path/to/ca.crt"
    namespace = "default"
    image = "alpine:latest"
```

This configuration informs the Runner to use Kubernetes, specifying the API endpoint, its credentials, and the default namespace and image for running jobs.

Another practical Executor is the VirtualBox Executor, which allows testing in virtual machine environments. This is particularly useful for cross-platform testing or for environments that require specific OS conditions.

Runners and Executors Configuration can be further fine-tuned based on project needs. Below is an example of a .gitlab-ci.yml configuration that targets specific Runners using tags:

```
stages:
  - build
  - test
  - deploy

build_job:
  stage: build
  script:
    - echo "Compiling the code..."
    - make
  tags:
    - docker

test_job:
```

```
  stage: test
  script:
    - echo "Running tests..."
    - pytest
  tags:
    - shell

deploy_job:
  stage: deploy
  script:
    - echo "Deploying the application..."
    - ./deploy.sh
  tags:
    - kubernetes
```

This configuration includes three jobs, each associated with different stages and tagged to run on different Executors. The build_job is tagged with docker, the test_job with shell, and the deploy_job with kubernetes, thereby directing these jobs to their respective Runners and Executors.

Understanding how to configure and utilize Runners and Executors effectively is essential for optimizing the CI/CD pipeline's performance. Proper configuration ensures jobs are executed in suitable environments, enhancing the build, test, and deployment efficiency.

5.9 Using Shared and Specific Runners

Runners in GitLab are the agents that execute the tasks defined in your CI/CD pipelines. Understanding how to effectively use shared and specific runners is critical for optimizing your pipeline execution and ensuring efficient resource utilization. This section details the configuration, differences, and use cases for both shared and specific runners, along with practical examples.

Runners Overview:

In GitLab, runners can be described as lightweight program structures that pick up and execute tasks based on the configurations defined in the .gitlab-ci.yml file. Each runner is responsible for executing jobs, and they can be deployed in various environments including virtual machines, physical machines, or even as simple Docker containers.

Shared Runners:

Shared runners are GitLab runners that are accessible to all projects hosted on a GitLab instance. They are typically configured by an administrator and can be an efficient way to leverage common resources for multiple projects. Shared runners are particularly useful for smaller projects or when you don't have specific requirements for job execution environments.

To register and configure shared runners, follow these steps:

```
$ sudo gitlab-runner register
Please enter the gitlab-ci coordinator URL (e.g. https://gitlab.com/):
https://gitlab.com/
Please enter the gitlab-ci token for this runner:
<YOUR_SHARD_RUNNER_TOKEN>
Please enter the gitlab-ci description for this runner:
[hostname] shared-runner
Please enter the gitlab-ci tags for this runner (comma separated):
shared,ci
Please enter the executor: shell, docker, ssh, kubernetes, custom:
docker
```

After registering, shared runners will automatically pick up jobs from any project without further configuration, making them a versatile tool for general usage but possibly leading to resource competition.

Specific Runners:

Specific runners are exclusive to individual projects or groups of projects. They offer nuanced control over the job execution environment and resources. Specific runners are ideal when your CI/CD jobs have unique requirements that generalized shared runners cannot meet. For instance, you might need specific dependencies or configurations unique to your project.

The registration process for specific runners is similar to that of shared runners, but must be tied to a specific project. In the project's Settings, you can retrieve your unique project token:

```
$ sudo gitlab-runner register
Please enter the gitlab-ci coordinator URL (e.g. https://gitlab.com/):
https://gitlab.com/
Please enter the gitlab-ci token for this runner:
<YOUR_PROJECT_SPECIFIC_TOKEN>
Please enter the gitlab-ci description for this runner:
[hostname] project-specific-runner
Please enter the gitlab-ci tags for this runner (comma separated):
specific,ci,project
Please enter the executor: shell, docker, ssh, kubernetes, custom:
docker
```

By configuring the runner with project-specific tokens, you ensure that the runner only picks up jobs from the designated project, enabling tighter control over the CI/CD environments.

Using Tags to Direct Jobs:

Tags in GitLab runners play a pivotal role in directing jobs to appropriate runners. Tags are defined during the runner registration process and must match the tags specified in your .gitlab-ci.yml file:

```
build-job:
  script:
    - echo "Building..."
  tags:
    - docker
deploy-job:
  script:
    - echo "Deploying..."
  tags:
    - shell
```

By associating specific tags with jobs, you can ensure that jobs are executed by runners with the corresponding capabilities and environment configurations. This tag mechanism is crucial for managing diverse workloads and maintaining efficient job execution.

Advantages and Considerations:

Using specific runners provides a range of advantages including dedicated resources, environment consistency, and reduced job wait times, but it also incurs higher administrative overhead for maintenance and setup. Conversely, while shared runners are easy to manage and ideal for general-purpose tasks, they may cause resource contention, influencing job execution times and reliability.

Monitoring and Managing Runners:

It is essential to monitor and manage both shared and specific runners to maintain the efficiency and performance of your CI/CD pipelines. GitLab provides built-in tools to track runner performance and utilization:

```
Project Settings -> CI / CD -> Runners
```

This interface displays vital information on registered runners, job allocation, and execution statuses. Regular monitoring enables proactive maintenance, ensuring runners are operating at optimal capacity and identifying any bottlenecks or underutilized resources.

Effectively managing the use of shared and specific runners can significantly enhance the performance of your CI/CD pipelines, offering the flexibility to meet project-specific needs while leveraging shared resources where appropriate.

5.10 Pipeline Visualization and Monitoring

Pipeline visualization and monitoring are critical for understanding and maintaining the health and efficiency of your Continuous Integration and Continuous Delivery (CI/CD) practices in GitLab. Through visualization, you can grasp the structure, state, and flow of pipelines, while monitoring allows you to catch issues early and optimize processes. This section will provide a thorough examination of the tools and techniques available in GitLab for visualizing and monitoring pipelines.

The pipeline view in GitLab provides a graphical representation of the CI/CD pipeline. Each stage and job is illustrated explicitly, showing their status and how they interconnect. This visualization enables users to ascertain whether a pipeline is running, passed, or failed, and identify at what step an issue occurred.

Accessing the Pipeline Graph: Navigate to your project in GitLab. Go to CI/CD > Pipelines. Click on the pipeline you wish to view. You will see a graphical representation of the pipeline, with each stage laid out horizontally and jobs within those stages displayed as labeled nodes.

Here is an example of how a simple pipeline visualization might look:

```
+-----------------+     +-------------------+
|      Build      |------->|       Test        |
+-----------------+     +-------------------+
         |                    |
         |                    |
         v                    v
+-----------------+     +-------------------+
| Security Scanning|     | Container Scanning |
+-----------------+     +-------------------+
         |                    |
         v                    v
+------------------------------+
|          Deployment             |
+------------------------------+
```

Pipeline Status Indicators: The status of each job within a pipeline is indicated by color codes:

- Green indicates a job that has passed.
- Red indicates a job that has failed.
- Blue indicates a job that is currently running.
- Yellow signifies a job that is pending.
- Gray indicates a job that is skipped.

Monitoring the Pipeline: Real-time monitoring in GitLab is facilitated using the Jobs page and pipeline views. Detailed logs for each job can be accessed directly from the pipeline graph interface. These logs provide insight into what occurred during each step, allowing for quick diagnosis and rectification of issues.

To check the logs:

- Click on any job within the pipeline graph.
- This action will open up the job details page.
- Click on Trace to view the logs.

An example of job logs might look like:

```
$ echo "Building the application..."
Building the application...
$ docker build -t myapp:latest .
Sending build context to Docker daemon 534.8kB
Step 1/7 : FROM ubuntu:18.04
 ---> 4e5021d210f6
Step 2/7 : RUN apt-get update && apt-get install -y ...
 ---> Using cache
 ---> 9fbda9994038
...
Successfully built 9fbda9994038
Successfully tagged myapp:latest
```

Pipeline Dashboard: The pipeline dashboard is an aggregated view of all pipelines within a project, accessible via CI/CD > Pipelines. This dashboard displays the status of each pipeline, the stages, and jobs within it, and details such as pipeline duration, when it was triggered, and by whom.

Pipeline Duration and Efficiency: GitLab provides insights on the duration of each pipeline and its constituent jobs. Identifying stages and jobs that consistently consume excessive time is crucial for optimizing pipeline efficiency. Comparative time tracking of different builds provides a clear indication of improvements or degradations in pipeline performance:

Pipeline	Duration (minutes)	Triggered by
Pipeline #1	10	User A
Pipeline #2	9	User B
Pipeline #3	11	User A

Notification and Alerts: GitLab supports various notification mechanisms to keep the development team informed about the pipeline status.

Users can configure GitLab to send email notifications on pipeline failures, or integrate with third-party services like Slack, Microsoft Teams, or custom webhooks for real-time incident response and monitoring.

An example of setting up notifications using webhooks:

- Go to your project's settings.
- Navigate to Settings > Integrations.
- Add a new webhook and configure the parameters like triggering events (e.g., pipeline failure).

Error Tracking and Troubleshooting: Effective error tracking involves drilling down into the logs produced at each stage of the pipeline. GitLab captures stdout/stderr outputs from all CI/CD jobs. Additionally, integrating tools like Sentry or Rollbar further enhances error tracking, offering more context and automated anomaly detection.

To conclude a more detailed view, investigating variables, job artifacts, and dependencies in the logs help isolate and resolve issues efficiently without guesswork. These practices in visualization and monitoring enable not just a reactive stance but also a proactive approach in maintaining robust CI/CD pipelines.

5.11 Artifacts and Caching in GitLab

Artifacts and caching play crucial roles in optimizing and preserving the outputs generated during the CI/CD pipeline execution in GitLab. Understanding these concepts is essential for efficient pipeline management.

Artifacts are files generated by jobs and preserved to be used by subsequent jobs or retrieved after pipeline completion. They serve as a mechanism to archive and share important assets, such as compiled binaries, test reports, or deployment packages.

The syntax to define artifacts in the .gitlab-ci.yml file is straightforward. The artifacts keyword is utilized within a job's definition to specify the list of files or directories to be saved as artifacts. Here is an example:

```
job:
  script:
    - make build
  artifacts:
```

```
  paths:
    - binaries/*.tar.gz
```

In this example, the job generates tar.gz files inside the binaries directory during the make build step. These files are then specified as artifacts using the paths key. GitLab preserves these paths for the job, and they can be accessed later in the pipeline or downloaded from the job's web interface.

Artifacts can also be configured with additional properties to control their behavior. Some commonly used properties include:

- expire_in: Defines how long GitLab keeps the artifacts before they expire and are automatically deleted. The time duration can be specified in human-readable formats, such as 1 week, 2 months, etc.
- when: Specifies when to save artifacts. Possible values are on_success (default), on_failure, and always. This can be useful for retaining logs or other diagnostics regardless of job success.
- reports: Used to designate artifacts known as reports, such as code coverage reports, JUnit test results, and security scanning results. These are displayed in GitLab's web interface for easy interpretation.

Here's an advanced example of artifact configuration, incorporating these additional properties:

```
job:
  script:
    - make build
  artifacts:
    paths:
      - binaries/*.tar.gz
    expire_in: 1 month
    when: always
    reports:
      junit: report.xml
```

This configuration ensures that the artifacts comprising binaries/*.tar.gz files are preserved for one month regardless of the job's success and includes a JUnit report report.xml that GitLab can present in its interface.

Artifacts can be confidential, often containing sensitive data. Best practices recommend limiting access to artifact paths according to the principle of least privilege. GitLab provides access controls to manage this.

Caching, on the other hand, is used to store dependencies or build outputs that remain unchanged across multiple pipeline runs, effectively accelerating subsequent executions by avoiding redundant work. The cache keyword is used to define caching behavior in the .gitlab-ci.yml file. The following example illustrates basic cache configuration:

```
job:
  script:
    - npm install
  cache:
    paths:
      - node_modules/
```

In this example, the node_modules directory is cached. When the job runs, GitLab checks its cache to see if the node_modules/ directory has already been stored. If so, it restores it, skipping the need to re-download and re-install the dependencies, considerably speeding up the execution.

Cache configurations can include more advanced options necessary for fine-grained control:

- key: Unique identifier of the cache. Supports using variables, allowing different cache keys for different branches or pipelines.
- policy: Policy controlling when the cache should be restored or updated. Options include pull (only fetch the cache), push (only update the cache), and pull-push (default, fetch and update).

Here is an example illustrating these options:

```
job:
  script:
    - npm install
  cache:
    key: "$CI_COMMIT_REF_SLUG"
    paths:
      - node_modules/
    policy: pull-push
```

This configuration sets a unique cache key based on the branch name, ensuring branch-specific caches. For instance, caches for master would be separate from those for a feature branch, preventing potentially conflicting caches across different branches.

It's possible to configure global caches or job-specific caches, providing flexibility. However, improper use of caching can lead to inconsistencies, especially in maintaining up-to-date dependencies or outputs.

Therefore, mindful management of cache expiration, clearing policies, and cache keys is imperative to harmonious CI/CD operations.

Artifacts and caching significantly enhance build efficiency and maintainability. Utilizing them correctly reduces build times, preserves valuable outputs, and ensures consistent artifact availability across pipeline stages. Understanding and employing these features effectively is key to leveraging the full potential of GitLab CI/CD pipelines.

5.12 Best Practices for CI/CD Pipelines

Effective implementation of Continuous Integration and Continuous Delivery (CI/CD) pipelines within GitLab requires adherence to tested best practices to ensure optimal performance, high reliability, and maintainability. These practices involve careful configuration and management of pipelines, jobs, stages, runners, and associated resources. Adopting these best practices can significantly enhance your development workflow, reduce errors, and accelerate your delivery cycles.

1. Modular Pipeline Design

Breaking down your CI/CD pipeline into modular, reusable components is crucial. By defining distinct stages and segregating tasks into smaller jobs, you can manage complexity and achieve better parallelism. For example, a typical sequence might include stages such as build, test, and deploy. Each stage can contain multiple jobs that handle specific tasks.

```
stages:
  - build
  - test
  - deploy

build_job:
  stage: build
  script:
    - echo "Building the application..."

test_job:
  stage: test
  script:
    - echo "Running unit tests..."

deploy_job:
  stage: deploy
  script:
    - echo "Deploying to production..."
```

2. Optimize Job Execution with Caching

Utilizing caching effectively can dramatically reduce job execution times by reusing dependencies and intermediary build artifacts. This avoids unnecessary downloads or recomputations, particularly useful for large projects.

```
cache:
  paths:
    - node_modules/
    - .m2/repository/

build_job:
  stage: build
  script:
    - npm install

test_job:
  stage: test
  script:
    - mvn test
```

3. Use Artifacts for Persisting Data Between Jobs

Artifacts allow the persistence of data between jobs and stages in the pipeline, facilitating the transfer of build outputs, test reports, and other essential files.

```
build_job:
  stage: build
  script:
    - mvn package
  artifacts:
    paths:
      - target/*.jar

deploy_job:
  stage: deploy
  script:
    - scp target/*.jar user@server:/deploy_dir
```

4. Implement Conditional Job Execution

In a CI/CD pipeline, certain jobs or stages might need to run conditionally based on specific circumstances such as branch selection, tags, or results of previous jobs. Utilizing the only and except keywords helps streamline the workflow.

```
deploy_job:
  stage: deploy
  script:
    - echo "Deploying..."
  only:
    - master
  except:
    - tags
```

5. Efficient Runner Management

Optimal configuration and choice of runners (shared or specific) align your pipeline requirements with the available computational resources. Runners should be adequately provisioned to handle the expected load, and specific runners can be used for specialized jobs requiring distinct environments.

```
build_job:
  stage: build
  tags:
    - docker
```

6. Pipeline Visualization and Monitoring

Leverage GitLab's in-built pipeline visualization tools to monitor the pipeline's status and progress actively. This helps in quickly identifying bottlenecks and failures, allowing for prompt resolution.

7. Securely Manage Secrets and Sensitive Data

Utilize protected variables and encrypted secrets to manage sensitive data within your pipeline. Ensure secrets are not hardcoded within pipeline definitions and regularly rotate them to mitigate potential security risks.

```
deploy_job:
  stage: deploy
  script:
    - echo "Deploying with secret..."
  variables:
    SECRET_KEY: $SECRET_KEY
```

8. Continuous Improvement and Iteration

Regularly review and refactor your CI/CD pipelines to adapt to project changes, technological advances, and process improvements. Continuous monitoring and feedback loops are essential to maintain an efficient pipeline.

Implementing these best practices will help create robust, scalable, and maintainable CI/CD pipelines that significantly enhance software development lifecycles. The modularization of pipeline tasks, effective caching, proper use of artifacts, conditional execution, efficient runner management, active monitoring, security practices, and continuous improvement collectively provide a cohesive framework for CI/CD excellence within GitLab.

Chapter 6

Advanced CI/CD Pipelines

This chapter explores advanced configurations and techniques for optimizing CI/CD pipelines in GitLab. It covers complex .gitlab-ci.yml configurations, managing pipelines across multiple environments, and using variables and secrets. You will learn about conditional and triggered pipelines, parent-child pipelines, and handling pipeline failures. The chapter also focuses on performance optimization, security, and compliance within pipelines, along with deployment strategies and integrations with third-party services. Real-world examples are provided to illustrate best practices.

6.1 Advanced .gitlab-ci.yml Configuration

The .gitlab-ci.yml file is the cornerstone for defining CI/CD pipelines in GitLab. Understanding the advanced configurations enables the creation of more efficient, secure, and scalable pipelines. We delve into advanced aspects, such as job dependencies, reusable configurations, using anchors and aliases, setting resource limits, and leveraging GitLab's caching mechanisms to optimize performance.

To begin with, the **job dependencies** are crucial for defining the order and prerequisites of different jobs. This can be managed using the needs keyword, which allows specifying which jobs are dependencies for the current job, facilitating parallel execution where possible.

```
job_a:
```

```
  stage: build
  script:
    - echo "Building the project"

job_b:
  stage: test
  needs: ["job_a"]
  script:
    - echo "Running tests"
```

In the above configuration, job_b explicitly depends on job_a. This configuration ensures that job_a completes before job_b starts. Leveraging job dependencies is essential for complex pipelines, helping optimize the pipeline execution time by running independent jobs in parallel.

Another powerful feature is the use of **anchors** and **aliases**. These features allow sections of the configuration to be reused across multiple jobs, minimizing repetition and potential inconsistencies. Anchors are defined using the & symbol, and aliases are referenced using *.

```
.default-job: &default_job
  script:
    - echo "This is a default script"

job_1:
  <<: *default_job
  script:
    - echo "Job 1 is running"

job_2:
  <<: *default_job
  script:
    - echo "Job 2 is running"
```

Here, .default-job serves as the anchor, containing a script that can be reused. Both job_1 and job_2 inherit this default script, demonstrating how to reuse parts of the configuration efficiently.

To improve the pipeline's performance and resource handling, set **resource limits** and manage the **cache** effectively. Resource limits can be specified using the resource_group keyword, preventing concurrent execution conflicts:

```
job_1:
  script:
    - echo "Running job 1"
  resource_group: my_resource_group

job_2:
  script:
    - echo "Running job 2"
  resource_group: my_resource_group
```

In this example, job_1 and job_2 share the same resource group, ensuring they do not run concurrently.

Caching can significantly reduce job execution time by preserving files between job runs. Define cache specifics using the cache keyword:

```
default:
  cache:
    paths:
      - .m2/repository

job_1:
  script:
    - mvn install

job_2:
  script:
    - mvn verify
```

The above configuration ensures that the Maven repository is cached between pipeline runs, reducing the need to download dependencies repeatedly. The cache can be further customized by specifying key and untracked settings for more granular control.

An additional consideration is configuring **artifacts**, which allow sharing files and directories between jobs and stages. Artifacts can be defined within jobs to ensure necessary files are present for subsequent phases.

```
build:
  stage: build
  script:
    - echo "Building the project"
    - mkdir build_output
    - touch build_output/file.txt
  artifacts:
    paths:
      - build_output/

test:
  stage: test
  script:
    - echo "Running tests"
    - ls build_output/
```

In this snippet, the build job creates an artifact in the build_output directory, which is then available to the test job.

Finally, leveraging **environment-specific configurations** can involve using variables and conditional statements to tailor the pipeline's behavior based on the target environment. For instance, you might want to define different settings for staging and production:

```
stages:
```

```
  - build
  - deploy

variables:
  STAGING_DEPLOY: "false"
  PRODUCTION_DEPLOY: "false"

build:
  stage: build
  script:
    - echo "Building project"

deploy_staging:
  stage: deploy
  script:
    - echo "Deploying to Staging"
  when: manual
  only:
    variables:
      - $STAGING_DEPLOY == "true"

deploy_production:
  stage: deploy
  script:
    - echo "Deploying to Production"
  when: manual
  only:
    variables:
      - $PRODUCTION_DEPLOY == "true"
```

In the above example, the deployment stages are manually triggered and conditionally executed based on environment variables, providing control and flexibility over the deployment process.

Incorporating these advanced features enhances the efficiency, maintainability, and clarity of your GitLab CI/CD pipelines, aligning them closely with complex real-world scenarios.

6.2 Pipelines for Multiple Environments

In advanced CI/CD usage, managing pipelines across multiple environments is essential for efficient and systematic deployment workflows. This section delves into configuration strategies and practices for handling multiple environments, such as development, testing, staging, and production, using GitLab CI/CD pipelines.

Environment Definitions and Usage

To manage pipelines effectively, defining distinct environments within the .gitlab-ci.yml file is crucial. Environments can be defined with a few simple configurations, specifying names and URLs.

```
stages:
  - build
  - test
  - deploy

build_job:
  stage: build
  script:
    - echo "Building the application..."

test_job:
  stage: test
  script:
    - echo "Running tests..."

deploy_dev:
  stage: deploy
  environment:
    name: development
    url: https://dev.example.com
  script:
    - echo "Deploying to development environment"

deploy_staging:
  stage: deploy
  environment:
    name: staging
    url: https://staging.example.com
  script:
    - echo "Deploying to staging environment"

deploy_prod:
  stage: deploy
  environment:
    name: production
    url: https://example.com
  script:
    - echo "Deploying to production environment"
```

The key here is the environment keyword, which defines the different environments such as development, staging, and production. Each environment is given a specific URL where it can be accessed.

Configuring Environment-Specific Variables

Environment-specific variables are crucial for differentiating settings and secrets across environments. These variables can be defined in the GitLab interface under Settings > CI/CD > Variables for each environment.

For instance, to set a development database URL:

```
Variable Key: DATABASE_URL
Variable Value: dev-database.example.com
```

This can then be accessed within the pipeline jobs.

```
deploy_dev:
  stage: deploy
```

```
  environment:
    name: development
    url: https://dev.example.com
  script:
    - echo "Deploying to development environment"
    - echo "Using database: ${DATABASE_URL}"
```

Similarly, separate variables can be defined for staging and production environments for seamless transition and referencing during pipeline execution.

Multi-Environment Deployment Strategies

In complex projects, deploying across multiple environments involves different strategies tailored to each environment's requirements. A common pattern is to deploy first to development, followed by testing, staging, and finally, production. Conditional execution based on successful deployment to prior environments ensures that the integrity of the application is preserved across transitions. This involves leveraging the `when` directive and artifacts to pass build assets.

```
stages:
  - build
  - deploy_dev
  - deploy_test
  - deploy_staging
  - deploy_prod

build_job:
  stage: build
  script:
    - echo "Building the application..."
    - mkdir dist
    - echo "Build artifacts" > dist/artifacts.txt
  artifacts:
    paths:
      - dist/

deploy_dev:
  stage: deploy_dev
  environment:
    name: development
    url: https://dev.example.com
  script:
    - echo "Deploying to development environment"
    - echo "Using database: ${DATABASE_URL}"
  dependencies:
    - build_job

deploy_test:
  stage: deploy_test
  environment:
    name: testing
    url: https://test.example.com
  script:
    - echo "Deploying to testing environment"
    - echo "Using database: ${DATABASE_URL}"
```

```
  dependencies:
    - deploy_dev
  when: on_success

deploy_staging:
  stage: deploy_staging
  environment:
    name: staging
    url: https://staging.example.com
  script:
    - echo "Deploying to staging environment"
    - echo "Using database: ${DATABASE_URL}"
  dependencies:
    - deploy_test
  when: on_success

deploy_prod:
  stage: deploy_prod
  environment:
    name: production
    url: https://example.com
  script:
    - echo "Deploying to production environment"
    - echo "Using database: ${DATABASE_URL}"
  dependencies:
    - deploy_staging
  when: on_success
```

Dynamic Environments

Dynamic environments facilitate feature-specific deployments, useful for review apps where each feature branch can deploy independently for testing.

```
deploy_review:
  stage: deploy
  environment:
    name: review/$CI_COMMIT_REF_NAME
    url: https://$CI_COMMIT_REF_SLUG.review.example.com
  script:
    - echo "Deploying to review environment: $CI_COMMIT_REF_NAME"
```

The environment name utilizes predefined variables like $CI_COMMIT_REF_NAME to dynamically create URLs and environments for each branch or merge request.

Monitoring and Cleanup

When using multiple environments, monitoring their status and performing regular cleanup is necessary to manage resources effectively. GitLab provides options for automatic environment deletion via stop commands.

```
stop_review:
  stage: cleanup
  environment:
    name: review/$CI_COMMIT_REF_NAME
```

```
  action: stop
script:
  - echo "Stopping review environment: $CI_COMMIT_REF_NAME"
```

Integrating these practices into CI/CD pipelines ensures robust management of multiple environments, facilitating smooth and controlled application development and deployment workflows.

49. Pipeline environments have now been added to your GitLab project.

6.3 Using Variables and Secrets

In GitLab CI/CD, variables and secrets are crucial for configuring pipelines, managing sensitive information, and ensuring the proper functioning of different jobs across various environments. Utilizing these elements effectively can significantly enhance the flexibility, security, and maintainability of your CI/CD pipelines. This section elucidates the process of defining and using variables and secrets within GitLab, delving into scope, protection, and use cases.

Variables in GitLab CI/CD can be scoped at different levels:

- **Instance-level** variables: Defined for the entire GitLab instance and accessible to all projects within the instance.
- **Group-level** variables: Defined for a specific group and accessible to all projects within that group.
- **Project-level** variables: Specific to a single project and configurable within the project's settings.
- **Pipeline-level** variables: Defined within the pipeline's YAML configuration or set during manual pipeline creation.

To access the project-level variables, navigate to **Settings** → **CI / CD** → **Variables**. Here, variables can be added, modified, or deleted. Each variable consists of a key-value pair, where the key is the variable's name and the value is its content.

To define a variable within the .gitlab-ci.yml file:

```
variables:
  PROJECT_VARIABLE: "value"
```

These variables are available throughout the pipeline and can be used in scripts, commands, or interpolated within other variables.

Secrets, on the other hand, encompass sensitive information such as API tokens, authentication credentials, and private keys. Managing these secrets securely is vital for maintaining the pipeline's integrity. GitLab offers protected variables for this purpose. Protected variables are hidden from logs and only accessible in protected branches and tags.

Defining a protected variable:

```
variables:
  SECRET_API_TOKEN:
    value: "secure-token"
    protected: true
```

To reference variables and secrets in pipeline jobs, use the $VARIABLE syntax. Below is an example of a job utilizing both a regular variable and a protected secret:

```
build:
  stage: build
  script:
    - echo "Project Environment: $PROJECT_VARIABLE"
    - echo "Performing secure operation with token: $SECRET_API_TOKEN"
```

Additionally, variables can be dynamically created and exported during a job's execution:

```
job_name:
  script:
    - export DYNAMIC_VAR="dynamic-value"
    - echo $DYNAMIC_VAR
```

To integrate variables defined at different scopes:

```
variables:
  PROJECT_VARIABLE: "project-scope-value"
  DYNAMIC_VAR: "dynamic-default"

job_name:
  script:
    - echo $PROJECT_VARIABLE
    - export DYNAMIC_VAR="overridden-dynamic-value"
    - echo $DYNAMIC_VAR
```

Masked variables offer another layer of security by ensuring that their values do not appear in job logs, whether in plain text or as part of commands. The values must match specific requirements, such as using only alphanumeric characters and certain symbols. To enable masking:

```
variables:
  MASKED_VAR:
    value: "sensitive-data"
    masked: true
```

GitLab CI/CD also provides predefined environment variables that convey contextual information about the current job, runner, and pipeline, such as:

- $CI_JOB_ID
- $CI_COMMIT_SHA
- $CI_PROJECT_NAME
- $CI_JOB_STAGE

For securing deployments and managing secrets efficiently, GitLab integrates with several secret management tools and services, including HashiCorp Vault. When using an external secrets manager like Vault, configure the secrets to be accessed in the pipeline using the corresponding GitLab CI/CD configuration syntax.

Implementing HashiCorp Vault:

```
vault:
  script:
    - echo "Using Vault to retrieve secrets"
    - export VAULT_TOKEN=$(vault login -token-only -method=github)
    - export SECRET=$(vault kv get -field=value secret/ci)
    - echo "Retrieved secret: $SECRET"
```

Proper handling of variables and secrets is essential for secure and effective CI/CD pipeline configurations. By leveraging the provided mechanisms, one can ensure sensitive information is protected and appropriately accessible within the scope of required jobs and stages.

6.4 Conditional and Triggered Pipelines

Conditional and triggered pipelines allow for sophisticated control over the execution flow of CI/CD processes in GitLab. By leveraging GitLab's robust syntax and features, one can achieve precise automation tailored to project needs and workflow requirements. It is essential to understand the mechanisms available for conditionally executing jobs and triggering pipelines based on external or internal events.

Conditions in .gitlab-ci.yml:
GitLab's CI/CD configuration file, .gitlab-ci.yml, supports conditionals primarily through the use of rules and only/except keywords. These directives enable fine-grained control over when jobs should run.

```
job:
  script:
    - echo "This job runs conditionally"
  rules:
    - if: '$CI_COMMIT_BRANCH == "main"'
    - if: '$CI_PIPELINE_SOURCE == "merge_request_event"'
      when: manual
```

In this example, the job will execute automatically if the pipeline runs on the main branch. Additionally, if the pipeline is triggered by a merge request event, the job will be set to manual, waiting for user intervention before proceeding.

Using rules vs only/except:
While the rules keyword provides extensive flexibility, GitLab also supports only and except keywords for more straightforward conditional execution.

```
job:
  script:
    - echo "This job runs based on only/except"
  only:
    - main
  except:
    - tags
```

This configuration ensures the job runs only on the main branch and excludes execution if the pipeline is for a tag. Although rules is recommended for new configurations due to its enhanced capabilities, understanding only/except remains useful for maintaining legacy pipelines.

Pipelines for Merge Requests:
A common pattern involves triggering pipelines when merge requests are created or updated. This ensures that changes are validated before integration into the target branch.

```
job:
  script:
    - echo "This job runs for merge requests"
  only:
    - merge_requests
```

The only: merge_requests directive simplifies job definitions for this purpose.

Triggered Pipelines:

GitLab supports pipeline triggers that can invoke a pipeline in a different project or within different contexts of the same project. Triggers can be manual or automated.

```
trigger_job:
  script: echo "This triggers another pipeline"
  trigger:
    project: my-group/other-project # Reference to the downstream project
    branch: main
```

In this scenario, when trigger_job runs, it triggers a pipeline in the my-group/other-project repository on the main branch. This facilitates cross-repository dependencies and coordinated workflows.

Handling Triggered Pipelines:
To handle triggered pipelines effectively, GitLab provides the CI_JOB_TOKEN. This token ensures secure and authenticated triggering of downstream jobs.

```
triggering_job:
  script:
    - curl --request POST --form "token=$CI_JOB_TOKEN" \
          "https://gitlab.example.com/api/v4/projects/<trigger_project_id>/trigger/
              pipeline"
```

Here, a manual API call is made to trigger a pipeline, passing the CI_JOB_TOKEN for authentication.

Pipeline Schedules:
Another method to trigger pipelines conditionally over a time interval involves pipeline schedules, often used for periodic tests or recurrent deployments.

```
schedule_job:
  script: echo "This job runs on a schedule"
  only:
    - schedules
```

GitLab UI allows configuring schedules under the CI/CD section, specifying intervals such as daily, monthly, etc.

Integrated Conditions:
Complex pipelines benefit from combining various conditional and triggering mechanisms. For example, one might want to conditionally trigger a pipeline based on a scheduled run and specific branch.

```
integrated_job:
  script:
    - echo "This job combines multiple conditions"
  rules:
    - if: '$CI_COMMIT_BRANCH == "develop"'
      when: on_success
```

```
    - if: '$CI_PIPELINE_SOURCE == "schedule"'
      when: on_success
```

This job executes for both scheduled runs and changes on the develop branch, providing a robust execution control mechanism.

The strategic use of conditional and triggered pipelines optimizes resource usage, enforces workflow policies, and ensures consistent quality across software development workflows.

6.5 Parent-Child Pipelines

Parent-child pipelines in GitLab provide a robust mechanism for organizing complex workflows and optimizing the execution of CI/CD tasks. They enable decomposition of a monolithic pipeline into manageable segments, improving readability, maintainability, and modularity. By leveraging parent-child pipelines, different parts of a project can be worked on independently while maintaining a coherent overall process.

Parent-child pipelines are defined within the .gitlab-ci.yml file. A parent pipeline spawns one or more child pipelines, each of which can execute specific stages or jobs. This architecture supports parallel execution and better failure isolation, since the failure of one child pipeline does not necessarily halt the parent pipeline or other child pipelines.

To configure parent-child pipelines, the needs and trigger keywords are instrumental. The trigger keyword in particular allows a job in the parent pipeline to start a child pipeline. Below is a detailed exploration of these configurations.

```
stages:
  - build
  - test
  - deploy

# Job in parent pipeline that triggers a child pipeline
build_job:
  stage: build
  script:
    - echo "Building the project..."
  trigger:
    include: path/to/child-pipeline.yml
    strategy: depend

# Continues with subsequent stages after the child pipeline
test_job:
  stage: test
  script:
    - echo "Running tests..."
```

```
  when: on_success

deploy_job:
  stage: deploy
  script:
    - echo "Deploying to production..."
  when: on_success
```

In the example above, build_job in the parent pipeline triggers the execution of a child pipeline defined in path/to/child-pipeline.yml. The strategy: depend option ensures that the parent pipeline waits for the completion of the child pipeline before proceeding to the next stage.

When defining child pipelines, the syntax is similar to that used in the main .gitlab-ci.yml file. Child pipelines can define their own stages, jobs, and rules independent of the parent pipeline.

```
stages:
  - child_build
  - child_test

child_build_job:
  stage: child_build
  script:
    - echo "Building inside child pipeline..."

child_test_job:
  stage: child_test
  script:
    - echo "Testing inside child pipeline..."
```

In this child pipeline example, there are two stages: child_build and child_test. These stages do not interfere with those of the parent pipeline, although their execution can influence the parent due to the strategy: depend option used in the parent's build_job.

- **Scalability**: Parent-child pipelines allow breaking down large CI/CD processes into smaller, manageable units. Each child pipeline can be developed, tested, and maintained independently.
- **Isolation**: Failures within a child pipeline do not propagate to other independent child pipelines. This isolation improves the resilience of the CI/CD process.
- **Concurrency**: Child pipelines can execute in parallel unless explicitly instructed to wait, thereby reducing the overall time required.
- **Modularity**: Different aspects of the CI/CD pipeline can be handled as modules, promoting reuse and simplifying maintenance.

Proper monitoring and debugging practices are vital for efficient use of parent-child pipelines. GitLab provides built-in pipeline visualization tools that display the hierarchy and status of parent and child pipelines. This feature is accessible through the pipeline view in the GitLab UI, where users can observe real-time progress and detailed logs.

To investigate issues, extensive logging within each stage or job is recommended. It enables pinpointing failures and bottlenecks in both the parent and the child pipelines. The output for executed commands can be observed directly from the GitLab projects' pipelines section.

A practical use case involves a software project with separate build, test, and deployment processes. A parent pipeline might handle preliminary build tasks and trigger child pipelines responsible for more detailed or environment-specific tasks.

```
# Parent Pipeline .gitlab-ci.yml
stages:
  - initial_build
  - trigger_child

initial_build_job:
  stage: initial_build
  script:
    - echo "Initial build step in parent pipeline..."

trigger_child_pipeline:
  stage: trigger_child
  trigger:
    include: child-pipelines/test-deploy.yml
    strategy: depend

# Child Pipeline test-deploy.yml
stages:
  - detailed_build
  - testing
  - deployment

detailed_build_job:
  stage: detailed_build
  script:
    - echo "Detailed build step in child pipeline..."

testing_job:
  stage: testing
  script:
    - echo "Running tests in child pipeline..."

deployment_job:
  stage: deployment
  script:
    - echo "Deploying from child pipeline..."
```

In this setup, the initial build step runs in the parent pipeline, and upon its success, a child pipeline defined in child-pipelines/test-deploy.yml is triggered. The child pipeline completes detailed build, testing, and deployment stages. Each step can be monitored independently, and any issues localized to a particular child pipeline are isolated from affecting the entire process.

Parent-child pipelines unlock advanced orchestration capabilities in GitLab CI/CD, enabling teams to design efficient, scalable, and maintainable workflows tailored to their project's needs.

6.6 Handling Pipeline Failures

In a Continuous Integration/Continuous Deployment (CI/CD) environment, handling pipeline failures effectively is crucial in maintaining the stability and reliability of software deployment. An advanced understanding of how to diagnose, mitigate, and prevent these failures is essential for ensuring a robust DevOps workflow. This section delves into the strategies and best practices for managing pipeline failures in GitLab CI/CD.

The first step in handling pipeline failures is to understand the common causes. Failures can arise from various sources, including syntax errors in the .gitlab-ci.yml file, issues with dependencies, misconfigurations, or bugs in the source code itself. Identifying the root cause is facilitated by GitLab's comprehensive logging and detailed error reporting, which can be examined in the job trace.

```
test:
  stage: test
  script:
    - echo "Running tests..."
    - exit 1
```

In the example above, the explicit exit 1 command forces the job to fail. The error message and exit status are logged, providing insights into the failure.

Addressing these failures involves both reactive and proactive measures. Reactively, it is imperative to set up notifications and alerts. GitLab can send notifications through various channels such as email and Slack. Configuring these notifications ensures that the appropriate stakeholders are informed of pipeline failures promptly.

Proactive measures include implementing retry logic, thereby allowing certain jobs to be retried automatically if they fail due to transient issues. This can be configured in the .gitlab-ci.yml file using the retry keyword.

```
deploy:
  stage: deploy
  script:
    - echo "Deploying to production..."
  retry: 2
```

In this configuration, the deployment job will be retried up to two additional times if it fails. While retrying can handle intermittent issues, it is important to examine the retry policy carefully to avoid masking underlying problems.

Another important aspect is setting appropriate pipeline exit statuses and using the allow_failure keyword for jobs whose failures should not affect the overall pipeline status. This is particularly useful for non-critical or experimental jobs.

```
lint:
  stage: test
  script:
    - echo "Running linter..."
    - eslint .
  allow_failure: true
```

Here, the linting job is marked with allow_failure, which means that its failure will not cause the entire pipeline to fail. This allows the pipeline to continue running subsequent stages.

Handling failures also necessitates the incorporation of debugging steps within the pipeline. Including verbose logging and breakpoints can aid significantly in diagnosing failures. Furthermore, using the artifacts keyword can store job outputs for later inspection.

```
test:
  stage: test
  script:
    - ./run-tests.sh
  artifacts:
    paths:
      - test-results/
```

This configuration ensures that the results of the test are stored and can be reviewed even after the pipeline execution.

GitLab's support for manual interventions through the use of protected environments and manual jobs can be strategically employed to halt pipeline execution at critical points and require manual approval before proceeding. This can be a crucial step in preventing the propagation of errors to production environments.

```
deploy_production:
  stage: deploy
```

```
script:
  - echo "Deploying to production..."
when: manual
environment:
  name: production
  url: https://production.example.com
```

For a comprehensive failure management strategy, implementing fallback and rollback mechanisms constitutes best practice. This can involve maintaining deployment scripts that automatically revert to a previous stable state in the event of a failure. This practice enhances the resilience of the deployment process and minimizes downtime.

Lastly, integrating monitoring and observability tools with GitLab pipelines contributes significantly to early detection and resolution of issues. Real-time monitoring and aggregating logs from all pipeline stages provide a holistic view of the pipeline health, aiding in the quick identification and resolution of failures.

Overall, handling pipeline failures adeptly requires a combination of reactive, proactive, and strategic measures. Leveraging GitLab's features, such as retries, manual interventions, verbose logging, and artifact storage, in conjunction with solid debugging practices and fallback mechanisms, can significantly enhance the reliability and robustness of CI/CD pipelines.

6.7 Optimizing Pipeline Performance

Efficient CI/CD pipelines are crucial for maintaining productivity and reducing the feedback loop in software development. Optimizing performance, therefore, involves various strategies that aim to minimize build times, improve resource utilization, and ensure that the pipeline scales effectively as the project grows.

One of the primary methods to enhance pipeline performance is to optimize the .gitlab-ci.yml file. This involves techniques such as parallel execution, proper use of caching, minimizing dependencies, and segmenting the pipeline into manageable stages.

```
stages: # List the stages in the pipeline
  - build
  - test
  - deploy

cache: # Use cache to speed up successive runs
  paths:
    - node_modules/
```

```
    - .m2/repository/

build: # Define a build job
  stage: build
  script:
    - npm install

test: # Define a test job
  stage: test
  script:
    - npm test

deploy: # Define a deploy job
  stage: deploy
  script:
    - npm run deploy
  only:
    - master
```

By defining a clear stage structure and utilizing caching, we prevent frequently used dependencies from being downloaded in every job run. This reduces network overhead and computation time.

Parallel execution is another key strategy. It allows independent jobs within the same stage to run concurrently, thus significantly decreasing the total pipeline duration. For example:

```
stages:
  - build
  - test

build-job1:
  stage: build
  script:
    - echo "Executing build job 1"

build-job2:
  stage: build
  script:
    - echo "Executing build job 2"

test-job1:
  stage: test
  script:
    - echo "Executing test job 1"

test-job2:
  stage: test
  script:
    - echo "Executing test job 2"
```

Here, build-job1 and build-job2 can run simultaneously, as can test-job1 and test-job2, thus taking full advantage of available CI runners.

Another critical aspect of pipeline optimization is the efficient use of artifacts. Artifacts can be used to share data between jobs and stages, eliminating the need to re-compute or re-download necessary files.

```
stages:
  - build
  - test

build:
  stage: build
  script:
    - npm install
    - npm run build
  artifacts:
    paths:
      - dist/

test:
  stage: test
  dependencies:
    - build
  script:
    - npm test
    - ls -la dist/
```

In this example, the build job generates a dist/ directory, which is then passed to the test job through artifacts. This prevents the test job from having to rebuild the dist/ directory, saving substantial time.

Effective resource allocation also plays a pivotal role. GitLab CI/CD supports the use of custom runners with specific hardware configurations to enhance performance. It is advisable to configure runners with appropriate specifications based on the computational needs of the project.

Employing job retries and allow_failure parameters can also indirectly impact performance by maintaining continuous workflow even when non-critical jobs fail, hence reducing unnecessary halts.

```
test:
  stage: test
  script:
    - npm test
  retry: 2 # Retry job up to two times if it fails

non_critical_test:
  stage: test
  script:
    - echo "This test is non-critical"
  allow_failure: true # Allow failures without affecting the pipeline status
```

Additionally, optimization extends to maintaining the pipeline environment. Integrating efficient source control practices like smaller, incremental commits allows for faster pipeline runs. Furthermore, leveraging conditional jobs using the rules keyword ensures unnecessary jobs are not executed, avoiding wasted resources.

```
deploy:
```

```
  stage: deploy
  script:
    - npm run deploy
  rules:
    - if: '$CI_COMMIT_REF_NAME == "main"'
```

In this instance, the deploy job runs only when the commit is pushed to the main branch, thus avoiding redundant deployment trials and conserving time and resources.

Finally, it is essential to regularly monitor pipeline metrics and logs to identify and resolve bottlenecks. GitLab CI/CD provides detailed logging and performance analytics tools that can be utilized to analyze job durations and pinpoint inefficiencies.

Through these optimization techniques, the effectiveness of your CI/CD process can be markedly improved, leading to reduced build times, efficient resource utilization, and ultimately, a more robust and maintainable deployment workflow.

6.8 Pipeline Security and Compliance

Ensuring security and compliance in CI/CD pipelines is paramount for maintaining the integrity and trustworthiness of software delivery. GitLab provides a suite of tools and configurations to enhance security and ensure compliance with various regulatory requirements. This section delves into key practices and techniques to fortify GitLab CI/CD pipelines against vulnerabilities and maintain strict adherence to compliance standards.

Secrets Management: Sensitive information such as API keys, passwords, and certificates must be handled securely. GitLab offers a secure way to manage secrets through protected variables. These variables can be stored at different levels—project, group, or instance—and their access can be restricted to protected branches or tags.

```
variables:
  SECRET_API_KEY: SECURE_STRING

stages:
  - build
  - test
  - deploy

build:
  stage: build
  script:
    - echo "Building..."
```

```
  only:
    - master

test:
  stage: test
  script:
    - echo "Running tests..."
  only:
    - master

deploy:
  stage: deploy
  script:
    - echo "Deploying with secret key $SECRET_API_KEY"
  only:
    - tags
    - branches
    - schedules
```

In this example, the SECRET_API_KEY variable is securely stored and used only during deployment. By limiting its usage to specific stages or conditions, the risk of exposure is minimized.

Role-Based Access Control (RBAC): GitLab's role-based access control helps define and enforce permissions for different users. Consistent application of RBAC ensures that only authorized personnel can modify pipeline configurations or access sensitive artifacts. Roles range from Guest to Owner, with each providing varying degrees of access.

Security Testing: Integrating security testing within CI/CD pipelines helps identify vulnerabilities early in the development cycle. GitLab supports several security testing techniques, including Static Application Security Testing (SAST), Dependency Scanning, and Dynamic Application Security Testing (DAST).

```
include:
  - template: SAST.gitlab-ci.yml
  - template: Dependency-Scanning.gitlab-ci.yml

stages:
  - build
  - test
  - scan

sast:
  stage: scan
  script:
    - echo "Running SAST..."
  only:
    - branches

dependency_scan:
  stage: scan
  script:
    - echo "Running dependency scanning..."
```

```
only:
  - branches
```

In this example, security scans are included in the pipeline by referencing predefined GitLab CI/CD templates. The results from these scans guide developers to remediate identified security issues.

Compliance Frameworks: To align with regulatory requirements like GDPR, HIPAA, or PCI-DSS, GitLab allows the creation of compliance frameworks. These frameworks can enforce specific pipeline configurations or job requirements to maintain compliance.

Audit Logging: GitLab's audit events feature logs user activities and changes within the system. These logs are crucial for compliance reporting and incident investigation.

```
Audit Logs in GitLab include:
- User login and logout
- Changes to project and group memberships
- Updates to repository data and CI/CD pipelines
```

Artifact Management: Artifacts produced during CI/CD processes, such as build outputs or reports, should be managed securely. GitLab provides access controls and expiration policies for artifacts to ensure that only authorized users can access them and that they are retained only as long as needed.

Manual Approvals: For sensitive stages, such as production deployment, incorporating manual approval steps enhances security. GitLab's manual jobs and environment-specific shielding provide a mechanism to pause the pipeline and require an authorized user to approve the continuation.

```
stages:
  - build
  - deploy

build:
  stage: build
  script:
    - echo "Building the application..."
  only:
    - master

deploy_to_production:
  stage: deploy
  script:
    - echo "Deploying to production..."
  when: manual
  only:
    - master
```

In this example, the deploy_to_production job waits for manual approval before executing. This practice ensures that critical deployments only occur with the explicit consent of responsible stakeholders.

Pipeline Code Review: Regular reviews of pipeline configurations (.gitlab-ci.yml) are essential. Code reviews help identify potential security flaws or misconfigurations that could lead to vulnerabilities or compliance issues. Using merge requests and enforcing mandatory code reviews by senior developers or security experts can significantly enhance the security posture of the pipeline configurations.

By systematically applying these practices, organizations can fortify their CI/CD pipelines against threats and ensure compliance with relevant standards. This not only protects the integrity of the development and deployment processes but also builds trust with users and stakeholders.

6.9 Pipeline as Code Best Practices

Effective CI/CD pipeline configuration is an essential component of modern DevOps practices. Adopting the principles of "Pipeline as Code" entails defining and managing your CI/CD pipeline configurations in a version-controlled, programmatic manner. This approach brings numerous advantages, including repeatability, transparency, ease of collaboration, and the ability to leverage configuration as part of the software development lifecycle.

A well-crafted .gitlab-ci.yml file can lead to predictable, maintainable, and efficient pipelines. Here, we will cover best practices to follow when defining pipelines as code in GitLab.

Use a Modular Approach: Break down your .gitlab-ci.yml configuration into smaller, reusable components. This can be achieved using Anchors and Aliases, which are part of the YAML specification. These tools allow you to define reusable snippets and include them in multiple places within your pipeline configuration file.

```
stages:
  - build
  - test
  - deploy

.default_template: &defaults
  image: python:3.8
  before_script:
    - pip install -r requirements.txt

build:
```

```
  <<: *defaults
  stage: build
  script:
    - python setup.py install

test:
  <<: *defaults
  stage: test
  script:
    - pytest

deploy:
  <<: *defaults
  stage: deploy
  script:
    - ssh user@server 'cd /path/to/app && git pull && service restart'
```

Parameterize Pipeline with Variables: Using predefined and custom variables allows you to parameterize different aspects of your pipeline. This enhances reusability and flexibility by enabling you to run the same pipeline in different environments or with different configurations.

```
variables:
  APP_ENV: "production"
  VERSION: "1.0"

stages:
  - deploy

deploy:
  stage: deploy
  script:
    - echo "Deploying version $VERSION to $APP_ENV environment"
```

Incorporate Conditional Workflow: Utilize the built-in rules for conditional execution of jobs. This can help in managing workflows dynamically based on branch names, tags, or the existence of certain files.

```
stages:
  - deploy

deploy:
  script:
    - echo "Deploying application"
  rules:
    - if: '$CI_COMMIT_BRANCH == "main"'
      when: always
    - if: '$CI_COMMIT_TAG =~ /^v\d+\.\d+\.\d+$/'
      when: always
```

Secure Secrets Management: Managing secrets securely is vital. Utilize GitLab's CI/CD secrets management by defining variables through GitLab's user interface under the project settings, ensuring sensitive data like API tokens and passwords aren't hard-coded in the .gitlab-ci.yml file.

Implement Error Handling and Retries: Incorporate error handling mechanisms by defining the allow_failure attribute and retries for jobs that might fail intermittently. This makes your pipelines more resilient, reducing the need for manual intervention.

```
stages:
  - test

test:
  stage: test
  script:
    - run-some-test
  allow_failure: true
  retry: 2
```

Optimize for Performance: Appropriate use of caching and artifact management can greatly enhance the performance of your pipelines. Specify cache and artifacts appropriately to avoid redundant computations and data transfers.

```
stages:
  - build
  - test

build:
  stage: build
  script:
    - make
  cache:
    key: ${CI_PROJECT_NAME}
    paths:
      - build/

test:
  stage: test
  script:
    - make test
  artifacts:
    paths:
      - test-results/
```

Structure Configurations for Readability: Maintain a clear, consistent structure and use comments where necessary to enhance readability and maintainability. Logical grouping and clear naming conventions will aid comprehension for anyone reviewing or modifying the configuration.

```
# Stages of the pipeline
stages:
  - build
  - test
  - deploy

# Build stage
build:
  stage: build
```

```
  script:
    - make

# Test stage
test:
  stage: test
  script:
    - make test

# Deploy stage
deploy:
  stage: deploy
  script:
    - scp -r ./* user@server:/path/to/app
```

Applying these best practices when designing your pipeline as code ensures a robust, efficient, and maintainable CI/CD process in GitLab.

6.10 Deployments with GitLab CI/CD

Deploying applications efficiently and reliably is a critical aspect of the software development lifecycle. GitLab CI/CD provides robust functionalities to manage deployments, ensuring that code changes are automatically tested, integrated, and deployed to various environments. This section delves into the strategies, configurations, and best practices for orchestrating deployments using GitLab CI/CD.

The .gitlab-ci.yml file, a cornerstone of GitLab CI/CD, defines the pipeline stages, jobs, and scripts necessary for deployment. Below, we review essential components and configurations to support deployments.

```
stages:
  - build
  - test
  - deploy

deploy_production:
  stage: deploy
  script:
    - echo "Deploying to production server"
    - rsync -avz --delete . user@production-server:/var/www/html/
  only:
    - master
```

In the example above, we define a deployment job named deploy_production within the deploy stage. The job executes a script to transfer files to the production server using rsync. The only keyword ensures this job runs only for the master branch, safeguarding against unintended deployments from other branches.

Multi-environment Deployments

Managing multiple environments such as development, staging, and production is a common practice. GitLab CI/CD facilitates this through environment-specific jobs and dynamic environments.

```
deploy_dev:
  stage: deploy
  script:
    - echo "Deploying to development server"
    - rsync -avz --delete . user@dev-server:/var/www/html/
  environment:
    name: development
    url: http://dev.example.com

deploy_stage:
  stage: deploy
  script:
    - echo "Deploying to staging server"
    - rsync -avz --delete . user@staging-server:/var/www/html/
  environment:
    name: staging
    url: http://staging.example.com

deploy_prod:
  stage: deploy
  script:
    - echo "Deploying to production server"
    - rsync -avz --delete . user@prod-server:/var/www/html/
  environment:
    name: production
    url: http://prod.example.com
  only:
    - master
```

Each deployment job specifies a unique environment, providing a clear separation of responsibilities and endpoints. The environment keyword defines the environment's name and URL, which GitLab uses to contextualize deployments.

Manual Deployments

Automated pipelines are powerful, but some stages, particularly deployments, may require manual approval to maintain control over production systems.

```
deploy_to_production:
  stage: deploy
  script:
    - echo "Deploying to production server"
    - rsync -avz --delete . user@prod-server:/var/www/html/
  only:
    - master
  when: manual
```

Setting the when keyword to manual ensures the job will not execute automatically, allowing project maintainers to trigger the deployment at an appropriate time via the GitLab web interface.

Rolling Deployments

To avoid disruptions during the deployment process, rolling deployments gradually replace instances of the running services.

```
rollout_job:
  stage: deploy
  script:
    - kubectl set image deployment/myapp myapp=myapp:
          v$CI_COMMIT_SHORT_SHA --record
  environment:
    name: production
    url: http://prod.example.com
  only:
    - master
```

Utilizing kubectl, the rollout_job updates the image of a Kubernetes deployment. This form of a zero-downtime deployment ensures that no service interruption occurs.

Using GitLab Environments and Deployment Tracking

GitLab environments provide an integrated view of the deployment landscape. Each environment can be monitored for deployment status, allowing seamless tracking of what version is deployed in which environment.

```
deploy_prod:
  stage: deploy
  script:
    - echo "Deploying to production server"
    - rsync -avz --delete . user@prod-server:/var/www/html/
  environment:
    name: production
    url: http://prod.example.com
  only:
    - tags
```

Deployments triggered by tags provide an extra layer of control, reinforcing that only tagged releases are deployed, enhancing stability and traceability.

Deployment Strategies

Several deployment strategies cater to different needs. Typical strategies include:

- **Blue-Green Deployments:** A two-environment setup where one environment (blue) is active while the other (green) is idle. The deployment switches between them.

- **Canary Deployments:** Gradual deployment to a small subset of users before a full scale rollout.
- **A/B Testing:** Running multiple variants simultaneously to compare performance and user engagement.
- **Feature Flags:** Toggling features on and off independently of deployments.

Blue-Green Deployment in GitLab can be configured as follows:

```
deploy_blue:
  stage: deploy
  script:
    - echo "Deploying to blue environment"
    - rsync -avz --delete . user@blue-server:/var/www/html/
  environment:
    name: blue
    url: http://blue.example.com

deploy_green:
  stage: deploy
  script:
    - echo "Deploying to green environment"
    - rsync -avz --delete . user@green-server:/var/www/html/
  environment:
    name: green
    url: http://green.example.com
```

Instantiating Feature Flags can be achieved by incorporating feature management tools:

```
feature_flags:
  stage: deploy
  script:
    - echo "Setting feature flags"
    - curl -X POST -H "Content-Type: application/json" -d '{"feature": "new-feature",
        "enabled": true}' http://feature-flags-service
```

By implementing these strategies, teams can maintain high availability and robustness of their applications.

Deployments with GitLab CI/CD offer flexibility and control, ensuring that the integration process is streamlined and robust. By carefully orchestrating deployment strategies and utilizing GitLab's features, development teams can achieve seamless and efficient software delivery.

6.11 Integrating Third-party Services

Integrating third-party services with GitLab CI/CD provides an avenue to extend the functionality of your CI/CD pipelines, streamline workflows, and enhance productivity. This section delves into the integration of various popular third-party services such as Slack, Jira, Docker Hub, Sentry, and Artifactory within GitLab CI/CD pipelines.

Slack integration in GitLab CI/CD enables notifications about pipeline events, thus keeping the entire development team informed and coordinated. To configure Slack notifications in your project, proceed to the project settings and navigate to 'Integrations'. Enable the Slack integration and configure the webhook URL obtained from your Slack workspace. The following integration snippet should be added to the '.gitlab-ci.yml' file:

```
slack_notify:
  script:
    - echo "Notifying Slack"
  after_script:
    - curl -X POST -H 'Content-type: application/json' --data '{"text":"Pipeline run
        completed for $CI_PROJECT_NAME at branch
        $CI_COMMIT_REF_NAME"}' $SLACK_WEBHOOK_URL
```

Jira integration allows for seamless interaction between GitLab issues and Jira tasks. To set up Jira integration, link your GitLab project to the Jira instance through the 'Integrations' section of the project settings. Once linked, you can use custom keywords to transition Jira tickets automatically in your pipeline script as shown below:

```
stages:
  - track

track_issue:
  script:
    - echo "Tracking Jira Issue"
  after_script:
    - curl -u $JIRA_USER:$JIRA_API_TOKEN -X POST --data '{"transition": {"id":
        "31"}}' -H 'Content-Type: application/json' https://your-jira-domain.
        atlassian.net/rest/api/2/issue/$CI_COMMIT_REF_NAME/transitions
```

For Docker Hub integration, GitLab CI/CD can automatically build and push Docker images. Authenticate Docker Hub by defining credentials in the '.gitlab-ci.yml' file or through GitLab CI/CD variables for security reasons:

```
variables:
  DOCKER_REGISTRY: docker.io
  DOCKER_USERNAME: $DOCKER_USER
  DOCKER_PASSWORD: $DOCKER_PASS

build_and_push:
  script:
    - docker login -u "$DOCKER_USERNAME" -p "$DOCKER_PASSWORD"
        $DOCKER_REGISTRY
    - docker build -t $DOCKER_REGISTRY/$CI_PROJECT_PATH:
        $CI_COMMIT_REF_SLUG .
```

```
    - docker push $DOCKER_REGISTRY/$CI_PROJECT_PATH:
          $CI_COMMIT_REF_SLUG
```

Sentry integration is crucial for monitoring and error tracking in your applications. By sending deployment and error information to Sentry, you can gain insights into application performance and issues. Configure Sentry by setting up the DSN (Data Source Name) in GitLab CI variables:

```
sentry_notify:
  script:
    - echo "Notifying Sentry"
  after_script:
    - curl -X POST -H 'Content-Type: application/json' -H "Authorization: Bearer
          $SENTRY_AUTH_TOKEN" --data '{"sha":"$CI_COMMIT_SHA", "
          environment":"$CI_ENVIRONMENT_NAME"}' https://sentry.io/api/0/
          projects/$SENTRY_ORG/$SENTRY_PROJECT/releases/
```

Artifactory integration allows storing, versioning, and managing build artifacts. To leverage Artifactory, authenticate and configure your repositories in GitLab CI pipeline scripts:

```
variables:
  ARTIFACTORY_URL: https://your-artifactory-domain
  ARTIFACTORY_USER: $ARTIFACTORY_USER
  ARTIFACTORY_PASSWORD: $ARTIFACTORY_PASS

upload_artifact:
  script:
    - curl -u $ARTIFACTORY_USER:$ARTIFACTORY_PASSWORD -T ./path/to/
          artifact.json "$ARTIFACTORY_URL/artifactory/repo-key/$(basename ./
          path/to/artifact.json)"
```

By integrating third-party services with GitLab CI/CD, these integrations facilitate automation, improve monitoring, and enhance the efficiency of development workflows. Each service expands GitLab's capabilities, allowing teams to maintain high standards of continuous integration and deployment practices.

6.12 Real-world CI/CD Pipeline Examples

To illustrate the concepts and practices discussed in this chapter, we will examine several real-world CI/CD pipeline examples. These examples demonstrate the implementation of complex pipeline configurations within GitLab, showcasing strategies to manage multiple environments, use variables and secrets effectively, optimize performance, and ensure security and compliance.

Example 1: A Multi-Environment Deployment Pipeline

Consider a project with separate development, staging, and production environments. The following .gitlab-ci.yml configuration manages deployments across these environments.

```
stages:
  - build
  - test
  - deploy

variables:
  DEV_IMAGE: myapp:dev
  STAGE_IMAGE: myapp:stage
  PROD_IMAGE: myapp:prod

build:
  stage: build
  script:
    - docker build -t $DEV_IMAGE .

test:
  stage: test
  script:
    - echo "Running tests..."
    - docker run --rm $DEV_IMAGE pytest

deploy_dev:
  stage: deploy
  environment:
    name: development
  script:
    - docker tag $DEV_IMAGE myregistry.com/$DEV_IMAGE
    - docker push myregistry.com/$DEV_IMAGE
  only:
    - develop

deploy_stage:
  stage: deploy
  environment:
    name: staging
  script:
    - docker tag $DEV_IMAGE myregistry.com/$STAGE_IMAGE
    - docker push myregistry.com/$STAGE_IMAGE
  only:
    - main

deploy_prod:
  stage: deploy
  environment:
    name: production
  script:
    - docker tag $DEV_IMAGE myregistry.com/$PROD_IMAGE
    - docker push myregistry.com/$PROD_IMAGE
  only:
    - tags
```

This configuration builds a Docker image in the build stage, runs tests in the test stage, and deploys the application to different environments based on the Git branch or tag. The only keyword ensures that deployments occur under specific conditions: the development environment deploys on develop branch, the staging environment on main branch, and the production environment when a tag is generated.

Example 2: Pipeline Optimized with Caching and Artifacts

To enhance CI/CD performance, caching dependencies and using artifacts to pass build results between stages can significantly reduce redundancy and build times.

```
stages:
  - install
  - build
  - test

cache:
  paths:
    - .npm/

install_dependencies:
  stage: install
  script:
    - npm install
  artifacts:
    paths:
      - node_modules/

build:
  stage: build
  script:
    - npm run build
  artifacts:
    paths:
      - dist/

test:
  stage: test
  script:
    - npm test
  dependencies:
    - install_dependencies
```

In this configuration, the cache keyword caches the .npm/ directory to preserve downloaded packages between pipeline runs. The artifacts keyword ensures that the node_modules/ directory is available to the build and test stages, improving pipeline efficiency by avoiding repetitive installations.

Example 3: Using Variables and Secrets for Secure Configurations

Managing secrets securely is paramount in CI/CD pipelines. GitLab CI/CD provides mechanisms for injecting secret variables into the pipeline without exposing them.

```
stages:
  - build
  - deploy

variables:
  DOCKER_TLS_CERT_PATH: "/etc/docker/certs"

before_script:
  - mkdir -p $DOCKER_TLS_CERT_PATH
  - echo "$CI_PRIVATE_KEY" | base64 -d > $DOCKER_TLS_CERT_PATH/client.
      key
  - echo "$CI_CERT" | base64 -d > $DOCKER_TLS_CERT_PATH/client.cert

build:
  stage: build
  script:
    - docker build -t myapp .

deploy:
  stage: deploy
  script:
    - docker login -u $CI_REGISTRY_USER -p $CI_REGISTRY_PASSWORD
        $CI_REGISTRY
    - docker push myapp
```

In this example, the before_script block decodes and configures TLS certificates for secure Docker operations, using variables (CI_PRIVATE_KEY and CI_CERT) stored securely in GitLab's variable settings. This prevents sensitive information from being hard-coded into the pipeline.

Example 4: Conditional and Triggered Pipelines for Complex Workflows

Advanced CI/CD pipelines often need conditional execution of jobs and triggering downstream pipelines based on specific criteria or events.

```
stages:
  - test
  - deploy

test:
  stage: test
  script:
    - echo "Running unit tests"
  only:
    - branches

deploy_staging:
  stage: deploy
  script:
    - echo "Deploy to staging"
  only:
    - /^staging-.*$/

trigger_downstream:
  stage: deploy
  script:
```

```
    - curl -X POST -F token=$TRIGGER_TOKEN -F ref=main https://gitlab.com/
        api/v4/projects/1234567/trigger/pipeline
```

This configuration includes a test job that runs for all branches, a deploy_staging job that runs only for branches matching the regex pattern \/ŝtaging-.*$/, and a trigger_downstream job that triggers a pipeline in another project using GitLab's API.

Example 5: Securing Deployment with Approval Gates

To ensure deployment security and compliance, using manual approvals can add an extra layer of governance before sensitive environments are affected.

```
stages:
  - build
  - deploy

build:
  stage: build
  script:
    - docker build -t myapp .

deploy_staging:
  stage: deploy
  script:
    - docker push myapp:staging
  only:
    - staging

deploy_production:
  stage: deploy
  script:
    - docker push myapp:prod
  only:
    - master
  when: manual
  environment:
    name: production
```

Here, the deploy_production job is marked as manual, requiring an explicit user action to proceed, which is useful for adding a human oversight step before deploying to production.

These examples collectively demonstrate various advanced configurations and techniques for optimizing CI/CD pipelines in GitLab by handling multi-environment deployments, utilizing caching and artifacts, managing secrets, setting conditional jobs, and enforcing approval gates.

Chapter 7

DevOps Practices with GitLab

This chapter examines the implementation of DevOps principles using GitLab. It addresses key aspects of DevOps culture, including continuous integration, continuous delivery, and continuous deployment. You will learn about infrastructure as code, monitoring, and logging within GitLab. The chapter also covers essential security practices, collaboration and communication techniques, and workflow automation. Practical case studies of successful DevOps implementations using GitLab are included to provide real-world context.

7.1 Introduction to DevOps

DevOps, a portmanteau of development (Dev) and operations (Ops), represents a cultural and technical movement that aims to enhance collaboration between software development and IT operations teams. This methodology promotes a synergistic effort to ensure the rapid and reliable delivery of high-quality software. Central to DevOps are concepts such as process automation, continuous delivery, and robust monitoring.

The traditional separation between development and operations often leads to inefficiencies. Development teams aim to introduce new features rapidly, while operations teams focus on system stability and uptime. This creates a conflict of interest, often referred to as the "wall of confusion". DevOps seeks to dismantle this barrier by fostering a culture where both teams work collectively towards shared objectives.

Central to DevOps is the principle of continuous integration (CI) and continuous delivery (CD). Continuous integration emphasizes the frequent and automated integration of code changes into a shared repository. Developers push their changes several times a day, which are integrated, built, and tested systematically. Continuous delivery extends this principle by ensuring that software can be released to production at any time. This systematizes the deployment process, ensuring swift, repeatable, and consistent releases.

In GitLab, CI/CD pipelines automate the testing, building, and deployment of applications. Here is an example of a basic GitLab CI/CD pipeline configuration using a '.gitlab-ci.yml' file:

```
stages:
  - build
  - test
  - deploy

build_job:
  stage: build
  script:
    - echo "Compiling the code..."
    - gcc -o my_app my_app.c

test_job:
  stage: test
  script:
    - echo "Running unit tests..."
    - ./run_unit_tests.sh

deploy_job:
  stage: deploy
  script:
    - echo "Deploying application..."
    - ./deploy.sh
```

In this example, the pipeline consists of three stages: *build*, *test*, and *deploy*. Each stage defines a job that executes specific scripts. The build stage compiles the code, the test stage runs unit tests, and the deploy stage deploys the application. These tasks are executed in a sequence, ensuring a smooth transition from development to deployment.

Another foundational element of DevOps is infrastructure as code (IaC). IaC treats infrastructure configuration in the same way as software code, using version control systems to manage configuration changes.

Tools such as Terraform, Ansible, and Chef make it possible to script the entire IT environment, from servers and networks to databases and storage. This approach increases transparency, simplifies infrastructure management, and mitigates configuration drift.

For instance, consider the following Terraform script to provision an AWS EC2 instance:

```
provider "aws" {
  region = "us-west-2"
}

resource "aws_instance" "my_instance" {
  ami = "ami-0c55b159cbfafe1f0"
  instance_type = "t2.micro"

  tags = {
    Name = "MyInstance"
  }
}
```

This script tells Terraform to use the AWS provider, configure the instance to use the 'us-west-2' region, and create a t2.micro EC2 instance based on the specified AMI.

Monitoring and logging are crucial for maintaining and improving system reliability and performance in a DevOps environment. Monitoring involves observing system performance and identifying potential issues, while logging records various events to provide a detailed history of system activities. These practices help teams quickly detect, diagnose, and resolve issues, as well as understand historical performance patterns.

Integrating monitoring tools such as Prometheus and Grafana with GitLab helps teams visualize critical metrics and set up alerts for potential anomalies. Below is an example of a basic Prometheus configuration to monitor application metrics:

```
global:
  scrape_interval: 15s

scrape_configs:
  - job_name: 'my_app'
    static_configs:
      - targets: ['localhost:9090']
```

This configuration sets up Prometheus to scrape metrics from the application running on 'localhost:9090' at 15-second intervals. When combined with Grafana, the metrics can be visualized to provide a graphical representation of the application's performance.

Security considerations are paramount within DevOps. The integration of security practices into the DevOps pipeline, often termed DevSecOps, ensures that security is a continuous, hands-on part of the development process. This involves automated security tests, static code analysis, and regular vulnerability assessments to prevent security risks and ensure compliance with standards.

The concept of Shift-Left testing encourages performing testing earlier in the development process, which includes security checks as part of the CI/CD pipeline. For example, integrating tools like SonarQube for static code analysis can identify code quality and security issues:

```
stages:
  - code_analysis

code_analysis_job:
  stage: code_analysis
  script:
    - sonar-scanner
```

In this pipeline, the *code_analysis* stage runs the 'sonar-scanner' command to perform static code analysis using SonarQube. This proactive approach ensures that security and quality issues are addressed early, reducing the risk of vulnerabilities in the production environment.

DevOps emphasizes a culture of collaboration and communication among teams. Tools like GitLab provide a platform for shared repositories, issue tracking, and merge requests, promoting transparency and accountability in the development process. Automated workflows enhance efficiency, reduce manual errors, and ensure consistent application delivery.

Understanding and implementing DevOps with GitLab involves a holistic approach, encompassing CI/CD, IaC, monitoring, and security practices. This methodology transforms the software development lifecycle, fostering a culture of continuous improvement and operational excellence. As we proceed through this chapter, we will delve deeper into each of these components, illustrating their practical application within GitLab.

7.2 DevOps Culture and Principles

DevOps, a portmanteau of "development" and "operations," is a culture and set of practices designed to bridge the gap between software development and IT operations. Its primary aim is to create an environment where building, testing, and releasing software can occur more rapidly, frequently, and reliably. Central to DevOps culture are various principles and values that ensure a collaborative, efficient, and transparent environment.

At the heart of DevOps culture is the promotion of shared responsibility. In traditional software development models, developers and operations teams often work in silos, leading to miscommunication and inefficiencies. DevOps advocates for these teams to work closely together, fostering a sense of collective ownership of the software and systems. This collaboration is facilitated by shared goals, metrics, and processes, which help align the objectives of both teams.

Key principles of DevOps include:

- **Collaboration and Communication**: DevOps encourages frequent and transparent communication between development, operations, and other stakeholders (e.g., QA, security). This can be achieved through regular meetings, shared communication channels, and collaborative tools like GitLab.
- **Automation**: Automating repetitive tasks such as testing, integration, and deployment allows teams to focus on more complex and value-adding activities. In DevOps, automation is paramount for achieving Continuous Integration (CI), Continuous Delivery (CD), and Continuous Deployment.
- **Continuous Improvement**: DevOps culture emphasizes the importance of iteratively refining and improving processes and systems. This involves regular feedback loops, retrospectives, and a commitment to learning from both successes and failures.
- **Measurement and Monitoring**: Utilizing metrics and monitoring tools ensures that teams can track performance, detect issues early, and make informed decisions. Data-driven insights help optimize both development and operational processes.
- **Customer-Centric Action**: All activities are guided by the goal of delivering value to the customer. This principle ensures that the team's efforts are aligned with end-user needs and expectations.
- **Resilience and Security**: A robust DevOps culture includes practices that enhance the resilience and security of systems. This involves proactive risk management, vulnerability assessments, and the integration of security practices into every phase of the software lifecycle.

Collaboration and Communication are fostered through various practices and tools. For instance, GitLab supports issue tracking, merge requests, and comments, which facilitate communication within the team. Collaborative tools such as these help synchronize efforts and resolve issues quickly.

For **Automation**, GitLab CI/CD pipelines play a crucial role. Pipelines automate the stages of building, testing, and deploying applications. Here is a basic example of a GitLab CI/CD pipeline definition:

```
stages:
  - build
  - test
  - deploy

build-job:
  stage: build
  script:
    - echo "Building the application..."
    - ./build_script.sh

test-job:
  stage: test
  script:
    - echo "Running unit tests..."
    - ./test_script.sh

deploy-job:
  stage: deploy
  script:
    - echo "Deploying the application..."
    - ./deploy_script.sh
```

The definition shows a pipeline with three stages: build, test, and deploy. Each job within the stages executes a specific script, streamlining the entire CI/CD process.

In line with the principle of **Continuous Improvement**, DevOps teams conduct regular retrospectives and use feedback mechanisms to iterate on their workflows. Tools such as GitLab's Value Stream Analytics help identify bottlenecks and optimize processes.

Measurement and monitoring tools are pivotal in adhering to the **Measurement and Monitoring** principle. GitLab integrates well with monitoring tools like Prometheus and Grafana, enabling teams to visualize metrics and log data. This helps in proactive issue detection and performance optimization. An exemplary configuration to set up Prometheus monitoring in GitLab might look like this:

```
prometheus:
  script:
    - apt-get update && apt-get install -y prometheus
    - systemctl start prometheus
```

```
    - systemctl enable prometheus
```

Consistently measuring and monitoring applications ensures early detection of anomalies and facilitates prompt remediation.

Customer-Centric Action is realized by integrating customer feedback loops into the DevOps process. This might involve monitoring user behavior, collecting feedback through surveys, and integrating this information into the development cycle. GitLab's analytics tools provide insights into user activity and can guide teams about areas needing improvement.

For enhancing **Resilience and Security**, DevOps teams implement practices like automated security testing and continuous vulnerability assessment. GitLab integrates various security scanning tools, such as SAST and DAST, into the CI/CD pipeline, ensuring that security is an integral part of the development process. A sample integration of SAST for security scanning would appear as follows:

```
sast:
  stage: test
  script:
    - echo "Running static application security testing..."
    - ./sast_script.sh
```

Securing the development pipeline and the final product is vital for building resilient systems that withstand potential threats and vulnerabilities.

Prominent among DevOps values are transparency and trust. By fostering a transparent environment where information is shared freely, teams build mutual trust and accountability. The end result is a more agile and responsive organization capable of adapting to changes rapidly and effectively.

In practice, the successful implementation of DevOps principles involves a combination of cultural shifts, process modifications, and the adoption of enabling technologies. As a unified and communicative team, development and operations work hand-in-hand to enhance software quality, deliver value more efficiently, and respond to customer needs swiftly. The principles and practices laid out in this section form the bedrock of a robust DevOps culture within any organization, providing a blueprint for improved collaboration, productivity, and innovation.

7.3 Implementing DevOps with GitLab

Within the landscape of DevOps, GitLab emerges as a powerful platform that seamlessly integrates diverse aspects of software development and operations. The implementation of DevOps using GitLab can be leveraged to streamline workflows, foster collaboration, and increase productivity. GitLab's comprehensive suite of tools takes developers through the entire software development lifecycle, facilitating features such as version control, continuous integration, continuous deployment, and more.

To successfully implement DevOps with GitLab, one must first understand GitLab's fundamental components and their roles within the DevOps pipeline. GitLab's architecture is built around repositories, pipelines, and runners. Each of these elements plays a crucial role in automating processes, enhancing collaboration, and ensuring code quality.

At the core of GitLab's functionality is the **repository**, a central location where code resides. It supports Git, a distributed version control system, enabling multiple team members to work concurrently on codebases. Each project in GitLab starts with the creation of a repository, which can be hosted either in the cloud or on-premises.

```
# Navigate to the GitLab dashboard
# Click on "New project"
# Provide a project name, description, and select the visibility level
# Click "Create project"
```

Following repository creation, it is essential to configure the **GitLab CI/CD** pipeline. Continuous Integration (CI) and Continuous Deployment (CD) are the backbones of the DevOps practice, allowing automatic building, testing, and deploying of applications. GitLab CI/CD pipelines are defined using a file named .gitlab-ci.yml, which resides in the root of the repository.

The .gitlab-ci.yml file contains a series of instructions and stages that our pipeline follows. For instance, a basic pipeline might consist of stages such as **build**, **test**, and **deploy**. Each stage can encompass multiple jobs, which are executed by GitLab Runners. Runners are lightweight, agent-like processes that execute CI/CD tasks.

```
stages:
  - build
  - test
  - deploy
```

```
build:
  stage: build
  script:
    - echo "Compiling the code..."
    - make

test:
  stage: test
  script:
    - echo "Running tests..."
    - make test

deploy:
  stage: deploy
  script:
    - echo "Deploying to production..."
    - make deploy
```

The above example elucidates a simple pipeline configuration. The build stage compiles the code, the test stage runs automated tests, and the deploy stage handles application deployment. This pipeline ensures that only code that passes all stages reaches production, significantly reducing the risk of defects.

GitLab Runners are critical in the execution of CI/CD jobs. They can be run on dedicated servers, virtual machines, or even containers. There are different types of runners, including shared runners (provided by GitLab) and specific runners (self-hosted by organizations). Configuring runners involves registering them with the GitLab instance and ensuring they are properly set up to execute pipeline jobs.

```
# Download and install the GitLab Runner
sudo apt-get install gitlab-runner

# Register the runner with the GitLab instance
sudo gitlab-runner register
# You will be prompted to provide the GitLab instance URL, registration token, and
    other details
```

Beyond the basic CI/CD pipelines, GitLab offers advanced features like **environments** and **review apps**. Environments allow you to deploy your applications to different stages, such as development, staging, and production. They provide a clear overview and control over the deployment process.

```
deploy_staging:
  stage: deploy
  script:
    - echo "Deploying to staging..."
    - make deploy-staging
  environment:
    name: staging
    url: https://staging.example.com
```

```
deploy_production:
  stage: deploy
  script:
    - echo "Deploying to production..."
    - make deploy-production
  environment:
    name: production
    url: https://example.com
```

Review apps are dynamically created environments for each merge request, providing a preview of changes before they are merged into the main branch. This feature enables stakeholders to visualize the impact of changes in real-time, facilitating faster and more informed decision-making.

```
review:
  stage: deploy
  script:
    - echo "Deploying review app..."
    - make deploy-review
  environment:
    name: review/$CI_COMMIT_REF_NAME
    url: https://review-$CI_COMMIT_REF_NAME.example.com
    on_stop: stop_review

stop_review:
  stage: clean_up
  script:
    - echo "Stopping review app..."
    - make stop-review
  when: manual
  environment:
    name: review/$CI_COMMIT_REF_NAME
    action: stop
```

Integrating GitLab with other DevOps tools can further enhance productivity and collaboration. GitLab supports integrations with popular tools like **Jira**, **Slack**, and **Kubernetes**. These integrations enable seamless tracking of issues, efficient communication among team members, and automated deployments to complex cloud environments.

```
# Example of Jira Integration
settings:
  issues:
    enabled: true
    tracker_id: 'jira'

# Example of Slack Integration
services:
  - name: slack_notifications
    settings:
      webhook: https://hooks.slack.com/services/...
      channel: #deployments
      username: gitlab-ci

# Example of Kubernetes Integration
kubernetes:
  api_url: https://kubernetes.example.com
  token: <token>
  ca_pem: <ca_pem>
```

By leveraging GitLab's comprehensive suite of tools and integrations, organizations can implement a robust DevOps strategy that enhances code quality, accelerates deployment cycles, and fosters collaboration. Through meticulous configuration of repositories, pipelines, and environments, along with strategic integrations, GitLab enables teams to adopt and thrive in a DevOps culture.

7.4 Continuous Integration (CI)

Continuous Integration (CI) is a fundamental DevOps practice that involves the systematic integration of code changes into a shared repository multiple times a day. Using GitLab for CI enables teams to detect errors quickly, ensure code quality, and reduce integration issues through automated testing and build processes.

At the core of CI in GitLab is the .gitlab-ci.yml file. This file contains the pipeline configuration that specifies the stages, jobs, and the corresponding scripts to be executed. A GitLab CI/CD pipeline runs every time code is pushed to the repository and follows the stages defined in this file.

Stages and Jobs

In a CI pipeline, stages represent the sequence of steps that need to be performed. A common arrangement includes stages like build, test, and deploy. Each stage encapsulates one or more jobs, which are the individual tasks to be run. Jobs within the same stage are executed in parallel, whereas stages are executed sequentially.

Example of a .gitlab-ci.yml file:

```
stages:
  - build
  - test
  - deploy

build-job:
  stage: build
  script:
    - echo "Compiling the code..."
    - make

test-job:
  stage: test
  script:
    - echo "Running tests..."
    - make test

deploy-job:
  stage: deploy
  script:
    - echo "Deploying the code..."
    - make deploy
```

Runners

GitLab CI uses runners to execute jobs. Runners are lightweight, scalable agents that run the code defined in the .gitlab-ci.yml file. They can be shared across multiple projects or dedicated to a single project. Runners come in different types, such as shell, docker, kubernetes, etc., which determine the environment in which the jobs run.

Example configuration for a runner:

```
[[runners]]
  name = "docker-runner"
  url = "https://gitlab.example.com/"
  token = "your-unique-token"
  executor = "docker"
  [runners.custom_build_dir]
  [runners.docker]
    tls_verify = false
    image = "docker:latest"
    privileged = true
    disable_entrypoint_overwrite = false
    oom_kill_disable = false
    disable_cache = false
    volumes = ["/cache"]
    shm_size = 0
```

Pipeline Execution

When code is pushed to the repository, the pipeline is triggered. GitLab displays the status of the pipeline, and users can access logs for each job to diagnose potential failures. Pipeline statuses are indicated by various badges such as passed, failed, and running.

Example of a pipeline status output:

```
Status  | Stage   | Job        | Duration
--------|---------|------------|----------
Passed  | build   | build-job  | 01:30
Failed  | test    | test-job   | 00:45
Skipped | deploy  | deploy-job | N/A
```

Artifacts and Caching

Artifacts are files generated by jobs and can be used by subsequent stages in the pipeline. These can include compiled binaries, test reports, logs, etc. Caching allows the reuse of dependencies and other files between pipeline runs to speed up the build process.

Example of configuring artifacts and caching in .gitlab-ci.yml:

```
build-job:
  stage: build
  script:
    - make
  artifacts:
    paths:
      - build/output/

test-job:
  stage: test
  script:
    - make test
  cache:
    paths:
      - .cache/
```

Notifications and Integrations

GitLab supports various integrations and notifications to inform team members about pipeline statuses. This ensures visibility and prompt action on issues. Integrations include email, Slack, and other third-party services.

Example of email notification configuration:

```
notifications:
  email:
    recipients:
      - "dev_team@example.com"
    on_success: always
    on_failure: always
```

Implementing CI with GitLab offers numerous advantages including early bug detection, improved code quality, and faster development cycles. By automating tests and builds, teams can focus on writing code, knowing that the integration process is continuously monitored and validated.

7.5 Continuous Delivery (CD)

Continuous Delivery (CD) is a software engineering approach in which teams produce software in short cycles, ensuring that the software can be reliably released at any time. This methodology involves the deployment of all code changes to a testing environment and, potentially, to a production environment after a build stage. The goal of CD is to make software development and release processes faster, safer, and more sustainable.

Key Concepts of Continuous Delivery

- **Automated Testing:** Automated tests are crucial in CD to ensure that new code changes do not break the existing system. These tests include unit tests, integration tests, and system tests.

- **Incremental Builds:** Each code change triggers an incremental build process that compiles and integrates the code, typically in a sandbox environment, to detect errors early.

- **Release Automation:** Automated deployment scripts ensure that code can be deployed without human intervention, reducing the possibility of manual errors.

- **Continuous Integration (CI):** CI is a prerequisite for CD. It involves the frequent integration of code into a shared repository, followed by automated builds and tests.

- **Version Control:** Proper version control is essential to manage changes and rollback if necessary. Using tools like GitLab helps in tracking version history and managing branches and merges.

The implementation of Continuous Delivery in GitLab is facilitated by GitLab CI/CD pipelines. Pipelines define a sequence of stages that include various jobs to be executed. This section elaborates on setting up a CD pipeline in GitLab, ensuring thorough testing, and deploying staged environments.

Setting Up a CD Pipeline in GitLab

GitLab CI/CD pipelines are defined in a .gitlab-ci.yml file placed at the root of your project repository. The following is an example of a basic CD pipeline configuration:

```
stages:
  - build
  - test
  - deploy

build-job:
  stage: build
  script:
    - echo "Compiling the code..."
    - mkdir -p build
    - gcc -o build/my_app src/*

test-job:
  stage: test
  script:
    - echo "Running automated tests..."
    - ./build/my_app --run-tests

deploy-job:
  stage: deploy
  script:
    - echo "Deploying to production..."
    - scp -r build/my_app user@server:/var/www/my_app
  environment:
    name: production
    url: https://www.example.com
```

Breakdown of the Example CD Pipeline

- stages: Defines the stages of the pipeline. In this example, we have three stages: build, test, and deploy.

- build-job: The build stage compiles the source code. It includes steps to create a build directory and compile the application using gcc.

- test-job: The test stage runs the automated tests. Here, the compiled application is executed with a testing flag to ensure functionality.

- deploy-job: The deploy stage transfers the built application to the production environment using scp. The environment key specifies the production environment's name and URL.

Automated Testing in CD

Effective automated testing is a continuous delivery pillar. Types of automated tests include:

- **Unit Tests:** Validate the behavior of individual units of code.

- **Integration Tests:** Ensure that combined units of code work together correctly.
- **System Tests:** Verify the overall behavior of the system and its interactions with external systems.
- **Acceptance Tests:** Confirm that the system meets the end-users' requirements.

Below is an example configuration of a test job in GitLab CI to perform unit testing using pytest for a Python project:

```
stages:
  - test

unit-test:
  stage: test
  script:
    - pip install -r requirements.txt
    - pytest tests/unit/
```

Deployment Strategies in CD

Deployment strategies in continuous delivery help minimize downtime and ensure new releases' robustness. Some common deployment strategies include:

- **Blue-Green Deployment:** Two environments, blue and green, are maintained. At any point, one environment (e.g., blue) runs the current production, while the other (e.g., green) is used for the new release. Switching environments is as simple as updating the route to point to the new environment.
- **Canary Releases:** A new release is first deployed to a small subset of users. If no issues are detected, the new release is gradually rolled out to all users.
- **Feature Toggles:** Allow new features to be deployed to production without being activated for all users. This strategy enables testing in production without exposing all changes to users.

Here is an example of a deploy job in GitLab CI for a blue-green deployment strategy:

```
stages:
  - deploy

blue-green-deploy:
```

```
  stage: deploy
  script:
    - echo "Deploying to green environment..."
    - scp -r build/my_app user@green-server:/var/www/my_app
    - echo "Switching route to green environment..."
    - ssh user@load-balancer 'sudo update-routing green'
  environment:
    name: green
    url: https://green.example.com
```

Monitoring and Debugging

Monitoring and logging are critical components of continuous delivery. Tools such as Prometheus for monitoring and Elasticsearch, Logstash, Kibana (ELK) stack for logging help maintain the application's health and performance. Integrate these tools with GitLab to observe metrics in real-time and gain insights into deployment issues.

Setting up monitoring with Prometheus in GitLab can be achieved with simple annotations in our .gitlab-ci.yml file:

```
monitoring-job:
  stage: monitoring
  script:
    - echo "Setting up monitoring..."
    - kubectl apply -f prometheus-setup.yaml
```

Combining these components effectively aligns with the principles of continuous delivery, ensuring that each change is validated through rigorous testing and automated deployment, thereby streamlining the path to production.

7.6 Continuous Deployment

Continuous Deployment (CD) represents an advanced and sophisticated evolution from Continuous Delivery (also abbreviated as CD). The primary objective of Continuous Deployment is to ensure that every code change passing the automated testing phase is automatically deployed into the production environment. This allows for an expedited delivery cycle, enabling development teams to achieve rapid iterations and releases, thereby promoting persistent feedback and enhancement.

The backbone of Continuous Deployment is an automated pipeline that validates and deploys each change in real-time. This pipeline facilitates immediate and accurate feedback, enabling developers to address any potential issues promptly. To build an effective Continuous Deployment pipeline in GitLab, it is crucial to integrate several technologies and workflows seamlessly.

The pipeline generally consists of the following stages:

- Build: This stage compiles the source code and creates build artifacts.
- Test: Comprehensive automated tests (unit, integration, end-to-end) are run to ensure the code is accurate and complete.
- Deploy: If the code passes all tests, it is automatically deployed to the production environment.

Pipeline Configuration

The GitLab CI/CD pipeline can be configured using a .gitlab-ci.yml file, which delineates the various stages, jobs, and commands needed to execute the pipeline efficiently. The core of this configuration leverages GitLab Runners, responsible for running the jobs defined within the pipeline.

Below is an example configuration of a .gitlab-ci.yml file for Continuous Deployment:

```
stages:
  - build
  - test
  - deploy

build_job:
  stage: build
  script:
    - echo "Compiling the code..."
    - ./gradlew build

test_job:
  stage: test
  script:
    - echo "Running unit tests..."
    - ./gradlew test

deploy_job:
  stage: deploy
  script:
    - echo "Deploying to production..."
    - ./deploy.sh
  only:
    - master
```

In this configuration:

- The build_job compiles the code.
- The test_job runs the unit tests.
- The deploy_job deploys the code to the production environment, but only if the 'master' branch is updated.

Environment Management

Managing different environments (e.g., development, staging, and production) is an essential aspect of Continuous Deployment. GitLab CI/CD facilitates environment management with ease. Environments can be specified within the .gitlab-ci.yml file.

Example of environment configuration:

```
deploy_development:
  stage: deploy
  script:
    - echo "Deploying to development..."
    - ./deploy.sh development
  environment:
    name: development

deploy_staging:
  stage: deploy
  script:
    - echo "Deploying to staging..."
    - ./deploy.sh staging
  environment:
    name: staging

deploy_production:
  stage: deploy
  script:
    - echo "Deploying to production..."
    - ./deploy.sh production
  environment:
    name: production
  only:
    - master
```

This configuration enables deploying to different environments using dedicated jobs for each. Deployments to 'production' occur only from the 'master' branch.

Rollback Strategies

Given the automation in Continuous Deployment, implementing rollback strategies is critical to mitigate potential issues after deployment.

The rollback strategy can be configured within the deployment scripts to revert to the previous stable release if the latest deployment fails.

Example of rollback configuration in a deployment script:

```
#!/bin/bash

DEPLOY_ENV=$1

deploy(){
  echo "Deploying to $DEPLOY_ENV environment..."
  # deployment commands here
}

rollback(){
  echo "Rolling back deployment in $DEPLOY_ENV environment..."
  # rollback commands here
}

deploy $DEPLOY_ENV
if [ $? -ne 0 ]; then
  echo "Deployment failed; initiating rollback..."
  rollback $DEPLOY_ENV
fi
```

Monitoring and Alerts

Continuous Deployment requires robust monitoring and alert mechanisms to ensure the health and performance of the deployed application. GitLab's integration with monitoring tools such as Prometheus and Grafana enables teams to set up detailed monitoring dashboards and alerting systems.

Implementing monitoring:

```
monitoring:
  stage: monitor
  script:
    - echo "Setting up monitoring..."
    - ./monitoring_setup.sh
  environment:
    name: production
```

Security in Continuous Deployment

Security is a paramount consideration in Continuous Deployment. Implementing Security Scanning mechanisms as part of the pipeline can identify vulnerabilities before code reaches production. GitLab's Security Dashboard and Dependency Scanning can be integrated effortlessly.

Example:

```
security_scan:
  stage: test
  script:
    - echo "Running security scans..."
    - ./security_scan.sh
```

By integrating the above approaches, Continuous Deployment in GitLab enables efficient, reliable, and secure deployment cycles.

7.7 Infrastructure as Code (IaC)

Infrastructure as Code (IaC) is a critical paradigm in modern DevOps practices, enabling the management and provisioning of computing infrastructure through machine-readable definition files, rather than physical hardware configuration or interactive configuration tools. With GitLab, IaC can be effectively implemented to ensure consistent and repeatable infrastructure deployments. This section delves into the core concepts of IaC, its advantages, and practical implementation using GitLab.

Core Concepts of IaC:

IaC is built upon several foundational principles that facilitate effective infrastructure management:

- **Declarative versus Imperative:** In the declarative approach, users specify the desired state of the infrastructure, leaving the IaC tool to determine how to achieve that state. The imperative approach, on the other hand, involves specifying the exact commands required to achieve the desired state. Declarative methods are generally preferred in IaC for their simplicity and clarity.

- **Idempotency:** Idempotent operations ensure that applying the same configuration multiple times will produce the same result. This is crucial for maintaining consistent infrastructure environments and reducing the risk of configuration drift.

- **Version Control:** Treating infrastructure definitions as code means they can be managed using version control systems like Git. This allows for better tracking of changes, collaboration, and rollback capabilities if necessary.

- **Automation:** Automating infrastructure provisioning reduces manual effort, speeds up deployments, and minimizes human error. Automation can be achieved through continuous integration and continuous delivery (CI/CD) pipelines.

Advantages of IaC:
Implementing IaC offers several benefits that align with the goals of DevOps practices:

- **Consistency:** By defining infrastructure in code, you ensure that every deployment is consistent with the last, reducing discrepancies between environments.
- **Scalability:** IaC makes it easier to scale infrastructure up or down based on demand, without the need for manual configuration changes.
- **Collaboration:** Teams can collaborate on infrastructure configurations just like they do on application code, improving efficiency and reducing misunderstandings.
- **Repeatability:** Infrastructure can be rebuilt from scratch reliably, which is particularly useful for disaster recovery or creating new environments for testing.
- **Auditability:** With infrastructure defined as code, it's easier to audit changes and understand the history of infrastructure configurations.

Practical Implementation using GitLab:

GitLab integrates IaC tools seamlessly, allowing for effective management of infrastructure within the same ecosystem used for application development. Below, we will explore the practical steps to implement IaC using GitLab CI/CD and popular IaC tools such as Terraform.

Setting up the GitLab Repository:

Start by creating a GitLab repository to store your IaC configuration files. Ensure that the repository is well-structured and includes directories for different environments (e.g., development, staging, production).

```
git init infrastructure-as-code
cd infrastructure-as-code
mkdir dev staging prod
```

Writing Terraform Configuration Files:

Next, create Terraform configuration files for your infrastructure. These files describe the required infrastructure using a declarative syntax.

```
# main.tf
provider "aws" {
  region = "us-west-2"
}

resource "aws_instance" "example" {
  ami = "ami-0c55b159cbfafe1f0"
  instance_type = "t2.micro"

  tags = {
    Name = "ExampleInstance"
  }
}
```

The **main.tf** file contains the provider configuration (AWS in this case) and a resource block defining an EC2 instance.

Integrating Terraform with GitLab CI/CD:

Define a GitLab CI/CD pipeline for automating the deployment of your infrastructure. Create a *.gitlab-ci.yml* file at the root of your repository.

```
stages:
  - validate
  - plan
  - apply

validate:
  stage: validate
  script:
    - terraform init
    - terraform validate

plan:
  stage: plan
  script:
    - terraform init
    - terraform plan -out=tfplan

apply:
  stage: apply
  script:
    - terraform apply tfplan
  when: manual
```

In this pipeline, the **validate** stage initializes and validates the Terraform configuration. The **plan** stage creates an execution plan, and the **apply** stage applies the plan to provision the infrastructure. The *when: manual* directive ensures that the application of changes is triggered manually, providing control over the deployment process.

Executing the Pipeline:

Once the .gitlab-ci.yml file is committed to the repository, GitLab CI/CD will automatically trigger the pipeline on any changes. The output of each stage can be monitored in the GitLab interface, providing visibility into the infrastructure provisioning process.

```
Job succeeded
Terraform has been successfully initialized!
Terraform validate: Configuration is valid.
Terraform plan: 1 to add, 0 to change, 0 to destroy.
Apply complete! Resources: 1 added, 0 changed, 0 destroyed.
```

Managing State:

Terraform uses state files to track the state of infrastructure resources. Store the state file securely, preferably using a remote backend such as AWS S3 or GitLab's built-in Terraform state management, to prevent conflict and ensure availability.

```
terraform {
  backend "s3" {
    bucket = "my-terraform-state"
    key = "state/terraform.tfstate"
    region = "us-west-2"
  }
}
```

This configuration stores the state file in an S3 bucket, ensuring that multiple users can collaborate without state conflicts.

With these steps, you can effectively manage your infrastructure as code using GitLab, bringing all the advantages of IaC to your development process. This approach not only ensures consistency and repeatability but also integrates seamlessly into the broader DevOps practices covered in this chapter.

7.8 Monitoring and Logging

Monitoring and logging are fundamental aspects of a robust DevOps strategy, enabling visibility into the system's performance and health. This section elucidates how GitLab facilitates effective monitoring and logging practices, ensuring that applications and infrastructure operate smoothly and issues are quickly identified and resolved.

Continuous monitoring provides real-time insights into the status of various components of the system. GitLab integrates with multiple monitoring tools, allowing teams to track metrics such as CPU usage, memory consumption, and network traffic. Logging captures detailed records of system events, which are invaluable for diagnosing issues, understanding system behavior over time, and auditing purposes.

Monitoring with GitLab

GitLab supports several monitoring tools and technologies, including Prometheus, Grafana, and Elasticsearch. These tools can be configured to collect, process, and visualize various metrics.

- **Prometheus:** An open-source monitoring and alerting toolkit. Prometheus collects metrics from configured targets at given intervals, evaluates rule expressions, and can trigger alerts if certain conditions are observed.
- **Grafana:** A multi-platform open-source analytics and monitoring web application. Grafana provides charts, graphs, and alerts for the web when connected to supported data sources.
- **Elasticsearch:** A distributed, RESTful search and analytics engine. Elasticsearch is used for log and time-series data analytics, discovering trends and finding anomalies.

To configure monitoring in GitLab, you need to set up the respective tools and connect them to your GitLab instance. The following example demonstrates how to set up Prometheus with GitLab.

```
# Add Prometheus as a service in your gitlab.yml
services:
- name: prometheus
  command: ["prometheus", "--config.file=/etc/prometheus/prometheus.yml"]
```

Once Prometheus is configured, you can define custom metrics to monitor specific aspects of your application. For instance, to monitor HTTP request duration, you might use the following Prometheus configuration:

```
scrape_configs:
- job_name: 'http_requests'
  static_configs:
  - targets: ['localhost:9090']
```

You can then visualize these metrics in Grafana by connecting it to your Prometheus data source and creating dashboards to display the metrics graphically.

Logging in GitLab

Logging is equally crucial for diagnosing issues and auditing system activities. GitLab integrates with logging solutions like Elasticsearch and

Logstash to manage and analyze logs efficiently. Here is an example of a Logstash configuration to index logs into Elasticsearch.

```
input {
  file {
    path => "/var/log/gitlab/gitlab-rails/production.log"
    start_position => "beginning"
  }
}

filter {
  grok {
    match => { "message" => "%{TIMESTAMP_ISO8601:timestamp} %{
          LOGLEVEL:loglevel} %{GREEDYDATA:logmessage}" }
  }
}

output {
  elasticsearch {
    hosts => ["localhost:9200"]
    index => "gitlab-logs-%{+YYYY.MM.dd}"
  }
  stdout { codec => rubydebug }
}
```

This configuration captures logs from the GitLab Rails production log, parses them using the grok filter, and then indexes them into Elasticsearch. With the logs indexed, you can use Kibana, another tool from the Elasticsearch stack, to search, analyze, and visualize the log data.

```
{
  "_index": "gitlab-logs-2023.09.21",
  "_type": "_doc",
  "_id": "1",
  "_score": 1,
  "_source": {
    "timestamp": "2023-09-21T13:32:01.123Z",
    "loglevel": "INFO",
    "logmessage": "User signed in"
  }
}
```

By implementing a monitoring and logging strategy using tools like Prometheus, Grafana, Elasticsearch, and Logstash with GitLab, teams can maintain high visibility into the operational status of their applications and infrastructure. This visibility enables proactive identification and resolution of issues, ensuring higher reliability and performance levels.

7.9 Security in DevOps

Security is a fundamental aspect of DevOps, often encapsulated in the term DevSecOps, which integrates security practices within the DevOps processes. This concept emphasizes that security is a shared responsibility, spanning the entire development lifecycle—from inception through deployment and beyond. The integration of security into DevOps aims to ensure that security is prioritized without compromising the agility and efficiency of the development cycle.

Shift-Left Security: The principle of "shift-left" within DevSecOps refers to the practice of integrating security measures and tests at the earliest possible stages of the software development lifecycle. This strategy contrasts with traditional approaches where security assessments occurred at the final stages. Early integration of security helps to identify vulnerabilities sooner, mitigate risks more effectively, and reduce the cost and complexity of fixing security issues.

A key component of shift-left security is code analysis. Static Application Security Testing (SAST) tools can scan source code for known vulnerabilities and coding standards violations. SAST can be integrated into the Continuous Integration (CI) pipeline using GitLab CI/CD. Below is an example of configuring SAST within a GitLab CI pipeline.

```
include:
  - template: Security/SAST.gitlab-ci.yml

sast:
  stage: test
  script:
    - echo "Running SAST Analysis"
  artifacts:
    reports:
      sast: gl-sast-report.json
```

The Security/SAST.gitlab-ci.yml template provides predefined jobs and rules to facilitate the integration of SAST into the CI pipeline. The results of the SAST analysis are stored in a JSON report, which GitLab can utilize to generate detailed security findings.

Dynamic Application Security Testing (DAST): While SAST analyzes static source code, Dynamic Application Security Testing (DAST) examines the running application. DAST simulates attacks against the application in its runtime environment, identifying potential vulnerabilities that may arise during operation such as SQL injection, Cross-Site Scripting (XSS), and insecure server configurations. Similar to SAST, DAST can be integrated into GitLab's CI/CD pipeline.

```
include:
  - template: Security/DAST.gitlab-ci.yml

dast:
  stage: test
  variables:
```

```
    DAST_WEBSITE: "http://your-application-url.com"
  script:
    - echo "Running DAST Analysis"
  artifacts:
    reports:
      dast: gl-dast-report.json
```

In this example, the DAST_WEBSITE environment variable defines the URL of the application to be tested. The Security/DAST.gitlab-ci.yml template allows the scheduled or event-triggered DAST scans, generating a report in JSON format detailing any security issues found during testing.

Dependency Scanning: Modern software development often involves using third-party libraries and packages, which can introduce security vulnerabilities. Dependency scanning tools can audit these dependencies for known vulnerabilities. GitLab provides built-in support for dependency scanning.

```
include:
  - template: Security/Dependency-Scanning.gitlab-ci.yml

dependency_scanning:
  stage: test
  script:
    - echo "Running Dependency Scanning"
  artifacts:
    reports:
      dependency_scanning: gl-dependency-scanning-report.json
```

By including the dependency scanning template, the CI pipeline automatically integrates dependency checks. The resulting report highlights any vulnerable dependencies, often offering recommendations for secure replacements or updates.

Container Security: Containerization is a common practice in modern DevOps workflows, providing consistency across different environments. However, containers bring unique security challenges, such as ensuring the integrity of container images. Tools such as Clair or Trivy can be used to scan Docker images for vulnerabilities.

```
scan_image:
  stage: test
  image: docker:stable
  services:
    - docker:dind
  script:
    - docker pull myregistry/myimage:latest
    - trivy image myregistry/myimage:latest
```

This code snippet demonstrates a CI job for scanning Docker images with Trivy. Including container security scans in the CI pipeline helps maintain secure container images.

Secrets Management: Mismanaging secrets like API keys, passwords, and certificates can expose systems to significant risks. Proper secrets management ensures that these sensitive pieces of information are stored and accessed securely. GitLab provides a secrets management system through CI/CD variables and Vault integration.

```
deploy:
  stage: deploy
  script:
    - echo "Deploying application"
    - ./deploy.sh --password=$CI_DEPLOY_PASSWORD
  variables:
    VAULT_ADDR: "https://vault.example.com"
```

Using CI/CD variables, secrets can be securely included in pipeline scripts without hardcoding them in the repository. Vault integration further enhances security by enabling dynamic secrets management and providing fine-grained access controls.

Security Monitoring and Logging: Continuous monitoring and logging are critical for maintaining security post-deployment. Tools like Prometheus and Grafana can be integrated with GitLab to provide insights into application performance and detect anomalous behavior. ELK stack (Elasticsearch, Logstash, Kibana) integration allows for centralized log management, facilitating the detection and investigation of security incidents.

```
monitoring:
  stage: monitor
  script:
    - echo "Setting up monitoring"
    - ./setup_monitoring.sh
metrics:
  image: prom/prometheus
  stage: monitor
  script:
    - ./start_prometheus.sh
```

Configuring monitoring in the CI/CD pipeline ensures that operational and security telemetry is collected systematically, providing visibility into potential security issues and assisting in compliance auditing.

Compliance and Governance: Adhering to industry regulations and standards such as GDPR, HIPAA, or ISO/IEC 27001 is vital. GitLab compliance management features assist in tracking and ensuring adherence to these standards through automated compliance pipeline templates and custom policies.

```
include:
  - project: 'compliance/pipelines'
    file: '/templates/security-compliance.yml'

compliance:
  stage: audit
  script:
    - echo "Running compliance checks"
```

Incorporating compliance checks as part of the CI/CD pipeline facilitates continuous compliance, reducing the risk of non-compliance and associated penalties.

By embedding security at every stage of the DevOps lifecycle, organizations can build robust and resilient systems. This proactive security approach not only mitigates risks but also fosters a secure and compliant development environment.

7.10 Collaboration and Communication

Effective collaboration and communication are foundational components of any successful DevOps practice. Within GitLab, a comprehensive suite of tools is provided to enhance team interoperability, streamline workflow processes, and ensure transparent, real-time collaboration among all stakeholders. These tools and associated practices promote a cohesive environment where developers, operations, and business units can work seamlessly towards shared objectives.

GitLab supports several features and best practices aimed at fostering an environment conducive to robust collaboration and communication:

- **Issue Tracking:** GitLab's built-in issue tracker allows teams to discuss requirements, enhancements, and bugs directly within the GitLab environment. Issues can be described in detail using Markdown, assigned to team members, annotated with labels and milestones, and organized into boards for visual clarity.

  Example: Creating a New Issue

  ```
  1. Navigate to your project's Issue section.
  2. Click on 'New Issue'.
  3. Fill in the title and description fields, using Markdown for formatting.
  4. Assign relevant team members.
  5. Apply necessary labels and milestones.
  6. Click 'Submit' to create the issue.
  ```

- **Merge Requests (MR):** Merge Requests facilitate code review and collaboration before changes are merged into the main branch. They provide a platform for discussing code changes, proposing modifications, and ensuring code quality through integrated CI pipelines running automated tests.

  Example: Creating a Merge Request

  ```
  1. Push changes to a new branch in the repository.
  2. Navigate to the Merge Requests tab.
  3. Click on 'New Merge Request'.
  4. Select source and target branches.
  5. Provide a detailed description of changes.
  6. Request reviews and assign relevant labels.
  7. Submit the merge request.
  ```

- **Comments and Discussions:** GitLab enables adding comments directly to issues, merge requests, and code snippets. This feature allows for asynchronous communication and documentation of key decisions and feedback.

- **To-Do Lists:** Each user in GitLab can manage personal to-do lists, which aggregate manually added tasks—like reviewing a merge request or updating documentation. These lists help in prioritizing daily work and ensuring no critical task is overlooked.

  Example: Managing a To-Do List

  ```
  1. Navigate to your dashboard.
  2. Click on 'To-Do List'.
  3. Add new tasks manually or convert issue/merge request tasks.
  4. Mark tasks as completed when done.
  5. Filter tasks by type or project.
  ```

- **Labels and Milestones:** Labels are powerful tools for categorizing issues and merge requests, providing a high-level view of project status. Milestones help track progress towards deadlines, encompassing multiple issues and merge requests, thus facilitating release planning and tracking.

  Example: Creating a Milestone

  ```
  1. Navigate to the project's Milestones tab.
  2. Click on 'New Milestone'.
  3. Provide a title, description, start date, and due date.
  4. Link relevant issues and merge requests.
  5. Click 'Create Milestone'.
  ```

- **Kanban Boards:** GitLab's issue boards offer a Kanban-style interface to visualize workflow states. They help project managers track progress and identify bottlenecks through customizable columns representing different stages of development.

Example: Creating a Kanban Board

```
1. Navigate to 'Boards' under the Issues section.
2. Click on 'Create new board'.
3. Define the board's name and description.
4. Add columns representing different workflow stages.
5. Customize column labels and their respective issue states.
6. Save the board.
```

- **Wikis and Documentation:** GitLab wikis allow project-specific documentations, accessible directly from the repository. These are useful for maintaining user guides, developer notes, or any documentation that requires base communication.

  Example: Creating a Wiki Page

```
1. Navigate to the 'Wiki' tab.
2. Click on 'New Page'.
3. Provide a title and content using Markdown.
4. Save the page.
5. Link the page from other documents for cross-referencing.
```

- **Integrations with Communication Tools:** GitLab integrates with several third-party communication tools like Slack, Microsoft Teams, and Mattermost. These integrations ensure real-time notifications and updates about important project events, thus bridging the gap between development and communication channels.

  Example: Integrating GitLab with Slack

```
1. Navigate to the project's 'Settings' > 'Integrations'.
2. Select 'Slack integration'.
3. Provide the Webhook URL from your Slack workspace.
4. Customize triggers for different events (e.g., new issue, merge request).
5. Click 'Save Changes' to enable integration.
```

- **CI/CD Pipelines Visualization:** GitLab's pipeline visualization provides a clear view of all stages and jobs involved in the continuous integration and deployment processes. This aids in quickly identifying issues, understanding pipeline flow, and improving transparency into DevOps metrics.

```
Example: Analyzing Pipeline Visualization
----------------------------------------

1. Navigate to your project's 'CI/CD' > 'Pipelines'.
2. Select a pipeline run from the list.
3. Visualize each job's status and logs by clicking on respective stages.
4. Use visualization to identify and resolve failed jobs.
```

These features collectively empower teams to maintain a high level of synchronization, effectively manage their workflow, and foster a culture of continuous feedback and improvement.

7.11 Automating Workflows

Automating workflows in a DevOps environment, particularly with GitLab, involves the integration of multiple processes, tools, and practices to create a seamless, efficient pipeline from code development to production deployment. This section delves into various techniques and tools available in GitLab to automate workflows, enhancing productivity and ensuring consistent quality.

One of the primary tools for workflow automation in GitLab is the GitLab CI/CD (Continuous Integration/Continuous Deployment) pipeline. This pipeline allows for the automation of code building, testing, and deployment processes, ensuring that changes are validated at every stage of the development lifecycle. The pipeline is defined using a .gitlab-ci.yml file, which includes a series of jobs to be executed.

Defining the GitLab CI/CD Pipeline

A typical .gitlab-ci.yml file might look as follows:

```
stages:
  - build
  - test
  - deploy

variables:
  SOME_VARIABLE: "value"

before_script:
  - apt-get update -y
  - apt-get install -y curl
  - echo "Running before_script"

build-job:
  stage: build
  script:
    - echo "Compiling the code..."
    - make

test-job:
  stage: test
  script:
    - echo "Running tests..."
    - make test
```

```
deploy-job:
  stage: deploy
  script:
    - echo "Deploying to production..."
    - make deploy
```

The stages keyword defines the sequence of stages that the pipeline will execute. Each job is associated with a stage and includes a specific script section that lists the commands to be run. The before_script section contains commands that are executed before each job, ensuring that necessary setup is performed across different stages.

Variables can also be defined globally or locally to adjust configurations without hardcoding values, enabling flexibility and reusability.

Pipeline Triggers

Pipeline triggers are mechanisms that allow the invocation of pipelines in response to certain events. GitLab supports triggering pipelines through various means such as commits, merge requests, schedules, and external webhooks. This capability ensures that pipelines are executed under appropriate conditions, facilitating automation.

For example, a pipeline can be scheduled to run daily by using the GitLab CI/CD schedules:

```
schedule:
  - cron: "0 0 * * *"
    script: "echo 'Daily pipeline triggered'"
```

This configuration leverages the CRON syntax to schedule a job to be executed at midnight every day.

Pipeline Conditions

The conditional execution of jobs can be handled using the rules keyword, enabling more sophisticated workflow automation. Conditions might include branch names, tags, the presence of files, or variables.

A job with specific rules might look like this:

```
deploy-job:
  stage: deploy
  script:
    - echo "Deploying to production..."
    - make deploy
  rules:
    - if: '$CI_COMMIT_BRANCH == "main"'
```

```
    - when: manual
```

This configuration ensures that the deployment job runs only on the main branch and requires manual approval, providing control over the automation process.

Artefacts and Caching

GitLab CI/CD supports sharing data between jobs using artefacts and caching mechanisms. Artefacts are files or directories generated by a job that can be passed to subsequent jobs. This feature is vital for ensuring continuity and availability of necessary files across different stages.

For example, to save build output as an artefact:

```
build:
  stage: build
  script:
    - make
  artefacts:
    paths:
      - build/
```

Caching allows for the reuse of dependencies or intermediate files, reducing redundancy and speeding up pipeline execution:

```
cache:
  paths:
    - node_modules/
    - .m2/repository/
```

This configuration caches directories like node_modules and Maven's local repository, minimizing repeated downloads.

Integrating with Third-Party Tools

GitLab provides extensive integration capabilities with various third-party tools such as Jenkins, Kubernetes, and Amazon Web Services (AWS), allowing for enhanced automation and extended DevOps practices.

For Kubernetes integration, for instance, GitLab can deploy applications directly to a Kubernetes cluster using GitLab's Kubernetes integration. This facilitates continuous deployment directly from GitLab CI/CD:

```
deploy-to-k8s:
```

```
  stage: deploy
  script:
    - kubectl apply -f k8s-deployment.yml
  environment:
    name: production
    url: http://production.example.com
  only:
    - main
```

In this configuration, code is deployed to a Kubernetes cluster upon merging into the main branch, demonstrated through the kubectl command that applies the Kubernetes deployment configuration.

Advanced Workflow Features

GitLab also supports advanced features such as parent-child pipelines and multi-project pipelines. Parent-child pipelines allow for the decomposition of complex workflows into more manageable sub-pipelines, enhancing modularity and maintainability.

A parent-child pipeline example:

```
main-pipeline:
  stage: build
  trigger:
    include: child-pipeline.yml
    strategy: depend
```

The child pipeline is defined in a separate YAML file and is triggered by the parent pipeline using the trigger keyword.

Multi-project pipelines enable orchestration across different repositories, facilitating comprehensive workflow automation across larger projects. This is particularly useful for microservices architectures where each service resides in a separate repository.

For instance, a cross-project pipeline can be defined as follows:

```
trigger-microservice:
  stage: deploy
  trigger:
    project: other-group/microservice
    branch: main
```

Here, the main project triggers a deployment pipeline in a microservice repository upon completion of the main pipeline.

The combination of these mechanisms equips GitLab users with robust tools to streamline and automate development workflows, ensuring continuous and efficient software delivery.

7.12 Case Studies: Successful DevOps Implementations

Organizations across various sectors have embraced DevOps practices to enhance their software development and deployment processes. This section will explore detailed case studies of successful DevOps implementations, focusing particularly on using GitLab. These real-world examples provide insight into how companies have leveraged GitLab's comprehensive toolset to improve efficiency, reliability, and collaboration in their DevOps workflows.

Case Study 1: E-commerce Platform Modernization

A leading e-commerce company sought to modernize its platform to handle increased traffic, improve deployment speed, and reduce downtime. The main challenges faced included:

- Slow deployment cycles
- High error rates during updates
- Lack of collaboration between development and operations teams

Upon migrating to GitLab, the company implemented several key DevOps practices:

Continuous Integration (CI):

They configured GitLab CI/CD pipelines to automate the testing and integration processes. The pipeline was defined in a `.gitlab-ci.yml` file:

```
stages:
  - build
  - test
  - deploy

build:
  stage: build
  script:
    - npm install
    - npm run build

test:
  stage: test
  script:
    - npm test

deploy:
  stage: deploy
```

```
script:
  - ./deploy.sh
  only:
    - main
```

The automated CI pipeline reduced the feedback loop, allowing developers to identify and fix issues early in the development cycle.

Continuous Delivery (CD):

For the deployment process, they utilized GitLab's CD features to ensure that new code changes could be delivered to production reliably and frequently. They adopted feature flags to slowly introduce new features into the production environment without affecting the entire user base.

Infrastructure as Code (IaC):

Infrastructure was managed using Terraform, and GitLab was configured to run Terraform scripts to provision resources automatically:

```
terraform-apply:
  stage: deploy
  script:
    - terraform init
    - terraform apply -auto-approve
  only:
    - main
```

This approach ensured that environments could be recreated consistently both locally and in production, reducing configuration drift.

Monitoring and Logging:

GitLab integrated monitoring tools like Prometheus and Grafana to provide real-time insights into system performance. Custom alarms and dashboards were set up to track key metrics and respond to incidents promptly.

Outcome:

The implementation led to a significant decrease in deployment times and a 40% reduction in post-deployment errors. The development and operations teams started working more cohesively, resulting in a more robust and scalable platform.

Case Study 2: Financial Services Automation

A financial services company aimed to automate its workflow to comply with stringent regulatory requirements while maintaining rapid development cycles. Key challenges were:

- Compliance with regulations
- Need for rapid development
- Maintaining high security

By leveraging GitLab, the company addressed these challenges effectively:

Automating Compliance Checks:

GitLab CI/CD was used to run automated compliance checks as part of the CI pipeline. Scripts were written to ensure code met regulatory requirements before merging:

```
compliance-check:
  stage: test
  script:
    - ./compliance_check.sh
  allow_failure: false
```

Security Integration:

Security scans were integrated into the pipeline using GitLab's built-in security features, which included Static Application Security Testing (SAST) and Dependency Scanning:

```
include:
  - template: Security/SAST.gitlab-ci.yml
  - template: Security/Dependency-Scanning.gitlab-ci.yml
```

These scans helped detect and mitigate vulnerabilities early in the development process.

Collaboration and Communication:

GitLab's Merge Requests (MRs) provided a platform for code review and collaboration. The use of comments and discussions in MRs improved the code quality and facilitated better cross-team communication.

Outcome:

The introduction of automated compliance checks and integrated security testing resulted in a 50% increase in regulatory audit pass rates. Development lead time was reduced considerably, and the security posture of the organization improved markedly.

Case Study 3: Real-Time Analytics Platform

A data analytics company needed to handle large volumes of real-time data while ensuring zero downtime and rapid iteration. The main obstacles included:

- Managing a large, scalable infrastructure
- Ensuring continuous availability
- Rapidly deploying updates

GitLab's capabilities supported the following solutions:

Scalable Infrastructure Management:

Kubernetes was used to manage the containerized applications, with GitLab CI/CD running the deployment pipelines. The .gitlab-ci.yml file included Kubernetes integration commands:

```
deploy-to-k8s:
  stage: deploy
  before_script:
    - echo "$KUBERNETES_CA_CERT" | base64 --decode > $CI_PROJECT_DIR/
        ca.crt
    - kubectl config set-cluster k8s-cluster --certificate-authority=$CI_PROJECT_DIR
        /ca.crt --server=$KUBERNETES_SERVER
    - kubectl config set-credentials k8s-user --token=$KUBERNETES_TOKEN
    - kubectl config set-context k8s-context --cluster=k8s-cluster --user=k8s-user
    - kubectl config use-context k8s-context
  script:
    - kubectl apply -f k8s/deployment.yaml
  only:
    - main
```

Ensuring Continuous Availability:

Canary deployments were implemented to gradually roll out updates to a subset of users. This approach enabled monitoring of new changes in a production environment, reducing the risk of widespread outages.

Outcome:

The deployment process became more resilient, and the company achieved near-zero downtime, even during peak data ingestion periods. The ability to perform canary deployments enabled rapid, safe iterations of the platform, enhancing its reliability and performance.

These case studies illustrate the transformative impact of integrating GitLab into DevOps workflows, highlighting how automation, collaboration, and continuous improvement can lead to significant operational enhancements across different industry sectors.

Chapter 8

GitLab Runner and Custom Executors

This chapter provides an in-depth look at GitLab Runner and custom executors. It covers the installation and registration of GitLab Runner, the difference between shared and specific runners, and configuring runners for various environments. The chapter details the types of executors available, such as Shell and Docker, and how to create custom executors. Additionally, it discusses scaling runners, optimizing their performance, and best practices for ensuring runner security.

8.1 What is GitLab Runner?

GitLab Runner is an essential component of GitLab's continuous integration/continuous deployment (CI/CD) infrastructure. At its core, GitLab Runner is an application used to execute jobs as defined in GitLab CI pipelines. It operates by scheduling and running build scripts as specified in the .gitlab-ci.yml file, facilitating the process of building, testing, and deploying code.

GitLab Runner can be installed as either a single binary or a Docker image, enabling flexibility in deployment options. Its primary purpose and functionality can be distilled into the following capabilities:

- **Job Execution:** GitLab Runner picks up and processes jobs defined in the pipeline configuration. It ensures that these jobs are executed according to the conditions and environment specified.

- **Scheduling:** It manages job queues, ensuring that jobs are run in the order they are queued and according to the availability of the assigned executors.

- **Environment Management:** Depending on the type of executor used, GitLab Runner can manage different environments, including shell, Docker, and custom environments.

- **Output and Logging:** During and after the execution of jobs, GitLab Runner streams real-time logs to the GitLab interface, allowing users to monitor job progress and debug issues efficiently.

- **Caching and Artifacts:** GitLab Runner can cache dependencies and upload job artifacts, optimizing the CI/CD pipeline execution by avoiding unnecessary re-computation and preserving build outputs for later stages.

The usage of GitLab Runner is tightly connected with the CI pipeline configuration specified in the .gitlab-ci.yml file. When a new commit is pushed to the repository, GitLab uses the definitions present in this file to create a pipeline, breaking it down into jobs and stages. GitLab Runner is then responsible for executing each job, adhering to the job's specific requirements.

```
# Example .gitlab-ci.yml configuration
stages:
  - build
  - test
  - deploy

build-job:
  stage: build
  script:
    - echo "Compiling the code..."
    - gcc -o myapp main.c

test-job:
  stage: test
  script:
    - echo "Running unit tests..."
    - ./run-tests.sh

deploy-job:
  stage: deploy
  script:
    - echo "Deploying the application..."
    - ./deploy.sh
```

In the example above, the .gitlab-ci.yml configuration defines a pipeline with three stages: build, test, and deploy. Each stage contains jobs with specific scripts that GitLab Runner will execute. When this configuration is processed, the pipeline will trigger jobs in their respective stages sequentially, ensuring that the build job completes before the test job begins, and the deploy job waits for the test job to finish.

GitLab Runner supports multiple types of executors, which are used to execute the defined scripts in various environments. The primary types of executors include:

- **Shell Executors:** Execute build scripts directly in the shell of the host system. This is the simplest executor type and does not require any additional configuration beyond having GitLab Runner installed on the system.

```
[[runners]]
  name = "shell-runner"
  executor = "shell"
```

- **Docker Executors:** Run jobs within Docker containers. This allows for greater environment isolation and dependency management. Docker executors can pull images from Docker Hub or any other container registry.

```
[[runners]]
  name = "docker-runner"
  executor = "docker"
  [runners.docker]
    image = "alpine:latest"
```

- **Custom Executors:** Enable the use of any arbitrary executor to run jobs. This is suitable for advanced use cases where control beyond typical executors is required.

```
[[runners]]
  name = "custom-runner"
  executor = "custom"
  [runners.custom]
    config_exec = "/path/to/custom-executor-config"
```

Shared runners and specific runners are two deployment models that determine how GitLab Runner instances are associated with projects and how they handle job execution:

- **Shared Runners:** Configured to handle jobs from any project within the GitLab instance. They are typically managed by GitLab administrators and are appropriate for general-purpose CI/CD tasks across multiple projects.

- **Specific Runners:** Dedicated to a specific project or group. They provide greater control over the execution environment and resources, making them ideal for projects with unique requirements or higher demand.

Regardless of the type, GitLab Runner plays a critical role in the CI/CD ecosystem, bridging the gap between code commits and deployment by automating the execution of build, test, and deployment scripts. Its flexibility in supporting various environments and executors ensures that it can meet the diverse needs of different projects and organizations.

8.2 Installing GitLab Runner

The process of installing GitLab Runner is a pivotal step towards leveraging continuous integration and deployment workflows within your projects. GitLab Runner is an open-source project that is written in Go and can run on various operating systems, such as Windows, macOS, and several distributions of Linux.

- **Supported Operating Systems:**
  - Linux distributions: Debian, Ubuntu, CentOS, and RHEL.
  - Windows: Windows Server 2016 and later versions.
  - macOS: macOS 10.12 and later versions.
- **Pre-requisites:** Ensure that you have administrative privileges on the system where you intend to install GitLab Runner.

Installation instructions differ slightly depending on the operating system in use. The subsequent sections provide a breakdown of installation steps for Ubuntu/Debian, CentOS/RHEL, Windows, and macOS.

Installation on Ubuntu/Debian:

1. Add the official GitLab Runner repository by executing the following commands in your terminal:

```
sudo apt-get update
sudo apt-get install -y curl
curl -fsSL https://packages.gitlab.com/install/repositories/runner/gitlab-runner/script.
      deb.sh | sudo bash
```

2. Install the GitLab Runner package:

```
sudo apt-get install gitlab-runner
```

After the package is installed, verify the installation by checking the version:

```
gitlab-runner --version
```

```
Version:      14.8.0
Git revision: c6bb62e8
Git branch:   14-8-stable
GO version:   go1.13.8
Built:        2022-01-18T09:36:45+0000
OS/Arch:      linux/amd64
```

Installation on CentOS/RHEL:

1. Add the official repository by creating a new file:

```
curl -fsSL https://packages.gitlab.com/install/repositories/runner/gitlab-runner/script.
      rpm.sh | sudo bash
```

2. Install the GitLab Runner package:

```
sudo yum install -y gitlab-runner
```

Verify the installation:

```
gitlab-runner --version
```

```
Version:      14.8.0
Git revision: c6bb62e8
Git branch:   14-8-stable
GO version:   go1.13.8
Built:        2022-01-18T09:36:45+0000
OS/Arch:      linux/amd64
```

Installation on Windows:

1. Download the binary from GitLab's official source:

```
https://gitlab-runner-downloads.s3.amazonaws.com/latest/binaries/gitlab-runner-
      windows-amd64.exe
```

2. Rename the downloaded binary to 'gitlab-runner.exe'.

3. Make 'gitlab-runner.exe' available in your system's 'PATH'. This can be done by moving the executable to a directory that is already in the

'PATH', or by modifying the 'PATH' environment variable to include the directory where 'gitlab-runner.exe' is located.

4. Register GitLab Runner as a service:

```
.\gitlab-runner.exe install
```

5. Start the service:

```
.\gitlab-runner.exe start
```

Installation on macOS:

1. Install GitLab Runner using Homebrew:

```
brew install gitlab-runner
```

2. Start the GitLab Runner service:

```
gitlab-runner start
```

To confirm the installation, check the version:

```
gitlab-runner --version
```

```
Version:      14.8.0
Git revision: c6bb62e8
Git branch:   14-8-stable
GO version:   go1.13.8
Built:        2022-01-18T09:36:45+0000
OS/Arch:      darwin/amd64
```

By following these installation steps, you enable your GitLab Runner to be functional and ready to be used for registration and subsequent configuration steps. This installation ensures the Runner is ready to execute jobs and helps maintain a consistent environment across different stages of project deployment.

8.3 Registering Runners with GitLab

Registering a GitLab Runner entails associating the Runner with a specific GitLab instance, project, or group. This procedure is critical for enabling Continuous Integration/Continuous Deployment (CI/CD) workflows. To begin this process, one must access the GitLab instance to obtain the required registration token. This token will be utilized during the Runner registration to assert connectivity and authentication.

To initiate the process, you can navigate to the **CI/CD** settings within your GitLab interface. Based on your preference for associating the Runner with an instance, group, or project, access the corresponding settings section to obtain the relevant registration token. Once the token is acquired, you are prepared to proceed with the registration on the machine where GitLab Runner is installed.

Follow these steps to register a GitLab Runner:

1. **Open the terminal** on the machine where GitLab Runner is installed.

2. **Execute the registration command**:

```
sudo gitlab-runner register
```

   You will be prompted to enter various configuration details sequentially.

The following interactive process includes several prompts:

- **Specify the GitLab instance URL:** You need to provide the URL of your GitLab instance (e.g., https://gitlab.example.com).
- **Enter the registration token:** Input the registration token you acquired from the CI/CD settings.
- **Provide a description for the Runner:** This is for informational purposes and can help identify the Runner (e.g., My-First-Runner).
- **Enter tags:** Tags help in assigning jobs to specific Runners. Tags should be comma-separated (e.g., linux,xenial,high-memory).
- **Define the executor:** Choose the executor that the Runner will use (e.g., docker, shell, custom). This choice determines the execution environment for the CI jobs.

```
Please enter the gitlab-ci coordinator URL (e.g. https://gitlab.com/)
https://gitlab.example.com
Please enter the gitlab-ci token for this runner
xxxxxxxxxxxxxxx
Please enter the gitlab-ci description for this runner
[hostname] My-First-Runner
Please enter the gitlab-ci tags for this runner (comma separated):
linux,xenial,high-memory
Please enter the executor: shell, docker, custom, etc.
docker
```

Depending on the chosen executor, additional configuration prompts may be presented. For instance, when selecting the Docker executor, you will need to supply details regarding the Docker environment, such as the default Docker image to use for running the jobs:

```
Please enter the default Docker image (e.g. ruby:2.6)
alpine:latest
```

After providing all necessary information, the Runner completes its registration and will appear in the GitLab **Runners** section of the instance, group, or project level settings, based on where the token was obtained. The GitLab UI confirms successful registration by listing the new Runner along with its details, such as tags and activity status.

For instance, if the Runner is registered successfully, the output resembles the following:

```
Runner registered successfully. Feel free to start it, but if it's running already the config should be automatically reloaded!
```

In case of configuration errors or unmet dependencies during the registration process, the error messages provide guidance for troubleshooting. These typically indicate missing software, incorrect URLs or tokens, or insufficient permissions. Carefully reviewing these messages aids in resolving issues promptly.

Example Use Case: Consider a CI/CD pipeline that requires using a specific Docker image for running tests. By registering a Docker-based GitLab Runner with the appropriate tags, developers can ensure jobs within their pipeline that match these tags will execute within the specified Docker environment.

Understanding the nuances of this process is critical for managing multiple Runners in diverse environments, ensuring efficient and secure CI/CD operations.

8.4 Shared vs. Specific Runners

In GitLab, runners are critical components responsible for executing the jobs defined in your pipeline configurations. Understanding the distinction between shared and specific runners allows you to better allocate resources, manage workload efficiently, and adhere to security practices.

Shared Runners are runners that are available to multiple projects simultaneously. They can be used by any project within a GitLab instance. These runners are ideal for small workloads, projects that need to quickly get a CI/CD pipeline up and running, or organizations looking to consolidate resource usage.

The primary benefits of using shared runners include:

- **Resource Efficiency**: Shared runners optimize the overall resource usage across multiple projects. They can handle jobs from different projects, reducing the idle time of runners and improving utilization rates.

- **Maintenance Simplicity**: As shared runners serve multiple projects, the effort required to maintain and update them is minimized. This centralized management makes it easier to apply updates, configure environments, and monitor performance.

- **Cost-Effectiveness**: For organizations that do not have heavy CI/CD demands, shared runners provide a cost-effective solution as they reduce the need for multiple dedicated machines.

However, there are also some drawbacks associated with shared runners:

- **Potential for Resource Contention**: Given that shared runners are available to multiple projects, there can be competition for resources. During peak times, jobs might queue up, leading to delays.

- **Security Concerns**: Since shared runners can execute jobs from different projects, ensuring that no job can interfere with another's environment becomes critical. There is an increased need for isolation and securing each project's data.

To configure a shared runner, the GitLab runner needs to be registered without specifying a project or group, thus making it globally available to the entire GitLab instance. Example registration command for a shared runner:

```
sudo gitlab-runner register --non-interactive \
  --url "https://gitlab.com/" \
  --registration-token "YOUR_REGISTRATION_TOKEN" \
  --description "Shared runner" \
  --tag-list "shared,linux,xenial" \
  --executor "docker" \
  --docker-image "alpine:latest"
```

Specific Runners, on the other hand, are dedicated to a single project or a single group of projects within GitLab. They are preferred when there's a need for greater control over the CI/CD pipeline execution environment or when jobs require specific configurations that shared runners cannot provide.

Advantages of specific runners include:

- **Guaranteed Resource Availability**: Specific runners are dedicated to a single project or group, ensuring that jobs do not experience delays due to resource competition.
- **Enhanced Security**: With specific runners, the risk of cross-project data leakage is significantly reduced. The isolation ensures that each project runs in its own environment, which can be strictly controlled and monitored.
- **Customization**: Specific runners can be tailored to meet the unique requirements of a project. This includes installing particular dependencies, customizing runner configurations, and optimizing the runner environment for the tasks at hand.

Nevertheless, there are some disadvantages to be aware of:

- **Increased Maintenance Effort**: Managing multiple specific runners requires more administrative work. Each runner needs to be individually monitored, updated, and maintained.
- **Higher Cost**: Provisioning dedicated runners for multiple projects or groups can lead to increased infrastructure costs, especially if the usage is uneven across the runners.

To configure a specific runner, the runner registration command must include the project or group token to limit its scope to the intended target. Example registration command for a specific runner:

```
sudo gitlab-runner register --non-interactive \
  --url "https://gitlab.com/" \
  --registration-token "SPECIFIC_PROJECT_REGISTRATION_TOKEN" \
  --description "Specific runner for project X" \
  --tag-list "specific,project-X,linux,xenial" \
  --executor "shell"
```

Understanding the trade-offs between shared and specific runners is essential for optimizing CI/CD workflows and maintaining a balance between resource usage, security, and performance. The selection of runner type should be guided by the specific needs of the projects and the overall CI/CD strategy of the organization.

8.5 Configuring GitLab Runner

Configuring GitLab Runner is a critical step to ensure optimal performance, compatibility with your projects, and alignment with organizational workflows. Proper configuration allows runners to execute jobs efficiently and securely, addressing the specific needs of different tasks and environments. This section explores the various aspects of configuring GitLab Runner, including preparation of the configuration file, setting job concurrency, defining cache locations, specifying runner tags, and configuring advanced networking options.

The primary configuration file for GitLab Runner is config.toml, located in the runner's directory. This file is generated automatically during the registration process but can be customized to meet specific requirements.

```
[[runners]]
  name = "my-runner"
  url = "https://gitlab.example.com/"
  token = "xxxxxxxxxxxxxx"
  executor = "shell"
  [runners.custom_build_dir]
  [runners.docker]
    tls_verify = false
    image = "ubuntu:16.04"
    privileged = true
    disable_entrypoint_overwrite = false
    oom_kill_disable = false
    disable_cache = false
    volumes = ["/cache"]
```

Setting Job Concurrency

Configuring job concurrency ensures that the runner does not become overwhelmed by too many parallel jobs, which can degrade performance. The concurrent parameter in config.toml defines the maximum number of jobs that can be handled simultaneously.

```
concurrent = 4
```

Defining Cache Locations

Caching can substantially improve job performance by storing reusable files like dependencies and libraries. The cache directive specifies where these files are stored.

```
[runners.cache]
  [runners.cache.s3]
    ServerAddress = "s3.amazonaws.com"
    AccessKey = "your_access_key"
    SecretKey = "your_secret_key"
    BucketName = "your_bucket_name"
    Insecure = false
```

Specifying Runner Tags

Runner tags help in assigning specific jobs to particular runners based on their capabilities or environment. Tags are defined within the config.toml file.

```
[[runners]]
  name = "my-tagged-runner"
  url = "https://gitlab.example.com"
  token = "xxxxxxxxxxxxxx"
  executor = "shell"
  tags = ["tag1", "tag2"]
```

Advanced Networking Options

In some instances, jobs may require advanced networking configurations such as custom DNS settings or specific network interfaces. These options can be set within the runner configuration.

```
[[runners]]
  name = "network-configured-runner"
  url = "https://gitlab.example.com"
  token = "xxxxxxxxxxxxxx"
  executor = "docker"
  [runners.docker]
    dns = ["8.8.8.8", "8.8.4.4"]
    network_mode = "bridge"
```

Resource Limits and Management

Resource management is crucial for maintaining runner stability and preventing resource exhaustion. This includes setting limits for CPU and memory usage.

```
[[runners]]
  name = "resource-limited-runner"
  url = "https://gitlab.example.com"
  token = "xxxxxxxxxxxxxx"
  executor = "docker"
  [runners.docker]
    cpus = "2"
    memory = "4g"
```

Implementing these configurations in the config.toml file allows you to tailor the GitLab Runner to better fit the needs of your CI/CD pipeline, providing a more efficient and robust environment for job execution.

8.6 Runner Executors Overview

GitLab Runner executors are crucial in orchestrating the execution of CI/CD jobs in various environments. An executor determines the environment and method by which jobs are executed. Understanding the different types of executors and their use cases is essential for optimizing CI/CD pipelines and ensuring efficient resource utilization.

GitLab Runner supports several types of executors, including **Shell**, **Docker**, **Docker Machine**, **Kubernetes**, **SSH**, **VirtualBox**, and custom executors. Each executor is suited for different scenarios and has its advantages and limitations. This section provides an overview of these executors, aiding in selecting the appropriate one based on specific requirements.

Shell Executor is the simplest form and is ideal for running jobs directly on the runner's host operating system. It uses the shell of the operating system (e.g., Bash on Linux, PowerShell on Windows) to execute commands. Configuration is straightforward, and it is an excellent choice for jobs that do not require isolation.

```
job:
  script:
    - echo "Executing job using Shell executor"
    - uname -a
```

However, the Shell executor has limitations, such as lack of environment isolation, which may lead to conflicts if multiple jobs run concurrently. Typically, it suits small projects or development environments where resource constraints are limited.

Docker Executor is popular due to its container-based isolation, ensuring that jobs run in a clean and consistent environment. It allows specifying different Docker images for different jobs, providing flexibility and reproducibility.

```
job:
  image: alpine:latest
  script:
    - echo "Executing job using Docker executor"
    - uname -a
```

This executor is highly scalable and can secure isolated environments for each job, making it suitable for most CI/CD pipelines. However, it necessitates Docker to be installed on the runner host, adding an additional layer of complexity.

Docker Machine Executor extends the Docker executor, allowing jobs to run on auto-provisioned Docker hosts using Docker Machine. This executor is beneficial for dynamically scaling the number of runners based on job load, ensuring resource optimization.

Kubernetes Executor leverages Kubernetes clusters to execute jobs, offering advanced scheduling, scalability, and container orchestration features. Jobs run in Kubernetes Pods, and the executor supports specifying custom Kubernetes resources and configurations.

```
job:
  image: alpine:latest
  script:
    - echo "Executing job using Kubernetes executor"
    - uname -a
```

Given Kubernetes' powerful orchestration capabilities, this executor is ideal for large-scale and complex CI/CD environments requiring sophisticated job scheduling and resource management.

SSH Executor allows running jobs on remote hosts accessible via SSH. It is useful when jobs need to run on specific hardware or configurations unavailable locally or in containers. However, it requires setting up SSH access and ensuring security practices are in place to protect remote hosts.

```
job:
  script:
    - echo "Executing job using SSH executor"
    - uname -a
```

VirtualBox Executor enables running jobs inside VirtualBox VMs, providing a high level of isolation and control over the job environment. This executor is less commonly used due to the overhead of managing virtual machines but is beneficial when jobs require specific or complex environments that containers cannot adequately provide.

Custom Executors are user-defined executors that provide maximum flexibility, allowing integration with virtually any execution environment. Implementing a custom executor involves creating a script or binary that follows the GitLab Runner executor API, enabling the utilization of niche or proprietary environments for job execution.

Selecting the right executor depends on various factors, including the need for isolation, environment consistency, resource availability, and specific job requirements. Proper configuration and management of executors enhance the efficiency, reliability, and security of CI/CD pipelines, catering to diverse project needs.

8.7 Using Shell Executors

Shell executors enable running CI/CD jobs directly on the host machine's shell environment. They provide a straightforward mechanism for executing scripts and commands without the complexity of containerization or virtualization. Configuring and utilizing shell executors involves several steps to ensure effective integration and smooth operation.

When registering a GitLab Runner with a shell executor, you need to select 'shell' as the executor type. The following command initiates the registration process:

```
sudo gitlab-runner register
```

During the registration, you will be prompted to enter the GitLab instance URL, registration token, description for the runner, and the tags associated with it. When asked to select an executor, you should choose 'shell'.

The primary configuration file for GitLab Runner is /etc/gitlab-runner/config.toml. For shell executors, the runner configuration within this file is relatively simple compared to other types of executors like Docker. Below is an example of a configuration for a shell executor:

```
[[runners]]
  name = "my-shell-runner"
  url = "https://gitlab.example.com/"
  token = "your-registration-token"
  executor = "shell"
```

In this configuration, the name specifies the human-readable name of the runner, url is the URL of your GitLab instance, token is the unique registration token obtained during the runner registration process, and executor is set to shell.

Shell executors execute jobs using the system shell (such as Bash on Unix-based systems or PowerShell on Windows). The scripts and commands specified in the CI/CD pipeline will run with the user permissions under which the GitLab Runner service is running. Consequently, any scripts included in the .gitlab-ci.yml file must be compatible with the shell environment on the runner host.

A simple .gitlab-ci.yml pipeline configuration for a shell executor might look like this:

```
stages:
  - build
  - test

build_job:
  stage: build
  script:
    - echo "Compiling the project..."
    - make

test_job:
  stage: test
  script:
    - echo "Running unit tests..."
    - make test
```

In the above example, the build_job includes commands to compile the project, and the test_job runs the unit tests. These jobs will be executed on the shell executor directly and will have access to the host machine's file system, networking, and system resources.

It's important to note the implications of running jobs in a shell executor, particularly in terms of security and resource isolation. Unlike containerized executors, shell executors do not provide intrinsic isolation between jobs. Therefore, it is critical to ensure that the scripts executed are safe and come from trusted sources. Ensuring restricted user privileges for the GitLab Runner service can mitigate some security risks.

To enhance security, one should consider:

- Running the GitLab Runner service under a dedicated, non-privileged user account.
- Applying strict file and directory permissions to limit access.
- Regularly updating the runner and system packages to mitigate known vulnerabilities.
- Using environment isolation techniques where feasible, such as chroot or tools like Firejail.

Using environment variables in your .gitlab-ci.yml is a common practice to manage configurations and secrets without hardcoding them in your scripts. Environment variables can be set globally in the gitlab-ci.yml file or at the job level. For example:

```
variables:
  DB_HOST: "localhost"
  DB_USER: "user"
  DB_PASS: "password"
```

```
test_job:
  stage: test
  script:
    - echo "Testing with database at $DB_HOST"
    - ./run_tests.sh
```

The example above sets database connection details using environment variables, which can then be referenced in job scripts. Sensitive information should be managed with GitLab CI/CD secrets or masked variables to prevent exposure.

Shell executors also support custom hooks for pre- and post-job execution using pre_clone_script and post_clone_script. These hooks execute custom scripts before and after job script execution respectively. Adding these hooks can be done directly in the config.toml file, for example:

```
[runners.custom_build_dir]
  pre_clone_script = "/path/to/pre_clone.sh"
  post_clone_script = "/path/to/post_clone.sh"
```

To conclude, shell executors provide a simple and efficient way to run CI/CD jobs directly on the host machine. Proper configuration and security measures are vital to ensure safe execution of jobs and protection of system resources.

8.8 Using Docker Executors

The Docker executor in GitLab Runner allows jobs to be executed inside isolated Docker containers. This provides a clean and reproducible environment for each job, which resolves issues related to dependencies and environment configuration that can arise in shared or specific runners. Docker executors are particularly powerful for CI/CD workflows as they facilitate consistency and scalability.

A Docker executor operates by pulling down a Docker image and running jobs within that container. This begins by specifying Docker as the executor type during runner registration and configuring it in the .gitlab-ci.yml file.

To use Docker as an executor, first register a GitLab Runner with Docker executor specified:

```
gitlab-ci-multi-runner register --non-interactive \
  --url "https://gitlab.example.com/" \
  --registration-token "REGISTRATION_TOKEN" \
  --executor "docker" \
```

```
--docker-image "alpine:latest"
```

In the above command, the –executor flag is set to docker, and –docker-image indicates the default Docker image to be used, here alpine:latest. This image will be pulled from Docker Hub unless otherwise specified.

A typical .gitlab-ci.yml file for a project leveraging Docker executors might look as follows:

```
image: python:3.8

services:
  - docker:19.03.12

variables:
  DOCKER_DRIVER: overlay2

before_script:
  - pip install -r requirements.txt

stages:
  - build
  - test

build-job:
  stage: build
  script:
    - python setup.py install

test-job:
  stage: test
  script:
    - pytest
```

In this example:

- image: python:3.8 specifies the base Docker image to be used for this job. All stages will use this Python 3.8 image unless overridden.
- services section specifies additional Docker services needed during the job, such as a Docker-in-Docker service for building Docker images.
- variables section sets environment variables required by Docker, here setting DOCKER_DRIVER to overlay2.
- before_script section defines commands to be executed before each job, installing project dependencies listed in requirements.txt.
- Stages define different parts of the CI/CD pipeline, with jobs defined in build-job and test-job using stage: build and stage: test

respectively.

- Each job's script section defines the commands to be run inside the Docker container.

Customizing Docker Executors

Customization of Docker executors includes configuring cache directories, specifying additional images, and setting authentication for private Docker registries. The following example demonstrates these advanced configurations:

```
image: custom:latest

services:
  - name: docker:19.03.12
    alias: docker

cache:
  paths:
    - ~/.cache/pip

variables:
  DOCKER_DRIVER: overlay2
  DOCKER_TLS_CERTDIR: ""

before_script:
  - docker info
  - docker login -u "$CI_REGISTRY_USER" -p "$CI_JOB_TOKEN"
       $CI_REGISTRY

build-job:
  stage: build
  script:
    - docker build -t $CI_REGISTRY_IMAGE:$CI_COMMIT_SHA .

test-job:
  stage: test
  script:
    - docker run --rm $CI_REGISTRY_IMAGE:$CI_COMMIT_SHA pytest
```

Important points in this script include:

- The cache section ensures that the pip cache is preserved between jobs, improving job efficiency.
- The variables section configures Docker TLS settings and the driver.
- The before_script section logs in to the Docker registry using GitLab CI/CD predefined variables.
- The build-job builds the Docker image and tags it with the commit SHA.

- The test-job runs tests using the image built in the previous job.

Runner Configuration for Docker Executors

A runner configuration file, typically located at /etc/gitlab-runner/config.toml, can further fine-tune Docker executors. Below is an example configuration:

```
[[runners]]
  name = "docker-runner"
  url = "https://gitlab.example.com/"
  token = "REGISTERED_RUNNER_TOKEN"
  executor = "docker"
  [runners.custom_build_dir]
  [runners.cache]
    [runners.cache.s3]
    [runners.cache.gcs]
  [runners.docker]
    tls_verify = false
    image = "docker:stable"
    privileged = true
    disable_entrypoint_overwrite = false
    oom_kill_disable = false
    disable_cache = false
    volumes = ["/cache"]
    shm_size = 0
```

Critical configuration parameters include:

- executor = "docker" defines the executor type.
- image = "docker:stable" sets the Docker image used for running jobs.
- privileged = true allows running Docker-in-Docker (dind) containers.
- volumes = ["/cache"] mounts shared volumes, such as for caching purposes.

By understanding and utilizing Docker executors efficiently, one can achieve significant improvements in CI/CD pipelines, including consistent build environments, isolation between jobs, and scalability across multiple platforms. Here is the corrected LaTeX text of the section, with all errors fixed and formatted according to the specified requirements:

8.9 Using Custom Executors

Custom executors in GitLab Runner provide a mechanism to define and use custom environments tailored to unique project requirements. This approach enables users to integrate specific tools, system configurations, or workflows that standard executors may not support natively.

To set up a custom executor, the primary requirement is to implement a series of predefined scripts that manage the lifecycle of the build environments. The lifecycle includes creating, preparing, running, and cleaning up the build environment. These scripts will be called by the GitLab Runner during the job execution process.

The necessary scripts for a custom executor include:

- config.sh - Configures the executor, typically defines settings or initializes necessary configurations.
- prepare.sh - Prepares the build environment, such as starting required services or configuring network settings.
- run.sh - Executes the job script.
- cleanup.sh - Cleans up the build environment after the job completes.

Here is an example of these scripts defined for a hypothetical custom executor:

```
#!/bin/bash
# Configuration settings
echo "Custom Executor: Configuration script executed."
```

```
#!/bin/bash
# Set up build environment
echo "Custom Executor: Preparing build environment."
# Example: Start a Docker container or a virtual machine
docker run -d --name custom_build_env your-docker-image
```

```
#!/bin/bash
# Execute the job script inside the prepared environment
echo "Custom Executor: Running job script."
# Example: Run the job in the Docker container
docker exec custom_build_env "$@"
```

```
#!/bin/bash
# Clean up the build environment
echo "Custom Executor: Cleaning up the build environment."
# Example: Stop and remove the Docker container
```

```
docker stop custom_build_env
docker rm custom_build_env
```

After creating these scripts, you need to configure your GitLab Runner to use them for job execution. Modify the config.toml file of your GitLab Runner to specify the custom executor's settings. Here is an example configuration:

```
[[runners]]
  name = "Custom Executor Runner"
  url = "https://gitlab.example.com"
  token = "YOUR_REGISTRATION_TOKEN"
  executor = "custom"
  [runners.custom]
    config_exec = "/path/to/your/executor/config.sh"
    prepare_exec = "/path/to/your/executor/prepare.sh"
    run_exec = "/path/to/your/executor/run.sh"
    cleanup_exec = "/path/to/your/executor/cleanup.sh"
```

Once these modifications are in place, restart the GitLab Runner service to apply the new configuration.

To verify everything is functioning correctly, you can create a simple GitLab CI pipeline to test your custom executor. Here is an example pipeline definition in your project's .gitlab-ci.yml file:

```
stages:
  - test

test_custom_executor:
  stage: test
  script:
    - echo "Executing job in custom executor."
```

When this pipeline runs, GitLab Runner will utilize the defined custom executor scripts for the job's execution.

Custom executors offer great flexibility and can be extended or modified as needed. You can incorporate additional scripts or commands to further tailor the build environment to your specific needs, such as establishing SSH connections, managing specialized hardware, or integrating with proprietary systems. The ability to control the entire lifecycle of the build environment provides substantial power and customization potential, making custom executors a robust feature in the GitLab Runner ecosystem.

8.10 Scaling Runners

Scaling runners in GitLab is a crucial task to ensure that CI/CD pipelines run efficiently and promptly, especially for large projects or high-frequency deployment cycles. Properly scaling your runners can help manage resources better, reduce waiting times for jobs, and handle peak loads effectively.

To begin with, scaling involves both vertical and horizontal scaling. Vertical scaling refers to upgrading the computational resources of a single runner, such as increasing its CPU, memory, or storage. Horizontal scaling, on the other hand, involves adding more runners to the pool to handle more jobs concurrently.

Horizontal Scaling

Horizontal scaling is typically more effective when it comes to handling larger workloads because it distributes the load across multiple runners. GitLab offers several strategies for horizontal scaling:

- **Static Configuration:** You can manually configure multiple runners by setting up each runner individually on different machines. This approach, while straightforward, can become labor-intensive as the number of runners increases.
- **Dynamic Scaling:** Leveraging orchestration tools such as Kubernetes can automate the process of scaling runners up and down based on demand. GitLab's Kubernetes executor can dynamically create and remove runners as needed.
- **Autoscaling with GitLab Runner:** GitLab Runner itself supports the autoscaling feature with certain executors like Docker Machine. This allows for the automatic creation of new runner instances when there is a high load and their removal when they are idle.

The configuration for each of these methods involves specific steps and considerations. For instance, using Docker Machine for autoscaling would require the following configuration in the config.toml file:

```
[[runners]]
  name = "docker-autoscaler"
  url = "https://gitlab.com/"
  token = "YOUR_RUNNER_TOKEN"
  executor = "docker+machine"
  [runners.custom_build_dir]
```

```
[runners.docker]
  image = "docker:19.03.12"
  privileged = true
[runners.cache]
  [runners.cache.s3]
  [runners.cache.gcs]
[runners.machine]
  IdleCount = 1
  IdleTime = 600
  MachineDriver = "google"
  MachineName = "auto-scale-%s"
  MachineOptions = [
    "google-project=YOUR_GOOGLE_PROJECT",
    "google-zone=us-central1-a",
    "google-machine-type=n1-standard-1"
  ]
```

In this configuration, IdleCount indicates the number of runners that remain available even when idle, and IdleTime specifies how long (in seconds) an idle instance remains before being terminated. The MachineOptions define the specifications for the autoscaled instances.

Vertical Scaling

For vertical scaling, if the runners are struggling with resource limitations (CPU, memory, etc.), increasing the allocated resources can significantly boost performance. This might include:

- Increasing the number of CPU cores allocated to the runner.
- Allocating more memory.
- Using faster storage options (e.g., SSDs instead of HDDs).
- Adjusting parallelism settings in the runner configuration.

Here is an example of modifying the config.toml file for vertical scaling:

```
[[runners]]
  name = "high-performance-runner"
  url = "https://gitlab.com/"
  token = "YOUR_RUNNER_TOKEN"
  executor = "shell"
  limit = 4
  [runners.custom_build_dir]
  [runners.cache]
    [runners.cache.s3]
    [runners.cache.gcs]
```

In this case, the limit parameter is set to 4, allowing this runner to handle up to four jobs concurrently. Ensure that sufficient resources are available on the host machine to handle this increased load efficiently.

Monitoring and Resource Management

Scaling runners also necessitates robust monitoring and resource management. Utilizing metrics and monitoring tools like Prometheus and Grafana, or GitLab's built-in monitoring capabilities, can provide valuable insights into the performance and usage of runners.

Establishing alerts for metrics such as CPU utilization, memory usage, disk I/O, and job queue lengths can help in proactive resource management:

```
# Prometheus configuration example for monitoring runners
scrape_configs:
  - job_name: 'gitlab_runners'
    static_configs:
      - targets: ['<runner_host>:9252']
```

The metrics collected can be visualized using Grafana to create dashboards that provide real-time insights.

Here's an example output from a Grafana dashboard that monitors GitLab runners:

```
---------------------------------------
|      GitLab Runner Metrics          |
---------------------------------------
| Runner Utilization    |  75%        |
| Pending Jobs          |  12         |
| Running Jobs          |  28         |
| CPU Usage             |  83%        |
| Memory Usage          |  65%        |
---------------------------------------
```

The balance between vertical and horizontal scaling depends on the specific needs of your CI/CD workloads, the available infrastructure, and the expected job load. Implementing a flexible scaling strategy ensures GitLab runners can handle varying demands efficiently, optimizing both performance and cost.

8.11 Runner Performance Optimization

Optimizing the performance of GitLab Runners is essential for efficient continuous integration and delivery pipelines. Achieving optimal runner performance involves several strategies, including resource management, concurrent job handling, caching, artifact management, and fine-tuning runner configurations. This section will delve into these strategies, providing comprehensive guidelines to enhance GitLab Runner performance.

Resource management is fundamental in ensuring that runners can handle assigned workloads efficiently. Allocating appropriate CPU and memory resources is crucial. To start, identify the available resources on the machine where the runner is executed. Overcommitting resources can lead to system instability and degraded performance. Ensure each runner instance has sufficient CPU and memory to perform operations without contention. This can be managed in the runner's configuration file:

```
[[runners]]
  name = "my-runner"
  url = "https://gitlab.example.com/"
  token = "your_runner_token"
  executor = "docker"
  [runners.custom_build_dir]
    run_dir = "/builds"
  [runners.docker]
    image = "python:3.8"
    privileged = true
    disable_entrypoint_overwrite = false
    oom_kill_disable = false
    disable_cache = false
    volumes = ["/cache"]
    shm_size = 0
  concurrent = 4
  check_interval = 0
```

In the above example, the concurrent setting specifies the maximum number of jobs the runner can execute concurrently. Adjust this number based on the system's capacity and the job's resource intensity. For instance, a high-concurrency setting may lead to performance bottlenecks if the underlying hardware cannot support multiple parallel jobs. Monitoring tools can aid in tracking resource utilization and identifying optimal concurrency levels.

Caching is another crucial aspect of runner performance optimization. Proper caching strategies reduce job execution times by preventing redundant compiling or downloading of dependencies. GitLab's caching mechanism can be configured within the .gitlab-ci.yml file:

```
job:
  script:
    - make
  cache:
    paths:
      - vendor/
      - .cache/pip/
```

In this example, the cache directive specifies directories to cache between job runs. This reduces the need to re-download dependencies, thus speeding up build times. Evaluate frequently used dependencies and toolchains to identify what should be cached. Additionally, utilize GitLab's distributed caching mechanisms to share cache between runners, optimizing overall performance.

Artifact management is closely related to caching. Artifacts are intermediate files generated by jobs, stored, and shared with subsequent jobs. Efficient usage of artifacts can significantly streamline pipelines. In the .gitlab-ci.yml file, artifacts can be defined as follows:

```
job:
  script:
    - make build
  artifacts:
    paths:
      - build/
    expire_in: 1 week
```

Here, the artifacts directive declares the paths to store as artifacts, and expire_in sets the lifetime of these artifacts, ensuring the storage system is not overloaded with outdated files. Consider the trade-off between storing artifacts for future use and the storage space consumed by these artifacts. Adjust the expire_in parameter based on the frequency of changes and the requirements of your CI/CD pipeline.

Fine-tuning runner configurations also plays a significant role in performance optimization. Adjusting configurations such as the shm_size (shared memory size), oom_kill_disable (disables out-of-memory killer), and allocating disk spaces can lead to performance improvements. Here's an example of a Docker runner configuration:

```
[runners.docker]
  image = "python:3.8"
  privileged = true
  disable_entrypoint_overwrite = false
  oom_kill_disable = true
  disable_cache = false
  volumes = ["/cache"]
  shm_size = 512000000
```

Setting oom_kill_disable to true prevents the out-of-memory killer from terminating the runner process. However, this should be done cautiously and in scenarios where the runner deals with large memory-intensive jobs. The shm_size parameter is set to increase the shared memory available, useful for jobs requiring substantial inter-process communication.

Efficient concurrent job handling is crucial. Balancing job queues and managing runner groups to segregate jobs based on resource requirements can mitigate resource contention. GitLab allows for runner grouping and specific job assignments within the CI/CD configuration:

```
stages:
  - build
  - test
  - deploy

build-job:
  stage: build
  tags:
    - build-runner

test-job:
  stage: test
  tags:
    - test-runner

deploy-job:
  stage: deploy
  tags:
    - deploy-runner
```

Tags enable assigning jobs to specific runners, thereby distributing the load based on runner availability and capabilities. By segregating runners for build, test, and deploy stages, resource allocation can be better managed to avoid bottlenecks. Using separate runners for different pipeline stages ensures that critical tasks do not compete for resources with less demanding jobs.

Monitoring and logging are vital components for continuous improvement of runner performance. GitLab provides detailed logging for runners, accessible through the GitLab UI. Analyze these logs to identify the root causes of performance degradation. Automated monitoring solutions like Prometheus and Grafana can be integrated with GitLab runners for real-time performance tracking and alerting.

```
[[runners]]
  executor = "docker"
  [runners.custom_build_dir]
    run_dir = "/builds"
  [runners.docker]
    image = "alpine"
    volumes = ["/var/run/docker.sock:/var/run/docker.sock", "/cache"]
  [runners.prometheus]
    url = "http://localhost:9090"
    listen_address = ":9252"
```

By specifying the prometheus section, runner metrics can be exposed to Prometheus. This integration allows in-depth performance analysis through custom dashboards and alerts set up in Grafana. Utilize these tools to monitor utilization patterns, identify bottlenecks, and optimize runner configurations proactively.

Finally, regular updates to GitLab Runner versions ensure that you benefit from the latest performance improvements and bug fixes. New versions might include enhancements in resource management, caching breadth, and overall efficiency.

To maintain an optimized runner infrastructure, consistently review and update your configuration, actively monitor performance metrics, and adapt to the changing demands of your CI/CD pipeline workloads.

8.12 Security Best Practices for Runners

Ensuring the security of GitLab Runners is paramount to maintaining the integrity and confidentiality of build processes and artifacts. This section outlines various techniques and considerations to enhance the security of GitLab Runners, whether deploying a simple shell executor or a complex custom setup.

Isolate Runner Environments

One of the fundamental principles in securing GitLab Runners is isolating the runner environments. Use distinct virtual machines or containers for each runner to prevent cross-contamination and ensure that each build runs in an isolated environment. For Docker executors, this is inherently managed, but for shell executors, using tools such as chroot or lightweight virtual environments like LXC can enhance isolation.

Minimize Runner Permissions

Only grant the minimum necessary permissions to the user under which the runner operates. Here are key recommendations:

- Run the GitLab Runner under a dedicated user account with restricted permissions.
- Avoid running the GitLab Runner with root privileges. If administrative access is required, use privilege escalation only where necessary and ensure it is tightly controlled.
- Limit network access to the runner, restricting it to only required endpoints and minimizing exposure to external networks.

Use Secure Storage for Tokens and Secrets

Utilize secure methods for storing any tokens, secrets, or sensitive information required by GitLab Runners:

- Store sensitive information in environment variables or secret management services like HashiCorp Vault or AWS Secrets Manager.

- Utilize GitLab's Secret CI/CD variables to store secure information instead of embedding them in pipeline configurations.

When defining these variables within the 'gitlab-ci.yml' file, ensure they are marked as protected and masked.

Regularly Update and Patch Software

Keep the GitLab Runner software and the underlying operating systems up-to-date. Regularly apply security patches to mitigate vulnerabilities:

- Regularly check for updates to the GitLab Runner and apply them promptly.

- Employ automated update tools for the operating system and security patches (e.g., apt-get for Debian-based systems or yum for Red Hat-based systems).

Configure Firewall and Network Security

Implement firewall rules and network controls to minimize unauthorized access:

- Use network segmentation to isolate Runners from the broader network.

- Configure firewalls to restrict incoming and outgoing traffic based on the principle of least privilege.

- Monitor network traffic for anomalies and potential intrusions.

Use Encrypted Communication

Ensure all communications between GitLab Runners and the GitLab instance are encrypted to protect against man-in-the-middle attacks:

- Configure GitLab and GitLab Runners to use HTTPS.

- Employ strong TLS configurations and disable weaker ciphers and protocols.

- Validate SSL certificates to prevent the use of self-signed or invalid certificates.

Monitor and Audit Runner Activity

Implement logging and monitoring to keep track of all runner activities and detect potential security issues:

- Enable logging for GitLab Runner and review logs regularly for unusual activity.
- Use log management solutions and security information and event management (SIEM) tools to analyze logs and detect anomalies.
- Set up alerts for suspicious activities and automate responses where appropriate.

Protect Against Build Directory Contamination

Ensure that the build directory is clean and not reused across jobs to prevent potential injection threats:

- Use the git clean command to remove untracked files and directories.
- Configure runners to use temporary directories and ensure they are wiped after each job.

Within the 'gitlab-ci.yml' file, the before_script and after_script can be configured to enforce such practices:

```
before_script:
  - git clean -fdx
after_script:
  - rm -rf build_directory
```

Run Jobs in Read-Only Mode (where possible)

Where applicable, run jobs in a read-only mode to prevent unauthorized alterations:

- For Docker executors, use read-only volume mounts for directories that do not require write access.
- Enforce file system permissions that restrict write capabilities to only essential files and directories.

Separate Staging and Production Runners

Deploy distinct runners for staging and production environments to minimize the risk of cross-environment contamination:

- Use environment-specific tags to segregate jobs.
- Configure separate runners with unique specifications and security policies for each environment.

Harden the Operating System

Apply best practices to harden the underlying operating system:

- Disable unnecessary services and close non-essential ports.
- Configure security-enhancing modules like SELinux or AppArmor.
- Enforce stringent user and group policies, including using strong authentication mechanisms.

Implementing the outlined security best practices will significantly enhance the security posture of your GitLab Runners. Integrating these measures proactively safeguards the build environment, ensuring reliable and secure operations.

Chapter 9

Security and Compliance in GitLab

This chapter focuses on the security and compliance features within GitLab. It covers user access management, two-factor authentication, and OAuth/SAML integration. The chapter examines securing repositories, CI/CD pipeline security, and vulnerability management. Code quality measures such as SAST and DAST, as well as container scanning, are discussed. It also addresses compliance management, including audit logs and reporting, ensuring alignment with industry standards and organizational policies.

9.1 Introduction to Security and Compliance

Security and compliance are critical components in the lifecycle of software development, especially within collaborative platforms such as GitLab. Ensuring that code repositories and CI/CD pipelines are secure not only protects intellectual property but also mitigates the potential risk of vulnerabilities being exploited in production environments. Additionally, adherence to regulatory compliance standards is fundamental in maintaining the integrity and trustworthiness of software products and the organizations that develop them.

Security in GitLab involves a multilayered approach to protect both the source code and the development process. This includes mechanisms to control user access, enforce authentication protocols, secure repositories, and manage potential vulnerabilities in the code and deployment processes. These security principles are vital to safeguarding against unauthorized access and malicious attacks.

Compliance within GitLab refers to the measures and practices that ensure the development process adheres to various industry standards and legal requirements. Compliance management involves maintaining audit logs, generating reports, and aligning with policies such as GDPR, HIPAA, and ISO standards. These protocols are designed to ensure that software development practices meet regulatory demands and promote transparency.

GitLab integrates a variety of features to support both security and compliance. The platform provides tools for managing user access and permissions, implementing two-factor authentication, and integrating with OAuth and SAML for single sign-on (SSO) capabilities. These features help in establishing a secure authentication framework and managing access controls effectively.

```
# Navigate to the user's profile settings
Settings > Account > Two-factor Authentication

# Click on Enable Two-factor Authentication

# Scan the QR code using an authenticator app

# Enter the generated code in GitLab to complete setup
```

Additionally, repository security in GitLab involves managing protected branches, mandatory code reviews, and access controls to ensure that only authorized personnel can modify critical parts of the codebase. Securing repositories includes implementing features like merge request approvals and enforcing code owner rules to maintain the integrity of the source code.

```
# Navigate to the repository's settings
Repository > Settings > Protected Branches

# Add a new protected branch
Branch name: main
Allowed to merge: Maintainers
Allowed to push: No one

# Save changes
```

CI/CD pipeline security encompasses several practices to secure the automated processes that build, test, and deploy code. These practices include the use of environment variables with limited scopes, ensuring the security of runners, and validating scripts to avoid execution of untrusted code. GitLab enables detailed configuration of CI/CD pipelines to enforce security at various stages of the development lifecycle.

```
# Define sensitive environment variables
variables:
  SECRET_KEY: "S3cr3t"

# Use protected runners
stages:
  - build
  - test
  - deploy

# Validate scripts and limit access
build:
  script:
    - ./validate.sh
  only:
    - protected
```

Vulnerability management in GitLab provides functionalities such as Static Application Security Testing (SAST), Dynamic Application Security Testing (DAST), and container scanning to identify and mitigate security risks in applications. These tools automate the scanning process and generate reports to help developers address vulnerabilities promptly.

```
# Include SAST template in .gitlab-ci.yml
include:
  - template: Security/SAST.gitlab-ci.yml

# Define SAST job
sast:
  stage: test
  script:
    - ./run-sast.sh
```

Maintaining compliance in GitLab involves generating and managing audit logs, and producing reports to demonstrate adherence to regulatory standards. Audit logs track user activities and changes in the repository, providing a transparent record of actions for compliance purposes.

```
# Navigate to the admin area
Admin Area > Audit Log

# Filter logs by event type or date
Event Type: User Login
Date Range: Last 30 days

# Export audit log for reporting
Export as CSV
```

By integrating these security and compliance features, GitLab provides a robust framework that helps organizations develop secure and compliant software. This ensures that all aspects of the development lifecycle are protected and aligned with industry standards, promoting a trustworthy and reliable development environment.

9.2 Security Features in GitLab

GitLab provides a robust set of security features designed to protect the integrity and confidentiality of code, safeguard user data, and ensure compliance with organizational policies. These features span across various aspects such as user authentication, authorization, repository protection, pipeline security, and vulnerability management.

User authentication within GitLab can be handled via multiple mechanisms to cater to different security needs. Administrators can enforce strong password policies, mandating complexity requirements and expiration periods. Two-factor authentication (2FA) adds an additional layer of security, requiring users to provide a second form of verification beyond their password. The 2FA process can be set up using authenticator apps like Google Authenticator or hardware security keys compliant with the Universal 2nd Factor (U2F) standard.

```
# Enabling 2FA in GitLab
1. Navigate to your account settings.
2. Click on "Account" and find the "Two-factor Authentication" section.
3. Follow the on-screen instructions to set up your 2FA with an authenticator app or
     hardware key.
```

Managing user access and permissions is crucial to ensuring that only authorized personnel can view or modify specific parts of the codebase. GitLab employs a role-based access control (RBAC) system, where permissions are granted based on predefined roles such as Guest, Reporter, Developer, Maintainer, and Owner. Each role determines the level of access within the project or group, restricting actions like code merges, edits, and administrative changes to specific users.

The protection of repositories is another critical aspect of GitLab's security features. Repository mirroring, protected branches, and protected tags are some of the functionalities that help in safeguarding code integrity. Administrators can mark certain branches and tags as "protected," thereby controlling who can push or merge code into these branches and who can create tags. This ensures that only trusted developers can make changes to critical parts of the codebase.

```
# Protecting a branch in GitLab
1. Navigate to your project and go to "Settings" > "Repository".
2. Scroll to the "Protected Branches" section.
3. Specify the branch you want to protect and define the allowed roles for pushing and
   merging.
4. Click "Protect" to enforce the protection rules.
```

Pipeline security is essential for maintaining the integrity of the Continuous Integration/Continuous Deployment (CI/CD) process. GitLab provides various features to secure pipelines, including:

- Secure variables: Sensitive information such as API keys and passwords can be stored as secure variables, which are masked in job logs and restricted from being accessible by unauthorized users.
- Pipeline integrity: GitLab validates pipelines before running them, ensuring consistency and preventing unauthorized modifications.
- Container registries: Secure container registries are integrated into GitLab, allowing safe storage and management of Docker images.

The maintenance of pipeline security is enhanced by using scanning tools integrated within GitLab. Static Application Security Testing (SAST) and Dynamic Application Security Testing (DAST) are used to detect vulnerabilities within the codebase and running applications, respectively. These tools are automated and can be incorporated into the CI/CD pipeline, providing real-time feedback on potential security issues.

```
# Example GitLab CI/CD configuration with SAST
stages:
  - build
  - test
  - deploy

include:
  - template: Security/SAST.gitlab-ci.yml

sast:
  variables:
    SAST_EXCLUDED_PATHS: "spec/"
```

```
Job Output:
$ sast
[INFO] Detected 3 vulnerabilities in the project:
  - High: SQL Injection in file src/db/query.js, line 42
  - Medium: XSS in file src/web/app.js, line 107
  - Low: Insecure Configuration in file config/settings.yml, line 14
```

Vulnerability management in GitLab is further enhanced by container scanning and dependency scanning, which checks for known vulnerabilities in container images and third-party dependencies respectively. These scans generate reports that provide detailed information about identified issues, including their severity levels and suggested mitigations.

Compliance management is a functional area where GitLab shines by offering features like audit logs and reporting. Every action taken within GitLab, such as logins, repository changes, and permission modifications, is recorded in audit logs. These logs can be examined to ensure compliance with industry standards and internal policies. GitLab also facilitates reporting, enabling organizations to generate compliance reports that summarize security posture and identify areas that need attention.

By integrating these security features, GitLab offers a comprehensive solution to meet the security and compliance needs of modern software development environments.

9.3 Managing User Access and Permissions

Effective management of user access and permissions is vital for ensuring the security and integrity of GitLab-based projects. The granular control over user roles and permissions minimizes the risk of unauthorized access and accidental alterations, thus safeguarding sensitive information and maintaining regulatory compliance. This section delves deeply into the various aspects of user access management, including user roles, permission levels, group memberships, and best practices.

In GitLab, user permissions can be managed through a combination of user roles and group memberships. Each role comes with a predefined set of capabilities, which are extended or restricted based on the individual requirements of a project or group.

User Roles:

- **Guest:** Users in the Guest role have limited access, primarily read-only, with the ability to create issues and leave comments.
- **Reporter:** The Reporter role grants read access to the repository, along with the ability to create and view issues, as well as download code.

- **Developer:** Users with the Developer role have extended permissions, including the ability to push and pull code, manage issues, and merge requests.
- **Maintainer:** Maintainers have comprehensive control over the repository, capable of managing settings, adding or removing members, and performing code merges.
- **Owner:** Owners possess the highest level of control, including all permissions of the Maintainer role, with additional administrative capabilities like group management and advanced project configurations.

Group and Project Memberships:

GitLab allows for the organization of users into groups, which can be assigned to specific projects. Group membership facilitates the streamlined management of user permissions across multiple projects. Permissions assigned at the group level are inherited by all projects within that group unless overridden by project-specific settings.

```
# Example command to add a user to a group with a specific role
gitlab-rails runner "group = Group.find_by_full_path('group_name'); user = User.
    find_by(username: 'new_user'); Members::GroupMemberCreator.new(group, user,
    GroupMember::DEVELOPER).execute"
```

Inherited and Explicit Permissions:

Inheritance of permissions can simplify user access management. A user assigned the Developer role in a parent group will inherently possess Developer access across all child projects. However, explicit permissions can be set at the project level to grant or restrict access as needed.

```
# Explicitly overriding permissions for a user in a specific project
gitlab-rails runner "project = Project.find_by_full_path('group_name/project_name')
    ; user = User.find_by(username: 'specific_user'); Members::
    ProjectMemberCreator.new(project, user, ProjectMember::REPORTER).execute"
```

Best Practices for Managing User Access and Permissions:

- **Principle of Least Privilege:** Assign users only the minimum permissions required to perform their roles. This reduces the risk of unintended actions that could compromise the repository.
- **Regular audits:** Periodically review user access logs and permissions. Remove or adjust permissions for users who change roles or leave projects.

- **Role-based access control (RBAC):** Use predefined roles effectively and avoid over-customizing roles, which can lead to complex and unmanageable permission settings.
- **Enforce two-factor authentication (2FA):** Ensure that 2FA is enabled for all users, adding an extra layer of security.
- **Document processes:** Maintain comprehensive documentation of access control policies and procedures, ensuring that all team members understand and adhere to them.

Automating Role and Permission Assignments:

To streamline the process of managing user access and permissions, automation scripts and hooks can be employed. For instance, when a new user is on-boarded, an automated script can be triggered to assign them the appropriate role based on their profile or team.

```
# Automated script example for user role assignment
#!/bin/bash

USER_NAME=$1
ROLE=$2
PROJECT_PATH=$3

gitlab-rails runner "user = User.find_by(username: '$USER_NAME'); project =
    Project.find_by_full_path('$PROJECT_PATH'); Members::
    ProjectMemberCreator.new(project, user, $ROLE).execute"
```

The output from the above script can be verified through GitLab's web interface or via additional command line queries.

```
$ ./assign_role.sh new_user Developer group_name/project_name

# Expected console output
User new_user successfully assigned as Developer to group_name/project_name
```

Effective management of user access and permissions is crucial in preventing unauthorized access, ensuring compliance with security policies, and maintaining the integrity of the project repository. By leveraging the built-in roles and customizable permissions in GitLab, alongside best practices, organizations can achieve a secure and efficient workflow.

9.4 Two-factor Authentication

Two-factor authentication (2FA) is a crucial security measure implemented in GitLab to ensure that user accounts remain secure even if their passwords are compromised. 2FA combines something the user knows (a password) with something the user has (a second factor like a smartphone app). This section explores the setup, configuration, and usage of 2FA in GitLab, providing a detailed understanding of how it enhances account security.

To begin setting up 2FA in GitLab, users must first navigate to their profile settings. This can be accomplished by clicking on the user avatar in the top right corner of the GitLab interface and selecting *Settings*. Within the settings menu, the user should locate the *Password* tab, where the 2FA configuration options are available.

Users will observe the *Two-factor Authentication* section, which includes the option to enable 2FA. Selecting this option will prompt users to secure their account with 2FA, starting with entering their current password to proceed.

GitLab supports several authentication apps for generating time-based one-time passwords (TOTPs). Some commonly used applications are Google Authenticator, Authy, and Microsoft Authenticator, all available for iOS and Android devices. The following outlines the step-by-step process to enable 2FA:

1. Open the 2FA application of choice on your mobile device.
2. Select the option to add a new account, typically indicated by a plus (+) symbol.
3. Scan the QR code provided on the GitLab 2FA setup page using the mobile device's camera, or alternatively, enter the secret key manually if scanning isn't possible.
4. The app will generate a one-time authentication code. Enter this code into the corresponding field on GitLab to verify the setup.

Upon successful entry of the one-time code, 2FA is now enabled for the user account. It's crucial to download and securely store the recovery codes provided by GitLab at this stage. These codes are essential in the event that the user's 2FA device is lost or unavailable.

```
1. Current password: ********
2. Scan QR code using authenticator app or enter secret key
3. Enter generated one-time password (OTP): 123456
4. Two-factor authentication enabled successfully!
5. Recovery codes (save these):
   - 1234-5678
   - 8765-4321
```

```
- 4321-8765
- 5678-1234
```

Authentication involving 2FA follows a straightforward process. Each time the user logs in, they must provide their username, password, and a verification code from their 2FA application. This significantly reduces the risk of unauthorized access.

There are specific scenarios where 2FA management becomes pertinent, such as recovery, disabling 2FA, and managing multiple devices. GitLab provides straightforward procedures for these situations:

Recovering Access using Recovery Codes: If a user loses access to their 2FA device, they can log in with their username and password, then use one of the previously saved recovery codes when prompted for the 2FA code. Each recovery code can only be used once.

```
1. Enter username and password
2. Enter recovery code: 1234-5678
3. Access granted
```

Disabling Two-factor Authentication: Users may need to disable 2FA, especially if switching to a new 2FA method or encountering persistent issues with their current setup. This is done through the GitLab profile settings under the *Account* section.

```
1. Navigate to Profile Settings > Account
2. Click "Disable Two-Factor Authentication"
3. Enter password to confirm
4. Two-factor authentication has been disabled
```

Managing Multiple Devices: Advanced users may prefer to register multiple devices for 2FA to ensure continuous access in the event one device is unavailable. This can be achieved by setting up 2FA on each device following the standard procedure. The key is to scan the QR code on each device before completing the verification process on GitLab.

The implementation of 2FA in GitLab substantially bolsters security, offering a robust defense against unauthorized access. By effectively managing 2FA settings and understanding recovery processes, users can maintain seamless access while ensuring their accounts remain secure.

9.5 OAuth and SAML Integration

GitLab provides integration with OAuth and SAML, which are industry-standard protocols for authorization and identity management. These protocols enhance security by leveraging existing user credentials and reducing the need for multiple passwords. This section explores the implementation and benefits of integrating OAuth and SAML within GitLab.

OAuth, which stands for Open Authorization, is an open-standard protocol that allows users to grant websites or applications access to their information without sharing their passwords. The primary advantage of OAuth is that it provides limited access without disclosing the user's credentials.

To integrate OAuth in GitLab, a registered application in GitLab is necessary. The configuration involves defining authorized redirect URIs and setting up scopes to specify permissions. Here is a sample configuration:

```
{
  "name": "Example Application",
  "redirect_uri": "https://example.com/auth/callback",
  "scopes": ["api", "read_user"],
  "confidential": true
}
```

Next, in the GitLab instance, navigate to the Admin Area and select the Applications section to register the new application. This process generates a Client ID and a Client Secret, which are essential for OAuth flow.

To illustrate, consider the following steps to initiate the authorization flow:

1. Redirect the user to the GitLab OAuth endpoint: https://gitlab.example.com/oauth/authorize?client_id=<client_id>&redirect_uri=<redirect_uri>&response_type=code&state=<state>

2. Upon user consent, an authorization code is returned to the redirect URI:

https://example.com/auth/callback?code=<authorization_code>&state=<state>

3. Exchange the authorization code for an access token:

```
POST https://gitlab.example.com/oauth/token
Content-Type: application/x-www-form-urlencoded
```

```
client_id=<client_id>&client_secret=<client_secret>&code=<authorization_code
    >&grant_type=authorization_code&redirect_uri=<redirect_uri>
```

This integration ensures that access to GitLab resources is controlled and based on the permissions granted by the user.

SAML, which stands for Security Assertion Markup Language, is an XML-based protocol used for exchanging authentication and authorization data between parties, predominantly between an identity provider (IdP) and a service provider (SP). SAML allows Single Sign-On (SSO) capabilities, facilitating a seamless and secure authentication experience across multiple applications.

GitLab supports SAML by acting as a service provider, enabling authentication via identity providers such as Okta, OneLogin, and others. Setting up SAML involves several steps, primarily configuration both on the GitLab side and the IdP side.

The SAML SP configuration in GitLab includes: - Assertion Consumer Service (ACS) URL: https://gitlab.example.com/users/auth/saml/callback - Entity ID: https://gitlab.example.com - Name ID format: Typically urn:oasis:names:tc:SAML:1.1:nameid-format:emailAddress

Here is a typical SAML configuration block for gitlab.rb:

```
gitlab_rails['omniauth_providers'] = [
  {
    'name' => 'saml',
    'args' => {
      assertion_consumer_service_url: 'https://gitlab.example.com/users/auth/saml/
          callback',
      idp_cert_fingerprint: '9F:C7:...',
      idp_sso_target_url: 'https://idp.example.com/sso',
      issuer: 'https://gitlab.example.com',
      attribute_service_name: 'GitLab',
      attribute_statements: {
        email: ['emailAddress'],
        name: ['name'],
        first_name: ['first_name'],
        last_name: ['last_name']
      }
    }
  }
]
```

On the IdP side, create a new application and provide the ACS URL, Entity ID, and Name ID format. The IdP will generate metadata, including a certificate fingerprint and the SSO URL, which needs to be populated in the GitLab configuration.

Upon successful configuration, users can sign in to GitLab via their

IdP, enhancing the security posture by centralizing authentication workflows.

OAuth and SAML integration within GitLab streamlines the user authentication process, improves security, and enhances user convenience. These protocols do not only provide efficient access management but also significantly reduce the risks associated with credential storage and handling.

9.6 Securing Repositories

In GitLab, repository security is paramount to ensuring the integrity and confidentiality of code and other stored artifacts. Effective repository security involves implementing a combination of access control measures, encryption mechanisms, and monitoring practices to safeguard the repository from unauthorized access and potential breaches.

Access Control

Access control is a critical component of repository security. In GitLab, access control is facilitated through a robust permissions model that allows administrators to fine-tune access levels for different users and groups. The primary access levels in GitLab are:

- **Guest:** Can create issues and comment on them but has no access to code.
- **Reporter:** Can clone and pull repository data but cannot push changes. They also have access to the repository's issue tracker.
- **Developer:** Can push changes and access repository branches but cannot manage repository settings.
- **Maintainer:** Has elevated privileges, including the ability to merge code, manage issues, and configure the repository.
- **Owner:** Full administrative access to the project and its repository.

Repositories can be further secured by enforcing branch protection rules. Protected branches are crucial for ensuring that critical branches, such as 'main' or 'master', are not modified directly by unauthorized users. This can be configured in the repository settings:

```
Settings > Repository > Protected branches
```

Here, you can specify which branches to protect and set conditions under which they can be modified. For instance, you can restrict direct pushes and require merge requests to be reviewed before integration.

Encryption

Encryption in transit and at rest is essential for securing data within repositories. GitLab supports HTTPS and SSH protocols for secure data transmission. To ensure all data transfers are encrypted, it is advisable to disable the HTTP protocol and enforce HTTPS.

```
Settings > Network > Allow only HTTPS
```

For SSH, ensure that users generate and configure their SSH keys properly. GitLab allows users to add their SSH public keys in their account settings:

```
Settings > SSH Keys > Add SSH Key
```

The encryption of data at rest is managed by the underlying storage mechanism used by GitLab. Enterprise installations can take advantage of encrypted storage solutions provided by hosting platforms or employ third-party encryption tools.

Monitoring and Logging

Monitoring and logging are indispensable for maintaining repository security. GitLab's built-in logging mechanisms capture events such as authentication attempts, repository access, and system changes. These logs are accessible via the GitLab interface:

```
Admin Area > Monitoring > Logs
```

Additionally, audit logs provide a detailed record of user activity within a repository. Audit logging can be crucial for forensic analysis and compliance requirements. These logs capture activities such as:

- User logins and logouts
- Permission changes
- Repository modifications
- Branch creation and deletion

These audit logs can be viewed and exported through:

```
Settings > Audit Events
```

Additional Security Measures

GitLab also provides security measures like IP whitelisting and integration with LDAP/AD for managing user access. IP whitelisting restricts repository access to specified IP addresses, significantly reducing the attack surface.

```
Settings > Network > Outbound Requests > Allow requests to the local network
```

Integration with LDAP or Active Directory allows for centralized authentication and user management, ensuring that only verified and authorized users can gain access to repositories.

Security Scanning

To further secure repositories, GitLab integrates Static Application Security Testing (SAST) and Dynamic Application Security Testing (DAST) directly into the CI/CD pipeline. These tools automatically scan code for vulnerabilities before they are merged into the repository, helping to identify and mitigate potential security risks early in the development cycle.

SAST can be enabled in the CI configuration file ('.gitlab-ci.yml') with the following snippet:

```
sast:
  stage: test
  script:
  - sast-tool scan my_project
```

DAST can be configured similarly, with additional settings specifying the target environment:

```
dast:
  stage: test
  script:
  - dast-tool scan http://my_project.example.com
```

These automated scans generate reports with identified vulnerabilities, which can be reviewed and addressed by developers. This process significantly improves the security posture of the repository by ensuring code quality and compliance with security standards.

By combining access control, encryption, monitoring, logging, and integrated security scanning, GitLab provides comprehensive mechanisms for securing repositories. Adopting these best practices can help mitigate risks and protect the valuable code and data contained within GitLab repositories.

9.7 CI/CD Pipeline Security

In the continuous integration and continuous deployment (CI/CD) paradigm, ensuring pipeline security is paramount to safeguard the integrity, confidentiality, and availability of both code and infrastructure. GitLab provides various mechanisms and best practices to secure CI/CD pipelines, minimizing the attack surface and mitigating potential threats.

The foundation of securing a CI/CD pipeline begins with understanding the pipeline's architecture. A typical pipeline consists of stages and jobs that define the build, test, and deployment steps. Each stage may execute scripts and commands in varying environments, making it a potential target for malicious activities. A structured approach to secure these pipelines involves proper configuration, using secure runners, and implementing checks and controls at every stage.

A pivotal aspect of pipeline security is the management and protection of secrets. Secrets such as API keys, passwords, and certificates are often essential to jobs within the pipeline. Leaking these secrets can lead to unauthorized access and significant security breaches. GitLab recommends multiple strategies to manage secrets:

- Use GitLab's built-in CI_VARIABLES to securely store and manage environment variables.
- Store secrets outside the repository to avoid accidental exposure through source code.
- Employ features like Masked Variables to prevent values from being logged in the CI/CD job logs.

For instance, to set a secret variable, navigate to the project settings, then to CI / CD > Variables, and add a new variable with the Masked option enabled. Here is an example:

```
# Example on how to configure CI/CD variables
# This should be done in the GitLab UI
CI_SECRET_KEY=123456abcdef
```

Ensuring that runners, which execute the pipeline jobs, are secure is another critical component. GitLab Runners can be of different types such as shared or group runners. It's vital to:

- Use the least privileged principle when configuring runners.
- Prefer private runners over shared runners for sensitive projects, ensuring dedicated resources.
- Regularly update runner software to the latest stable versions, benefiting from security patches.

An example configuration for a secure runner can be set up in the config.toml file:

```
[[runners]]
  name = "secure-runner"
  url = "https://gitlab.example.com/"
  token = "RUNNER-TOKEN"
  executor = "shell"
  [runners.custom_build_dir]
  [runners.ssh]
  [runners.docker]
    tls_verify = false
    image = "alpine:latest"
    privileged = false
    disable_cache = false
```

To fortify the pipeline stages, it's also recommended to use secure coding practices and automated tools to scan for vulnerabilities. GitLab integrates static application security testing (SAST) and dynamic application security testing (DAST) into the pipeline processes. These tests analyze code and applications for potential vulnerabilities, providing reports that can be acted upon promptly.

Enable SAST in your .gitlab-ci.yml script as follows:

```
include:
  - template: Security/SAST.gitlab-ci.yml
```

This integrates SAST scanning into the pipeline with minimal configuration. Similarly, DAST can be activated using:

```
dast:
  stage: test
  image: dast_image
  script:
    - /path/to/dast --auth-url=http://example.com/login
```

Moreover, permissions need precise management. GitLab's role-based access control ensures that only authorized personnel can trigger pipeline execution, alter configurations, or make changes to the pipeline stages. By controlling access tightly, the risk of unauthorized alterations, which could compromise pipeline security, is mitigated.

Implementing robust logging and monitoring practices is essential. GitLab allows users to view job logs to audit activities, detect anomalies, and respond swiftly to incidents. Logs can be exported and analyzed using external tools for comprehensive insights:

```
$ cat /var/log/gitlab-ci-runner.log
$ export LOGS=$(cat /var/log/gitlab-ci-runner.log)
$ echo $LOGS | grep "ERROR"
```

Lastly, it is advisable to use isolated environments for different stages of the pipeline. This practice reduces the risk of contamination from one environment to another and restricts the scope of potential attacks. Techniques include leveraging Docker containers for isolation and employing Kubernetes namespaces for environment segregation.

Ensuring CI/CD pipeline security in GitLab requires a multi-faceted approach involving the secure management of secrets, proper runner configuration, continuous vulnerability scanning, stringent access controls, comprehensive logging, and environment isolation. Following these strategies fortifies the pipelines against potential threats, maintaining the integrity and reliability of the CI/CD process.

9.8 Vulnerability Management

Vulnerability management is a crucial aspect of maintaining the security and stability of any software project. GitLab provides a range of tools and features designed to identify, track, and mitigate vulnerabilities within your codebase and infrastructure. This section delves into the multifaceted aspects of vulnerability management, discussing features such as integrated vulnerability scanning, dependency scanning, and container scanning.

GitLab integrates several automated scanners to detect various types of vulnerabilities during the software development lifecycle. These scanners can be configured to run at different stages of the CI/CD pipeline, ensuring that potential security issues are identified and addressed as early as possible.

Integrated Vulnerability Scanning

Integrated vulnerability scanning in GitLab includes Static Application Security Testing (SAST), Dependency Scanning, and Dynamic Application Security Testing (DAST). SAST scans your source code for known vulnerabilities, while Dependency Scanning checks for vulnerabilities in your project dependencies, and DAST tests your running web applications for exploitable conditions.

The following code snippet demonstrates how to configure a SAST scan in your .gitlab-ci.yml file:

```
stages:
  - build
  - test
  - deploy
  - dast # dynamic security testing stage

include:
  - template: SAST.gitlab-ci.yml
  - template: Dependency-Scanning.gitlab-ci.yml
  - template: DAST.gitlab-ci.yml

sast:
  stage: test
  script:
    - echo "Running SAST scans"

dependency_scanning:
  stage: test
  script:
    - echo "Running Dependency Scanning"

dast:
  stage: dast
  script:
    - echo "Running DAST checks"
```

The include keyword in the .gitlab-ci.yml file incorporates templates provided by GitLab that contain the necessary configurations for running SAST, Dependency Scanning, and DAST tests. Each scanning tool runs as part of the test stage, ensuring that vulnerabilities are detected before the deployment stage.

Dependency Scanning

Dependency Scanning identifies vulnerabilities in your project's dependencies. Since modern applications often rely on multiple third-party libraries, monitoring these dependencies for known vulnerabilities is vital. By integrating dependency scanning in the CI/CD pipeline, GitLab automatically checks against vulnerability databases and notifies you if any vulnerabilities are found.

```
$ dependency_scanning job report:
- Critical: 0
- High: 2
- Medium: 5
- Low: 12
- Unknown: 0
```

Dynamic Application Security Testing (DAST)

DAST analyzes your running application to identify potential vulnerabilities that an attacker could exploit. Unlike SAST, which examines the source code, DAST interacts with the deployed application and tests it in real-time, simulating attacks to find security weaknesses.

The following code snippet shows a sample DAST configuration in your .gitlab-ci.yml file:

```
dast:
  stage: dast
  script:
    - export DAST_WEBSITE=${CI_ENVIRONMENT_URL}
    - echo "Starting DAST scan on $DAST_WEBSITE"
    - ./dast-scan --url $DAST_WEBSITE --report dast-report.json
  artifacts:
    reports:
      dast: dast-report.json
```

This configuration sets up a DAST job within the dast stage. The environment variable DAST_WEBSITE points to the URL of the deployed application. The ./dast-scan command performs the scan and generates a report, which is then available as an artifact.

Managing and Viewing Vulnerabilities

Upon completing the scans, GitLab provides a detailed report of the identified vulnerabilities. These reports are accessible from the Merge Requests (MR) and through the Security Dashboard. They categorize vulnerabilities based on their severity levels, such as critical, high, medium, and low.

Example snippet displaying output of a SAST scan:

```
SAST vulnerabilities:
- Critical: 1
- High: 3
- Medium: 7
- Low: 15
```

The vulnerability details include descriptions, locations in the code, and recommended remediation steps. Security teams can assign, track, and manage these vulnerabilities directly within GitLab, ensuring efficient resolution and compliance with security policies.

Automated Remediation and Policies

GitLab also supports automated remediation for certain types of vulnerabilities, specifically within dependency scanning. When a known vulnerability is found in a dependency, GitLab can automatically generate merge requests with updated, secure versions of the affected dependencies.

Additionally, GitLab allows the definition of security policies that enforce specific rules and checks as part of your CI/CD pipeline. These rules can block deployments if critical vulnerabilities are detected or enforce that all code changes undergo security scanning.

```
security_scan:
  stage: test
  script:
    - echo "Running Comprehensive Security Scanning"
  rules:
    - if: '$CI_COMMIT_MESSAGE =~ /SECURITY/i'
      when: always
    - when: on_success
    - changes:
      - "**/*.js"
      - "**/*.py"
```

The above example shows a security scanning job configured with specific rules to run scans based on commit messages or changes in specific files. This ensures that critical security checks are not bypassed and adhere to organizational policies.

Advanced features in GitLab's vulnerability management toolkit, such as guided remediation, security dashboards, and compliance reporting, render a comprehensive security infrastructure, thereby reducing the risk of unaddressed vulnerabilities in your codebase.

9.9 Code Quality and SAST

Code quality in software development is paramount, ensuring that the codebase is maintainable, readable, and less prone to errors. GitLab provides an integrated solution to monitor and enhance code quality through Static Application Security Testing (SAST). SAST involves analyzing the source code for security vulnerabilities without executing the program, making it an essential component of a comprehensive security strategy.

GitLab's SAST feature supports several languages and frameworks, offering a robust mechanism for detecting vulnerabilities early in the development cycle. This proactive approach enables developers to address security issues before they reach production, thereby reducing potential risks and improving overall software quality.

To utilize SAST in GitLab, ensure that the GitLab CI/CD pipeline is properly configured. The example provided below demonstrates the configuration process for enabling SAST within a project's pipeline:

```
include:
  - template: Security/SAST.gitlab-ci.yml
```

This configuration snippet includes the default GitLab SAST template in your .gitlab-ci.yml file, activating the SAST analyzers for supported languages and frameworks.

When a pipeline that includes SAST runs, it analyzes the codebase for potential vulnerabilities. The results are integrated into the GitLab interface under the Security Dashboard, providing detailed insights into identified issues, their severity, and suggested remediation steps.

Consider adding specific configurations to fine-tune SAST according to project requirements. An example configuration with added parameters is provided below:

```
sast:
  stage: test
  variables:
    SAST_EXCLUDED_PATHS: "spec,tests"
    SAST_TIMEOUT: "10m"
  artifacts:
    reports:
      sast: gl-sast-report.json
```

In this example, SAST_EXCLUDED_PATHS specifies directories to exclude from analysis, and SAST_TIMEOUT sets a maximum duration for the SAST job. The results are saved in gl-sast-report.json, which GitLab uses to generate the vulnerability report.

SAST integrates with various programming languages, and it is crucial to understand the specific analyzers supported by GitLab. Some of the supported languages and tools include:

- **Python**: Bandit
- **Ruby**: Brakeman
- **JavaScript/TypeScript**: ESLint
- **Java**: SpotBugs

- **Go**: gosec
- **C/C++**: Flawfinder

Each analyzer comes with its default rules and configurations, which can be customized to suit the project needs. For instance, specific ESLint rules for JavaScript can be configured in an .eslintrc.json file. An example configuration might look like this:

```
{
  "env": {
    "browser": true,
    "es2021": true
  },
  "extends": [
    "eslint:recommended",
    "plugin:react/recommended"
  ],
  "parserOptions": {
    "ecmaFeatures": {
      "jsx": true
    },
    "ecmaVersion": 12,
    "sourceType": "module"
  },
  "rules": {
    "no-console": "warn",
    "no-unused-vars": "error"
  }
}
```

This ensures that the SAST analyzers adhere to the coding standards and security requirements specific to the project.

Integrating SAST with the GitLab CI/CD pipeline not only enhances security but also promotes best coding practices by encouraging developers to write cleaner and safer code. The continuous analysis helps catch vulnerabilities early, facilitating easier and cheaper remediation.

Users can also extend SAST capabilities using custom analyzers or integrating external tools. GitLab provides a flexible environment to incorporate additional security tools if the default set does not meet all project requirements.

Running a SAST job within the GitLab CI/CD might produce the following output in case of identified vulnerabilities:

```
[INFO] Analyzing code...
[INFO] Found 2 security issues
[LOW] Suspicious function name (src/app.js:45)
[HIGH] SQL Injection vulnerability (src/db.js:99)
```

The pipeline will display the summary of identified issues along with their severity levels in the GitLab UI, allowing developers to prioritize and address these issues promptly.

Adopting SAST within GitLab as part of the CI/CD pipeline ensures an ongoing review process, strengthening the security posture of the codebase. Early detection and remediation of vulnerabilities bolster the overall resilience of the software against potential attacks, fostering a culture of security-first development among teams.

Effective use of SAST necessitates regular updates to the analyzers and rulesets, ensuring they stay current with evolving security threats. It is recommended to periodically review and manage the SAST configurations, keeping them aligned with the latest security standards and best practices.

9.10 DAST and Container Scanning

Dynamic Application Security Testing (DAST) and Container Scanning are essential components in ensuring the security and integrity of web applications and their runtime environments. This section delves into these two critical aspects, describing their functionalities, integrations within GitLab, and best practices for their effective utilization.

DAST is a security testing methodology that analyzes web applications in their runtime environment. Unlike Static Application Security Testing (SAST), which scrutinizes the source code, DAST inspects the application as it is running. This approach helps identify vulnerabilities that are only apparent during execution, such as issues related to authentication, authorization, and logic flaws.

In GitLab, DAST is seamlessly integrated into the CI/CD pipeline, allowing automated security testing as part of the development workflow. The integration leverages GitLab's built-in DAST analyzers, which are based on OWASP ZAP (Zed Attack Proxy), a widely used open-source web application security scanner.

To include DAST in your GitLab pipeline, the following configuration can be added to the .gitlab-ci.yml file:

```
dast:
  image: "registry.gitlab.com/gitlab-org/security-products/dast"
  stage: test
  script:
    - /analyze
  artifacts:
    reports:
      dast: gl-dast-report.json
```

This configuration utilizes the DAST Docker image provided by GitLab and runs the analyzer during the test stage of the pipeline. The results are output as a JSON report, which GitLab can process to display vulnerabilities within the merge request or pipeline results interface.

A typical output of a DAST scan might include vulnerabilities such as SQL injection, cross-site scripting (XSS), and security misconfigurations. Here's an example of how vulnerabilities are reported:

```
{
  "site": {
    "@name": "http://example.com",
    "alerts": [
      {
        "pluginid": "40012",
        "alert": "XSS",
        "name": "Cross Site Scripting (Persistent)",
        "riskcode": "3",
        "confidence": "3",
        "desc": "Cross-Site Scripting can be used to hijack sessions.",
        "solution": "Filter input and escape output.",
        "url": "http://example.com/login",
        ...
      }
    ]
  }
}
```

Container Scanning, on the other hand, focuses on examining Docker images for vulnerabilities. As organizations increasingly deploy applications using containerized environments, ensuring the security of these containers becomes paramount. GitLab's Container Scanning feature uses tools like Clair and Trivy to detect vulnerabilities in the packages and layers within Docker images.

To enable Container Scanning, you can add the following to your .gitlab-ci.yml file:

```
include:
  - template: Security/Container-Scanning.gitlab-ci.yml
```

This inclusion leverages GitLab's predefined CI/CD template for container scanning, which sets up the scanning job to execute during the test stage. It scans Docker images specified in the container_scanning job and reports any vulnerabilities detected.

Below is an example entry in gitlab-ci.yml for a custom container scanning configuration:

```
container_scanning:
  image: "docker:latest"
  stage: test
  services:
    - docker:dind
```

```
variables:
  DOCKER_DRIVER: overlay2
script:
  - docker pull $CI_REGISTRY_IMAGE:$CI_COMMIT_REF_SLUG
  - docker scan $CI_REGISTRY_IMAGE:$CI_COMMIT_REF_SLUG
artifacts:
  reports:
    container_scanning: gl-container-scanning-report.json
```

When executed, the scan results are compiled into a report that GitLab renders within the pipeline interface, highlighting vulnerabilities such as outdated packages, known exploits, and configuration flaws.

Effective use of DAST and Container Scanning requires more than just enabling these scans. It involves regular monitoring, updating the security definitions, and prioritizing remediation efforts based on the criticality of the vulnerabilities found. Integrating these tools within GitLab facilitates a proactive security posture, embedding security into the DevOps lifecycle and addressing issues as early as possible.

The continuous monitoring and assessment of applications and their containerized environments align with industry standards and best practices, ensuring robust security measures are in place throughout the software development process.

9.11 Compliance Management

Compliance management in GitLab entails the consistent adherence to industry standards, legal and regulatory requirements, and organizational policies. GitLab provides various features to help organizations ensure that their software development and delivery processes comply with these guidelines. This not only mitigates risk but also helps in maintaining a secure software development lifecycle. Several aspects contribute to comprehensive compliance management in GitLab: project_level_controls, audit trails, flexible roles and permissions, and mandatory security practices.

Project-Level Controls

GitLab facilitates compliance by enforcing project-level controls. These controls ensure that specific compliance requirements are adhered to at the project level, thereby maintaining the integrity and security of your repositories.

- **Protected Branches:** By configuring protected branches, organizations can ensure that only authorized users have the ability to merge code. This mitigates the risk of unauthorized changes that could compromise compliance.

- **Merge Request Approvals:** Setting mandatory approvers for merge requests guarantees that code changes are reviewed by a designated person or group. This shared responsibility model ensures that no single developer can introduce changes without oversight.
- **Push Rules:** GitLab allows the creation of push rules that can enforce stringent commit guidelines, like requiring commit messages to follow specific patterns or prohibiting force pushes to certain branches.

Audit Trails

Maintaining detailed and immutable audit trails is crucial for compliance. GitLab provides audit logs that capture a wide range of activities to ensure transparency and accountability.

- **Logged Events:** Activities such as user logins, permission changes, repository access, and code changes are logged with detailed information including user identity, timestamps, and affected assets.
- **Search and Filtering:** The audit logs are equipped with robust search and filtering functionalities to help administrators quickly locate events of interest. This allows for more efficient monitoring and forensic investigations.
- **API Access:** Audit log data can be accessed via the GitLab API, facilitating integration with other security information and event management (SIEM) systems used for comprehensive security monitoring and compliance reporting.

Flexible Roles and Permissions

Fine-grained control over user roles and permissions is essential for compliance. GitLab's role-based access control (RBAC) system allows for precise definition of what users can and cannot do, reducing the risk of unauthorized actions.

- **Predefined Roles:** GitLab provides predefined roles like Guest, Reporter, Developer, Maintainer, and Owner, each with varying levels of access.

- **Custom Permissions:** Beyond predefined roles, you can create custom permissions to better suit specific compliance needs. For example, you may restrict certain roles from merging code, creating projects, or deleting repositories.
- **Group Memberships:** Users can be assigned to one or multiple groups with defined roles, enabling centralized and efficient permission management across projects.

Mandatory Security Practices

GitLab enforces security practices that align closely with compliance requirements, ensuring a secure development environment.

- **Two-Factor Authentication (2FA):** Requiring 2FA ensures that only authenticated users can gain access, significantly reducing the risk of unauthorized access.
- **Code Quality and Security Scans:** Automated security and code quality scans, including static application security testing (SAST) and dynamic application security testing (DAST), help detect vulnerabilities early in the development lifecycle.
- **Dependency Scanning:** Regularly scanning dependencies for known vulnerabilities ensures that third-party libraries and modules do not introduce security risks.

Compliance Reporting

Effective compliance management involves generating detailed reports that demonstrate adherence to policies and regulations. GitLab facilitates this through its robust reporting tools.

- **Compliance Dashboards:** GitLab provides out-of-the-box compliance dashboards that offer a visual representation of the organization's compliance status, highlighting areas that need attention.
- **Audit Reports:** Detailed audit reports can be generated based on audit logs, providing evidence of compliance activities over time. These reports can be tailored to meet specific regulatory requirements.
- **Pipeline Compliance:** CI/CD pipeline compliance status helps in monitoring whether the executed pipelines adhere to the defined compliance rules, including passing all required tests and checks.

9.12 Audit Logs and Reporting

Audit logs and reporting functionalities are essential components of any robust security and compliance framework within GitLab. These features provide granular visibility into user activities, system changes, and compliance adherence, helping organizations swiftly detect and respond to any potential security incidents.

Audit logs in GitLab capture a comprehensive record of alterations and actions performed by users. This data includes login attempts, repository modifications, permission changes, and other significant events. Accessing and inspecting these logs is crucial for compliance and security oversight, as they can identify unauthorized access and irregular activities that might compromise system integrity.

To access audit logs, perform the following steps:

```
1. Log in to your GitLab instance with administrative privileges.
2. Navigate to the 'Admin Area'.
3. Click on the 'Audit Logs' section.
```

The logs are displayed in a chronological format, detailing the exact time and nature of each event. The logs include metadata such as the user who performed the action, their IP address, and the specific project or resource affected.

GitLab provides the following key audit log events:

- **User Events**: Logins, logouts, password changes, and profile updates.
- **Project Events**: Repository creates, deletes, access permissions changes, branch deletions, and merges.
- **Group Events**: Modifications to group membership, group settings, and subgroup configurations.
- **Administrative Events**: System-wide configuration changes, user creation, and privilege modifications.

To enhance the audit logs' usability, GitLab includes filtering capabilities. Filters can be applied to search for specific types of events or those related to particular users. This is especially helpful when auditing large systems where the volume of logs could be overwhelming.

```
Example:
```

~~~~
- To filter logs by username:
  ```bash
  /admin/audit_logs?user_username=<username>
  ```
- To filter logs by event type:
  ```bash
  /admin/audit_logs?action=<event_type>
  ```
~~~~

Administrators can also export audit logs for external analysis or long-term storage. These logs can be downloaded in JSON format, which facilitates integration with other security information and event management (SIEM) systems. To export logs:

```
1. Navigate to 'Audit Logs'.
2. Select the 'Export' button.
3. Choose the desired time range and export format.
```

Reporting complements the audit logging capability by synthesizing data into actionable insights. GitLab's built-in analytics features can produce comprehensive reports on user activity, code repository changes, CI/CD pipeline performance, and security vulnerabilities.

Reports are generated from the data gathered in various logs and system metrics. They can be configured to cover different scopes, such as project-centric reports, group activity reports, or organization-wide summaries. Generating a report usually involves:

- **Defining the scope**: Selecting projects, groups, or users.
- **Choosing the metrics**: Identifying what information needs to be included, such as login attempts, failed build jobs, or vulnerability counts.
- **Scheduling the report**: Setting up periodic generation of reports, which could be daily, weekly, or monthly.

To create an automated report:

```
1. Go to the 'Analytics' section of the GitLab instance.
2. Select 'Create New Report'.
3. Define the scope and metrics.
4. Choose the schedule for automatic generation and delivery.
```

Furthermore, integrated dashboards offer visual representations of these reports, enabling administrators to quickly grasp key security and compliance indicators. The dashboards can be customized with various widgets that track specific events or metrics in real-time.

Example of a GitLab Analytics Dashboard:
- Widget for daily failed login attempts.
- Graph representation of code changes and commit frequency.
- Trend charts showing the occurrence of security vulnerabilities over time.

Effective utilization of audit logs and reporting tools in GitLab provides a structured approach to maintaining visibility, ensuring compliance, and reacting proactively to security incidents.

Chapter 10

Scaling GitLab in the Cloud

This chapter addresses the strategies and best practices for scaling GitLab in cloud environments. It covers the benefits of cloud deployment, selecting a cloud provider, and the setup of GitLab on platforms like AWS, Google Cloud, and Azure. The chapter also explores networking and security considerations, automating deployment, and leveraging Kubernetes for container orchestration. Additional topics include high availability, disaster recovery, performance tuning, and managing costs for efficient cloud operations.

10.1 Introduction to Cloud Computing

Cloud computing represents a paradigm shift in the way information technology services are delivered. This section will detail the foundational aspects of cloud computing, outlining essential concepts, infrastructure, and service models that undergird this technology.

At its core, cloud computing is the delivery of computing services, including servers, storage, databases, networking, software, analytics, and intelligence, over the Internet ("the cloud") to offer faster innovation, flexible resources, and economies of scale. Users typically pay only for cloud services they use, helping lower their operating costs, run their infrastructure more efficiently, and scale as the business needs change.

Cloud computing environments primarily feature three key service models: Infrastructure as a Service (IaaS), Platform as a Service (PaaS), and Software as a Service (SaaS).

Infrastructure as a Service (IaaS) provides basic computing resources such as virtualized physical hardware, networking features, and data storage space. These resources are available on-demand and are managed over the internet, allowing users to build VMs (Virtual Machines) and other essential infrastructure components. For example, AWS EC2 and Google Compute Engine offer scalable computing capacity that can be configured and managed by users.

Platform as a Service (PaaS) offers a higher level of abstraction by providing a framework that developers can build upon to develop or customize applications. This model eliminates the complexities of infrastructure management, allowing for efficient development and deployment of applications. Services such as Google App Engine and Microsoft Azure App Services exemplify PaaS, allowing developers to focus on coding and logic without worrying about underlying hardware or software infrastructure.

Software as a Service (SaaS) delivers software applications over the internet, on a subscription basis. Users can access applications such as email, customer relationship management (CRM), or collaboration software via web browsers. Services like Google Workspace, Microsoft Office 365, and Salesforce are prevailing examples of SaaS, providing comprehensive software solutions that are fully managed by the provider.

Additionally, cloud computing is delineated into different deployment models, primarily Public Cloud, Private Cloud, Hybrid Cloud, and Multi-Cloud.

Public Cloud is a cloud environment where services and infrastructure are provisioned for open use by the general public. They are owned and operated by third-party cloud service providers, delivering resources and services over the internet. Examples include AWS, Google Cloud Platform (GCP), and Microsoft Azure.

Private Cloud is a cloud environment exclusively used by a single organization. It can be physically located at the organization's on-site data center or can be hosted by a third-party provider but offers dedicated resources and infrastructure for a single organization. Private clouds are typically utilized by financial institutions, governmental organizations, and any organization requiring a high level of security and control over their IT resources.

Hybrid Cloud combines public and private clouds, allowing data and applications to be shared between them. By enabling data and application portability, the hybrid cloud model offers greater flexibility and optimization of the existing infrastructure, security, and compliance requirements. It strategically balances workloads between public and private clouds according to changing demands and costs.

Multi-Cloud refers to the use of multiple cloud computing services from different cloud providers in a single heterogeneous architecture. By incorporating services and resources from various providers, organizations can avoid vendor lock-in, leverage the best technologies from each cloud provider, and ensure redundancy and resilience.

In cloud computing, key concepts such as scalability, elasticity, and flexibility are crucial. Scalability refers to the ability of the system to handle a growing amount of work or its potential to be enlarged to accommodate that growth. Elasticity, closely related, is the system's ability to automatically adapt to workload changes by provisioning and de-provisioning resources dynamically. Flexibility pertains to the ease with which a system or environment can change to support different levels of workloads and shifting business needs.

Cloud computing fundamentally transforms how enterprises approach IT infrastructure, driving innovations and efficiencies. As we delve further into scaling GitLab in the cloud, it becomes imperative to harness these underlying principles and models, ensuring optimized deployment and management of resources. The subsequent sections of this chapter will explore specific implementations, configurations, and best practices for deploying GitLab in various cloud environments, equipped with the necessary understanding of cloud computing foundations.

10.2 Benefits of Scaling GitLab in the Cloud

Scaling GitLab in the cloud presents numerous advantages, delivering enhanced performance, reliability, and flexibility. Cloud deployment aligns with modern software development practices, leveraging distributed computing resources to optimize operations. This section elucidates these benefits, providing a nuanced understanding crucial for informed decision-making.

Enhanced Performance and Elasticity

One of the principal benefits of cloud deployment for GitLab is enhanced performance. Cloud providers like AWS, Google Cloud, and Azure offer scalable infrastructure that can efficiently handle varying loads. Elastic computing resources enable seamless scaling of compute power, memory, and storage based on demand. This elasticity is crucial for operations characterized by unpredictable workloads, reducing the likelihood of performance bottlenecks.

```
# Example AWS EC2 auto-scaling command
aws autoscaling create-auto-scaling-group \
    --auto-scaling-group-name my-gitlab-asg \
    --launch-configuration-name my-gitlab-lc \
    --min-size 1 --max-size 10 --desired-capacity 2 \
    --availability-zones us-west-2a us-west-2b
```

The elasticity of cloud resources ensures that GitLab instances can automatically expand and contract as needed, maintaining optimal performance during peak usage while reducing costs during off-peak periods.

High Availability (HA) and Reliability

Cloud platforms offer inherent high availability and reliability features that are more challenging to implement in on-premises setups. By distributing GitLab services across multiple geographic regions and availability zones, cloud deployment mitigates the risk of downtime due to hardware failures, natural disasters, or other localized incidents.

```
# Example AWS RDS configuration for multi-AZ deployment
aws rds create-db-instance \
    --db-instance-identifier gitlab-db \
    --allocated-storage 20 \
    --db-instance-class db.m5.large \
    --engine postgres \
    --master-username admin \
    --master-user-password secret99 \
    --availability-zone us-west-2a \
    --multi-az
```

Using a multi-availability zone configuration can dramatically increase the robustness of the GitLab service, ensuring continuous availability and minimal downtime.

Cost Efficiency

Cloud computing offers significant cost advantages. Traditional on-premises installations require substantial upfront investment in hardware and software, alongside ongoing maintenance and operational costs. In contrast, cloud services follow a pay-as-you-go model, enabling organizations to align expenditures with actual usage. This financial model enhances cost predictability and efficiency.

Consider an organization migrating its GitLab instance to an AWS EC2-based setup. The flexibility to scale resources based on current needs allows the organization to optimize costs continuously. Additionally, reserved instances and spot instances can further reduce expenses.

```
# Example of purchasing a reserved instance
aws ec2 purchase-reserved-instances-offering \
    --instance-count 1 \
    --reserved-instances-offering-id a1b2c3d4-5678-90ab-cdef-11111EXAMPLE
```

Enhanced Security Features

Cloud providers invest significantly in security infrastructure and practices, often surpassing the capabilities of individual organizations. These providers offer advanced security features, including data encryption, network firewalls, and compliance certifications, thus enhancing the overall security posture of a GitLab deployment.

For instance, using AWS's Identity and Access Management (IAM) services, administrators can define granular access permissions, ensuring that only authorized users can access sensitive data.

```
# Example IAM policy creation in AWS
aws iam create-policy \
    --policy-name GitLabReadOnlyAccess \
    --policy-document file://readonly-policy.json
{
  "Version": "2012-10-17",
  "Statement": [
    {
      "Effect": "Allow",
      "Action": "s3:GetObject",
      "Resource": "arn:aws:s3:::my-gitlab-bucket/*"
    }
  ]
}
```

Employing such security best practices in a cloud environment enhances data protection and access control, thus mitigating the risk of breaches.

Disaster Recovery

Cloud platforms also offer robust disaster recovery (DR) solutions. These services allow organizations to create comprehensive DR plans, ensuring the swift recovery of GitLab instances in the event of failure.

```
# Example command to create an EBS snapshot for DR
aws ec2 create-snapshot \
    --volume-id vol-0abcd1234efgh5678 \
    --description "Snapshot for GitLab DR"
```

By leveraging such capabilities, organizations can implement efficient backup and recovery mechanisms, minimizing the impact of potential data loss incidents.

Global Collaboration and Accessibility

Cloud-based GitLab instances facilitate global collaboration by providing easy access to a distributed workforce. Developers located in different regions can access the same GitLab resources without latency issues, promoting seamless collaboration and continuous integration/-continuous deployment (CI/CD) processes.

Using CDN (Content Delivery Network) and acceleration services provided by cloud vendors further enhances accessibility, ensuring that all team members can effectively contribute to repositories regardless of their geographical location.

Integration with Other Cloud Services

Lastly, scaling GitLab in the cloud avails myriad integration possibilities with other cloud services. For example, integrating with AWS Lambda for serverless operations, leveraging Google Cloud Pub/Sub for messaging services, or using Azure DevOps for end-to-end development pipelines can significantly expand GitLab's functionality.

```
# Example AWS Lambda function creation for CI/CD
aws lambda create-function \
    --function-name my-gitlab-lambda \
    --runtime python3.8 \
    --role arn:aws:iam::account-id:role/service-role/MyGitLabRole \
    --handler lambda_function.lambda_handler \
    --zip-file fileb://function.zip
```

Strategically combining GitLab with complementary cloud services enhances operational efficiency and provides a competitive edge in software development environments.

10.3 Choosing a Cloud Provider

The selection of an appropriate cloud provider is critical for the effective scaling of GitLab. This decision hinges upon various factors including service offerings, pricing, reliability, and integration capabilities. The primary cloud providers discussed in this chapter are Amazon Web Services (AWS), Google Cloud Platform (GCP), and Microsoft Azure. Each provider brings a unique set of features and constraints that must be meticulously evaluated to ensure they meet the specific needs of an organization.

Service Offerings and Ecosystem

Each cloud provider offers a comprehensive suite of services that cater to different cloud computing needs. AWS provides a vast array of offerings including computing power, storage solutions, networking capabilities, and managed database services. The prominence of AWS in the market is supported by its extensive and mature ecosystem and its early market entry. Google Cloud Platform excels in data analytics, machine learning integrations, and high-performance computing. Google's robust network infrastructure also makes GCP a favorable option for latency-sensitive applications. Azure, with its strong enterprise integrations, is particularly well-suited for organizations heavily invested in Microsoft products. Azure's seamless integration with Windows Server, Active Directory, and other Microsoft tools provides a unified cloud experience for such enterprises.

Pricing Models

Pricing is another pivotal consideration when selecting a cloud provider. Each cloud provider uses a different pricing model which generally includes pay-as-you-go, reserved instances, and spot instances. AWS uses an on-demand pricing model but offers discounts for reserved instances and spot instances, which allow leveraging unused capacity at reduced rates. GCP provides sustained use discounts for long-running workloads and committed use contracts for cost savings on predictable workloads. Azure follows a similar pricing strategy with pay-as-you-go options, reserved VM instances, and spot VMs for non-critical workloads.

Accurate and real-time cost estimation tools provided by these cloud services can assist in planning and maintaining budget control. However, organizations should also consider other hidden costs such as data egress fees, especially when dealing with multi-cloud strategies.

Reliability and Compliance

Uptime, data durability, and compliance with industry standards are crucial elements to appraise. AWS guarantees a monthly uptime percentage of 99.99% (four nines) for its compute services, with extensive compliance certifications including SOC 1, SOC 2, and ISO 27001. GCP also provides similar uptime guarantees and supports compliance standards including GDPR, HIPAA, and PCI DSS. Azure offers a financially-backed SLA of 99.95% (three nines) for its compute services, and is compliant with a host of regulatory standards, making it suitable for enterprises in regulated industries.

Networking and Global Presence

Network performance and the geographical distribution of data centers significantly impact service latency and redundancy. AWS operates in multiple availability zones across various regions worldwide, which helps in building highly available and fault-tolerant applications. GCP's global network is well-regarded for its performance and includes nearly the same number of regions and zones as AWS. Azure's extensive global footprint includes a substantial number of regions, each subdivided into multiple availability zones, thereby facilitating improved resilience and disaster recovery options.

Integration and Ecosystem Compatibility

The integration capabilities and ecosystem compatibility of a cloud provider with existing company infrastructure are vital for achieving smooth operations and interoperability. AWS is known for its ability to integrate with a wide variety of third-party services and on-premises systems. GCP's Kubernetes Engine remains highly regarded for container orchestration, and its BigQuery service is a potent tool for SQL-like data analysis. Azure stands out with its Azure DevOps Services, which integrate seamlessly with existing GitLab CI/CD pipelines, and its Active Directory services for identity management.

Community and Support

The level of community support and availability of technical assistance can greatly influence the ease of implementing and maintaining cloud solutions. AWS boasts a robust community, vast documentation, and numerous tutorials, alongside comprehensive support plans. GCP has an active community, bolstered by detailed documentation and various support channels. Azure also offers extensive support options, including direct support from Microsoft engineers and a strong community base.

Choosing a cloud provider necessitates a nuanced examination of these factors to align the provider's strengths with the organization's specific technological and business requirements. This meticulous cloud selection process ensures not only the successful scaling of GitLab but also the realization of optimal performance, cost efficiency, and compliance adherence.

10.4 Setting Up GitLab on AWS

Setting up GitLab on Amazon Web Services (AWS) involves several steps including selecting the appropriate AWS services, configuring networking, and deploying GitLab itself. This section will guide you through a step-by-step process to ensure a successful and scalable deployment.

Firstly, ensure that you have an active AWS account and necessary permissions to create and manage AWS resources.

Step 1: Selecting AWS Services

1. **EC2 Instances:** Choose Elastic Compute Cloud (EC2) instances to host your GitLab application. The instance type should depend on your expected load. For small teams or testing purposes, a t3.medium instance might suffice, while larger deployments may require m5.large or higher.

2. **EBS Volumes:** Utilize Elastic Block Store (EBS) for persistent storage. Allocate sufficient space based on your repository size and expected data growth. Prefer SSD-backed volumes (gp2) for better performance.

3. **RDS for PostgreSQL:** Offload the database to Amazon Relational Database Service (RDS) with a PostgreSQL engine for better maintenance and scalability.

4. **S3 Buckets:** Amazon S3 (Simple Storage Service) can be used for storing artifacts, backups, and other static files.

5. **VPC and Networking:** Set up a Virtual Private Cloud (VPC) to manage networking and security aspects.

Step 2: Preparing the Environment

1. **Create a VPC:** Define a VPC along with subnets, route tables, and internet gateways.

```
aws ec2 create-vpc --cidr-block 10.0.0.0/16
aws ec2 create-subnet --vpc-id vpc-xxxxxx --cidr-block 10.0.1.0/24
aws ec2 create-internet-gateway
aws ec2 attach-internet-gateway --vpc-id vpc-xxxxxx --internet-gateway-id igw-xxxxxx
aws ec2 create-route-table --vpc-id vpc-xxxxxx
aws ec2 associate-route-table --subnet-id subnet-xxxxxx --route-table-id rtb-xxxxxx
aws ec2 create-route --route-table-id rtb-xxxxxx --destination-cidr-block 0.0.0.0/0 --
    gateway-id igw-xxxxxx
```

2. **Security Groups:** Set up security groups to manage access to your instances.

```
aws ec2 create-security-group --group-name GitLab-SG --description "Security group for
        GitLab" --vpc-id vpc-xxxxxx
aws ec2 authorize-security-group-ingress --group-id sg-xxxxxx --protocol tcp --port 22 --
       cidr 0.0.0.0/0
aws ec2 authorize-security-group-ingress --group-id sg-xxxxxx --protocol tcp --port 80 --
       cidr 0.0.0.0/0
aws ec2 authorize-security-group-ingress --group-id sg-xxxxxx --protocol tcp --port 443
       --cidr 0.0.0.0/0
```

3. **EC2 Key Pair:** Create or use an existing key pair to access your instances.

```
aws ec2 create-key-pair --key-name GitLabKey --query 'KeyMaterial' --output text >
       GitLabKey.pem
chmod 400 GitLabKey.pem
```

Step 3: Launching EC2 Instances

1. **Spin Up the Instance:** Launch an EC2 instance with the required configurations.

```
aws ec2 run-instances --image-id ami-xxxxxxxx --count 1 --instance-type t3.medium --
       key-name GitLabKey --security-group-ids sg-xxxxxx --subnet-id subnet-xxxxxx
```

2. **Elastic IP Address:** Allocate and associate an Elastic IP address to ensure consistent access.

```
aws ec2 allocate-address
aws ec2 associate-address --instance-id i-xxxxxx --allocation-id eipalloc-xxxxxx
```

Step 4: Installing Docker and GitLab

1. **Installing Docker:** Install Docker on your EC2 instance.

```
sudo amazon-linux-extras install docker
sudo service docker start
sudo usermod -a -G docker ec2-user
```

2. **Running GitLab Container:** Pull and run the GitLab Docker container.

```
sudo docker run --detach \
  --hostname <your-domain-name> \
  --publish 443:443 --publish 80:80 --publish 22:22 \
  --name gitlab \
  --restart always \
  --volume /srv/gitlab/config:/etc/gitlab \
  --volume /srv/gitlab/logs:/var/log/gitlab \
  --volume /srv/gitlab/data:/var/opt/gitlab \
  gitlab/gitlab-ce:latest
```

Step 5: Configuring GitLab

1. **Initial Setup:** Access the GitLab instance via the browser using the

Elastic IP or domain name. Utilize the default root password (printed during setup) to log in and then set your own password.

2. **Email Setup:** Configure SMTP settings to enable email notifications.

```
/etc/gitlab/gitlab.rb:
external_url 'http://<your-domain-name>'
gitlab_rails['smtp_enable'] = true
gitlab_rails['smtp_address'] = "smtp.gmail.com"
gitlab_rails['smtp_port'] = 587
gitlab_rails['smtp_user_name'] = "<your-email>"
gitlab_rails['smtp_password'] = "<your-password>"
gitlab_rails['smtp_domain'] = "smtp.gmail.com"
gitlab_rails['smtp_authentication'] = "login"
gitlab_rails['smtp_enable_starttls_auto'] = true
```

3. **SSL Certificates:** Implement SSL for secure communication, either by using Let's Encrypt or by providing custom SSL certificates.

```
/etc/gitlab/gitlab.rb:
letsencrypt['enable'] = true
letsencrypt['contact_emails'] = ['<your-email>']
letsencrypt['auto_renew'] = true
nginx['redirect_http_to_https'] = true
```

Execute 'sudo gitlab-ctl reconfigure' after making these changes.

Step 6: Database Configuration

1. **RDS Setup:** Configure and launch a PostgreSQL instance in Amazon RDS. Secure and manage access using appropriate security groups.

```
aws rds create-db-instance \
  --db-instance-identifier gitlab-db \
  --db-instance-class db.t3.medium \
  --engine postgres \
  --allocated-storage 20 \
  --master-username <username> \
  --master-user-password <password>
```

2. **GitLab Connection:** Modify the GitLab configuration to point to the RDS PostgreSQL instance.

```
/etc/gitlab/gitlab.rb:
gitlab_rails['db_adapter'] = 'postgresql'
gitlab_rails['db_encoding'] = 'unicode'
gitlab_rails['db_database'] = 'gitlabhq_production'
gitlab_rails['db_pool'] = 10
gitlab_rails['db_username'] = '<username>'
gitlab_rails['db_password'] = '<password>'
gitlab_rails['db_host'] = '<rds-endpoint>'
```

Execute 'sudo gitlab-ctl reconfigure' to apply the changes.

Step 7: Additional Configurations

1. **Backup and Restore:** Set up automated backups using S3 for disaster recovery.

```
/etc/gitlab/gitlab.rb:
gitlab_rails['backup_path'] = "/var/opt/gitlab/backups"
gitlab_rails['backup_archive_permissions'] = 0644
gitlab_rails['backup_keep_time'] = 604800
```

Automate backups with a cron job:

```
0 2 * * * gitlab-rake gitlab:backup:create CRON=1
```

2. **Logging and Monitoring:** Utilize CloudWatch for logging and monitoring GitLab's performance metrics.

By systematically following these steps, GitLab can be effectively deployed and managed on AWS, ensuring scalability, reliability, and security.

10.5 Setting Up GitLab on Google Cloud

When deploying GitLab on Google Cloud Platform (GCP), one can leverage the myriad of services and robust infrastructure provided by Google to ensure a scalable, reliable, and high-performance GitLab instance. This section will delve into the steps necessary to set up GitLab on GCP, including provisioning the virtual machine, configuring the necessary dependencies, and finalizing the GitLab installation.

Firstly, it is essential to have a Google Cloud account with billing enabled. Once the account setup is complete, follow the steps below:

1. **Create a Google Cloud Project**:
   - Navigate to the Google Cloud Console.
   - Click on the project dropdown menu at the top of the page and select New Project.
   - Provide a name for the project and click Create.
2. **Enable Required APIs**:
   - Go to the APIs & Services section in the Google Cloud Console.

- Enable the following APIs: Compute Engine API, Cloud DNS API.

3. **Provision a Virtual Machine Instance**:

   - Navigate to the Compute Engine dashboard.
   - Click on Create Instance.
   - Configure the instance with the following details:
     - **Name**: Enter a unique name for your VM instance.
     - **Region/Zone**: Select a region close to your users for lower latency.
     - **Machine Type**: Choose a machine type that meets the requirements of your GitLab deployment. For a standard setup, an n1-standard-2 instance may be sufficient.
     - **Boot Disk**: Select Change to configure the boot disk. Choose Ubuntu 20.04 LTS from the list of operating systems.
     - **Networking**: Configure the network settings. By default, the instance will be created with one external IP address.
   - Click Create to provision the VM.

4. **SSH into the Virtual Machine**:

   - In the Google Cloud Console, navigate to the VM Instances page.
   - Click SSH to open a terminal window connected to your new VM instance.

Once you are logged into your VM instance, proceed with the following steps to install GitLab:

1. **Update and Install Required Dependencies**:

```
sudo apt-get update
sudo apt-get upgrade -y
sudo apt-get install -y curl openssh-server ca-certificates tzdata perl
sudo apt-get install -y postfix
```

2. **Add the GitLab Package Repository**:

```
curl https://packages.gitlab.com/install/repositories/gitlab/gitlab-ee/script.deb.
    sh | sudo bash
```

3. **Install GitLab**:

```
sudo EXTERNAL_URL="http://$(curl -s api.ipify.org)" apt-get install gitlab-
    ee
```

4. **Configure GitLab**:

   - Open the configuration file using a text editor such as nano.

   ```
   sudo nano /etc/gitlab/gitlab.rb
   ```

   - Ensure the external_url is correctly set to the public IP address of the VM instance or a domain name if you have configured DNS.
   - Save the file and reconfigure GitLab.

   ```
   sudo gitlab-ctl reconfigure
   ```

Upon completing the reconfiguration, you can access your GitLab instance in a web browser by navigating to the external URL you configured. The first-time setup will prompt you to set the root password.

Setting Up GitLab on Google Cloud provides a robust and scalable environment. Google Cloud's managed services and tools ensure that your GitLab instance remains performant and secure as it scales with your development needs.

10.6 Setting Up GitLab on Azure

Setting up GitLab on Microsoft Azure involves several steps that include provisioning resources, configuring virtual machines, setting up networking, and securing the environment. The following instructions provide a detailed guide to effectively deploy GitLab on Azure.

Initially, ensure that your Azure account is active and you have the necessary permissions to create resources.

- Login to the Azure portal: https://portal.azure.com
- Navigate to the Resource groups service to organize related resources.

Create a new resource group by providing a name and selecting an appropriate region close to your user base.

```
az group create --name GitLabResourceGroup --location eastus
```

Provision a Virtual Network (VNet), which will hold the virtual machines and other resources for your GitLab setup.

```
az network vnet create --resource-group GitLabResourceGroup --name GitLabVNet --
    subnet-name GitLabSubnet
```

After creating the VNet, provision a Virtual Machine (VM) where GitLab will be installed. For this, choose an appropriate size that matches your expected load. A general-purpose VM like Standard DS3 v2 is a good starting point.

```
az vm create \
   --resource-group GitLabResourceGroup \
   --name GitLabVM \
   --vnet-name GitLabVNet \
   --subnet GitLabSubnet \
   --image UbuntuLTS \
   --size Standard_DS3_v2 \
   --admin-username azureuser \
   --generate-ssh-keys
```

With the VM provisioned, connect to it using SSH to begin the GitLab installation.

```
ssh azureuser@<public-ip-of-GitLabVM>
```

Update the package lists and install necessary dependencies:

```
sudo apt-get update
sudo apt-get install -y curl openssh-server ca-certificates
```

Add the GitLab package repository and install GitLab:

```
curl https://packages.gitlab.com/install/repositories/gitlab/gitlab-ee/script.deb.sh |
    sudo bash
sudo EXTERNAL_URL="http://<public-ip-of-GitLabVM>" apt-get install gitlab-ee
```

After installation, GitLab's web interface will be accessible via the VM's public IP address. Before accessing the web UI, configure the following firewall rules to allow HTTP/HTTPS traffic:

```
az network nsg rule create --resource-group GitLabResourceGroup --nsg-name
    GitLabNSG --name allow-http --priority 100 --destination-port-ranges 80 --access
    Allow --protocol Tcp --description "Allow HTTP"
az network nsg rule create --resource-group GitLabResourceGroup --nsg-name
    GitLabNSG --name allow-https --priority 110 --destination-port-ranges 443 --
    access Allow --protocol Tcp --description "Allow HTTPS"
```

Navigate to the GitLab web interface at http:

//<public-ip-of-GitLabVM>. The initial login screen will prompt the creation of an admin account.

For enhanced security and performance, consider the use of Azure Managed Disks and ensuring VM backups. Azure offers Azure Backup and Azure Site Recovery services that can be configured for disaster recovery and business continuity.

Also, ensure SSL/TLS encryption for the GitLab instance. Utilize Azure Key Vault to store and manage keys and secrets including SSL certificates securely:

- Provision an Azure Key Vault resource.
- Upload your SSL/TLS certificate to the Key Vault.
- Access and bind the certificate to GitLab configuration.

Configure GitLab to use the SSL/TLS certificate:

```
external_url "https://<gitlab.yourdomain.com>"
nginx['ssl_certificate'] = "/etc/gitlab/ssl/gitlab.yourdomain.com.crt"
nginx['ssl_certificate_key'] = "/etc/gitlab/ssl/gitlab.yourdomain.com.key"
```

Remember to configure DNS settings to point your domain to the public IP of the GitLab VM. Automate these processes using Azure's ARM templates or Terraform configurations for repeatable deployments:

```
resource "azurerm_resource_group" "example" {
  name = "GitLabResourceGroup"
  location = "East US"
}

resource "azurerm_virtual_network" "example" {
  name = "example-vnet"
  address_space = ["10.0.0.0/16"]
  location = azurerm_resource_group.example.location
  resource_group_name = azurerm_resource_group.example.name
}
# Additional configuration to provision the rest of the resources
```

By following these steps, you achieve a basic yet functional GitLab instance on Microsoft Azure. Evaluate your specific needs, including expected user load and required integrations, to optimize and scale the deployment accordingly. Implement monitoring and logging using Azure Monitor and Azure Log Analytics to maintain operational efficiency.

10.7 Networking and Security in the Cloud

Networking and security are critical components when deploying GitLab in cloud environments. A robust network setup ensures reliable connectivity and performance, while comprehensive security measures protect against potential vulnerabilities and attacks. This section delves into networking concepts, security best practices, and specific configurations to optimize your GitLab deployment.

Networking Basics for Cloud Deployment

Cloud networking involves the interconnection of virtual networks, subnets, and routing mechanisms within a cloud provider's infrastructure. Each cloud environment, such as AWS, Google Cloud, and Azure, offers various networking services and tools to manage traffic and ensure secure communication.

Key concepts include:

- **Virtual Private Cloud (VPC)**: A logically isolated section of the cloud where resources can be deployed. It provides control over a virtual networking environment.
- **Subnets**: Subdivisions within a VPC used to segment network traffic, typically categorized into public and private subnets.
- **Routing Tables**: Direct network traffic between subnets and external networks.
- **Network Access Control Lists (ACLs)**: Stateless filters for controlling inbound and outbound traffic at the subnet level.
- **Security Groups**: Stateful virtual firewalls that control inbound and outbound traffic to resources like virtual machines.

Configuring Networking for GitLab

For efficient GitLab operation, a typical cloud network setup involves segregating services into different subnets based on security requirements and connectivity needs. A common configuration might include:

- **Public Subnet**: Contains publicly accessible resources such as load balancers or bastion hosts.
- **Private Subnet**: Hosts internal resources, including GitLab application servers, database instances, and other backend services.

The interaction between these subnets is managed through routing tables and security groups, ensuring that public-facing components can communicate with private resources while restricting unauthorized access.

VPC Configuration Example on AWS

The following example demonstrates creating a basic VPC with public and private subnets on AWS using the CLI:

```
# Create VPC
aws ec2 create-vpc --cidr-block 10.0.0.0/16

# Create Subnets
aws ec2 create-subnet --vpc-id vpc-0abcd1234efgh5678 --cidr-block 10.0.1.0/24 --
    availability-zone us-east-1a
aws ec2 create-subnet --vpc-id vpc-0abcd1234efgh5678 --cidr-block 10.0.2.0/24 --
    availability-zone us-east-1a

# Create Internet Gateway and attach to VPC
aws ec2 create-internet-gateway
aws ec2 attach-internet-gateway --vpc-id vpc-0abcd1234efgh5678 --internet-gateway-id
    igw-0abcdef1234567890

# Create Route Table for Public Subnet and associate
aws ec2 create-route-table --vpc-id vpc-0abcd1234efgh5678
aws ec2 create-route --route-table-id rtb-0abcdef1234567890 --destination-cidr-block
    0.0.0.0/0 --gateway-id igw-0abcdef1234567890
aws ec2 associate-route-table --subnet-id subnet-0abcdef1234567890 --route-table-id rtb
    -0abcdef1234567890
```

Enhancing Security for GitLab Deployment

Security measures in cloud environments are vital to safeguard your GitLab instance and data. Some essential security practices include:

- **Use Security Groups and Network ACLs**: Define strict inbound and outbound rules to limit exposure. Allow traffic only from known sources and required ports (e.g., SSH, HTTP/S).
- **Implement Bastion Hosts**: Use bastion hosts for secure SSH access to instances in private subnets. Prevent direct SSH access to GitLab servers.
- **Enable Encryption**: Employ encryption for data at rest and in transit. Use cloud provider services such as AWS KMS for key management and TLS certificates for HTTPS.
- **Regular Security Audits**: Perform regular security audits and vulnerability assessments. Use tools like AWS Inspector or Google Cloud Security Command Center.

- **Multi-Factor Authentication (MFA)**: Enforce MFA for user access to cloud services and GitLab itself to enhance authentication security.

Implementing Security Groups on AWS

Configuring a security group for a GitLab instance to allow HTTP and HTTPS traffic from the internet and restrict SSH access can be accomplished as follows:

```
# Create Security Group
aws ec2 create-security-group --group-name gitlab-sg --description "Security group for
    GitLab" --vpc-id vpc-0abcd1234efgh5678

# Allow HTTP (80) and HTTPS (443) traffic from anywhere
aws ec2 authorize-security-group-ingress --group-id sg-0abcd1234efgh5678 --protocol tcp
    --port 80 --cidr 0.0.0.0/0
aws ec2 authorize-security-group-ingress --group-id sg-0abcd1234efgh5678 --protocol tcp
    --port 443 --cidr 0.0.0.0/0

# Allow SSH (22) traffic from a specific IP (e.g., your office IP)
aws ec2 authorize-security-group-ingress --group-id sg-0abcd1234efgh5678 --protocol tcp
    --port 22 --cidr XX.XX.XX.XX/32
```

This setup grants HTTP and HTTPS access to the GitLab instance while restricting SSH access to a specific source IP address, which heightens security.

Advanced Security Practices

Beyond basic configurations, advanced security practices are crucial for protecting your GitLab deployment:

- **Use IAM Roles**: Assign least-privilege IAM roles to restrict permissions. Avoid using root accounts or overly permissive policies.
- **Network Security Monitoring**: Utilize network monitoring tools to detect unusual patterns or potential threats. Services such as AWS GuardDuty or Google Cloud VPC Flow Logs can be beneficial.
- **Regular Patch Management**: Ensure that all instances and services are updated with the latest security patches. Automate patch management where possible to reduce administrative overhead.
- **Incident Response Plan**: Develop and routinely update an incident response plan. Practice drills to ensure readiness in the event of a security breach.

These practices collectively contribute to a secure and robust environment for running GitLab in the cloud, balancing both networking and security considerations efficiently.

10.8 Automating GitLab Deployment

Automation of GitLab deployment is a critical facet of modern software development, enabling rapid and reliable deployments, minimizing human errors, and promoting consistency across various environments. This section outlines the necessary procedures and tools for automating GitLab deployment in cloud environments.

Automation can be approached using several tools and methodologies, with Infrastructure as Code (IaC) being a prominent technique. This method involves managing and provisioning computing resources through machine-readable configuration files. Some popular tools for IaC include Terraform, Ansible, and AWS CloudFormation.

- **Terraform:** A tool for building, changing, and versioning infrastructure safely and efficiently.
- **Ansible:** An open-source automation tool for configuration management, application deployment, and task automation.
- **AWS CloudFormation:** A service that gives developers and businesses an easy way to create collections of related AWS and third-party resources, and provision and manage them in an orderly and predictable fashion.

For the purpose of this section, we will focus on Terraform and Ansible due to their widespread adoption and versatility across different cloud providers.

Using Terraform to Deploy GitLab

Terraform allows you to define cloud and on-premises resources in human-readable configuration files that you can version, reuse, and share. Its key feature is the ability to manage resources across various cloud services via a unified configuration language. The basic structure of a Terraform configuration consists of providers, resources, and modules.

A typical Terraform configuration file to deploy GitLab on AWS could be structured as follows:

```
provider "aws" {
  region = "us-west-1"
}

resource "aws_instance" "gitlab_server" {
  ami = "ami-0c55b159cbfafe1f0"
  instance_type = "t2.micro"
  tags = {
    Name = "GitLab-Server"
  }
}

resource "aws_security_group" "gitlab_sg" {
  name = "gitlab_sg"
  description = "Allow inbound traffic"

  ingress {
    from_port = 80
    to_port = 80
    protocol = "tcp"
    cidr_blocks = ["0.0.0.0/0"]
  }

  egress {
    from_port = 0
    to_port = 0
    protocol = "-1"
    cidr_blocks = ["0.0.0.0/0"]
  }
}
```

This configuration sets up an AWS EC2 instance that will serve as the GitLab server. It assigns a security group allowing inbound HTTP traffic. The AMI ID corresponds to a base Amazon Linux image; you will need to modify it based on your specific GitLab installation requirements.

Provisioning with Ansible

Ansible's simplicity and agentless architecture make it a desirable choice for automating the configuration of machines. Ansible playbooks are written in YAML and describe a set of tasks to bring a system to a desired state.

Below is an example of an Ansible playbook to configure and deploy GitLab on a previously provisioned server:

```
- name: Configure GitLab server
  hosts: gitlab
  become: yes

  tasks:
    - name: Install dependencies
```

```
    apt:
      name:
        - curl
        - openssh-server
        - ca-certificates
        - tzdata
      state: present
      update_cache: yes

  - name: Add GitLab's official repository
    apt_repository:
      repo: 'deb https://packages.gitlab.com/gitlab/gitlab-ce/ubuntu/ bionic main'
      state: present

  - name: Install GitLab
    apt:
      name: gitlab-ce
      state: present

  - name: Configure GitLab
    shell: |
      gitlab-ctl reconfigure
```

This playbook performs several tasks:

- Installs essential dependencies required for GitLab.
- Adds the GitLab package repository to the server.
- Installs the GitLab Community Edition package.
- Runs the `gitlab-ctl reconfigure` command to configure GitLab.

To run this playbook, create an inventory file (e.g., `hosts.ini`) with the IP address of your GitLab server:

```
[gitlab]
192.168.1.10
```

Execute the playbook using the following command:

```
ansible-playbook -i hosts.ini gitlab-playbook.yml
```

CI/CD Pipelines for Automated Deployment

Integrating CI/CD pipelines with GitLab itself can further streamline the deployment process. GitLab CI/CD allows for defining deployment pipelines in a `.gitlab-ci.yml` file within the repository. For automated deployment, you may define a pipeline stage that triggers an Ansible playbook or Terraform script.

```
stages:
  - deploy

deploy:
  stage: deploy
  script:
    - apt-get update -qy
    - apt-get install -y ansible
    - ansible-playbook -i inventory/hosts.ini gitlab-playbook.yml
  only:
    - main
```

This CI/CD definition includes a single stage named deploy that runs an Ansible playbook whenever changes are pushed to the main branch. It ensures that the GitLab server is kept up-to-date with the latest configuration and code.

Best Practices

Adopting best practices for automating GitLab deployment can significantly impact the efficiency and reliability of your operations. Some best practices include:

- **Version Control:** Store all IaC and configuration files in version control systems like Git to enable traceability and collaboration.
- **State Management:** Use remote state storage for Terraform to allow multiple team members to work on the same infrastructure safely.
- **Idempotency:** Ensure that deployment tasks are idempotent, meaning running the same script multiple times should yield the same results.
- **Secrets Management:** Securely manage sensitive data, such as passwords and API keys, using tools like AWS Secrets Manager, HashiCorp Vault, or GitLab's own secrets management.
- **Testing:** Regularly test your automation scripts in staging environments before applying them to production.

These methodologies and techniques ensure that your GitLab deployment is not only automated but also robust and secure, allowing you to focus on development without worrying about the underlying infrastructure.

10.9 Using Kubernetes with GitLab

Kubernetes is an open-source platform designed to automate deploying, scaling, and operating application containers. Using Kubernetes with GitLab enhances the platform's ability to handle complex, containerized applications at scale. Deploying GitLab on Kubernetes also provides benefits such as self-healing capabilities, automatic rollouts and rollbacks, and secret and configuration management.

GitLab leverages Kubernetes through its integration with GitLab CI/CD, allowing for seamless deployment pipelines directly to Kubernetes clusters. This section details setting up and managing GitLab with Kubernetes, including creating a Kubernetes cluster, connecting GitLab to the cluster, and deploying applications using GitLab CI/CD.

Setting Up a Kubernetes Cluster

Creating a Kubernetes cluster can be performed on multiple cloud providers or on-premise environments. For cloud deployment, managed Kubernetes services like Google Kubernetes Engine (GKE), Amazon Elastic Kubernetes Service (EKS), and Azure Kubernetes Service (AKS) simplify the setup process. This example illustrates using Google Kubernetes Engine.

First, install the Google Cloud SDK and authenticate:

```
gcloud auth login
gcloud config set project YOUR_PROJECT_ID
```

Next, create a Kubernetes cluster:

```
gcloud container clusters create gitlab-cluster \
    --zone us-central1-a \
    --num-nodes 3
```

Retrieve the cluster credentials for kubectl:

```
gcloud container clusters get-credentials gitlab-cluster
```

Connecting GitLab to Kubernetes

Once the cluster is operational, the next step is to connect it to GitLab. Navigate to your GitLab instance, open the project you wish to integrate with Kubernetes, and follow the steps below:

1. Go to *Settings > CI/CD > Clusters*. 2. Click *Add Kubernetes cluster*.

3. Enter the cluster details such as API URL, CA certificate, and Token. These can be found using:

```
kubectl config view
```

4. Click *Add Kubernetes Cluster*.

After the cluster is added, GitLab uses it to run CI/CD jobs, deploy applications, and manage resources.

Deploying Applications with GitLab CI/CD

Define the deployment pipeline in your repository's .gitlab-ci.yml file. Here is an example of a basic deployment pipeline for a Docker image:

```
stages:
  - build
  - deploy

build:
  image: docker:latest
  services:
    - docker:dind
  script:
    - docker build -t $CI_REGISTRY_IMAGE:$CI_COMMIT_SHA .
    - docker push $CI_REGISTRY_IMAGE:$CI_COMMIT_SHA
  only:
    - master

deploy:
  image: lachlanevenson/k8s-helm:latest
  script:
    - helm upgrade --install my-app ./helm-chart --set image.tag=$CI_COMMIT_SHA
  environment:
    name: production
    url: http://my-app.example.com
  only:
    - master
```

In the above file: - The build stage constructs a Docker image and pushes it to the GitLab container registry. - The deploy stage utilizes Helm (a package manager for Kubernetes) to update and install the application.

Kubernetes Runner

For large projects or multiple deployments, setting up a GitLab Runner within Kubernetes itself can be advantageous. Here are the steps involved in deploying a Kubernetes-based GitLab Runner:

1. Install Helm:

```
curl https://raw.githubusercontent.com/helm/helm/master/scripts/get-helm-3 | bash
```

2. Add the GitLab Helm repository:

```
helm repo add gitlab https://charts.gitlab.io
```

3. Install the GitLab Runner:

```
helm install --name gitlab-runner -f values.yaml gitlab/gitlab-runner
```

The values.yaml file configures the Runner, where you can specify values like the GitLab URL, Runner registration token, and other preferences.

Managing Secrets with Kubernetes

Handling sensitive information is crucial for security. Kubernetes provides a mechanism for managing secrets. Create a secret in your Kubernetes cluster using the following command:

```
kubectl create secret generic my-secret --from-literal=DATABASE_PASSWORD=
    my_password
```

Reference this secret in your deployment files:

```
apiVersion: apps/v1
kind: Deployment
metadata:
  name: my-app
spec:
  template:
    spec:
      containers:
      - name: my-container
        image: my-image
        env:
        - name: DATABASE_PASSWORD
          valueFrom:
            secretKeyRef:
              name: my-secret
              key: DATABASE_PASSWORD
```

Utilizing Kubernetes, GitLab benefits from robust orchestration capabilities, enabling scalable, manageable, and secure deployments. This integration allows seamless CI/CD pipelines from code commit to production deployment, leveraging containers' flexibility and efficiency.

10.10 High Availability and Disaster Recovery

High availability (HA) and disaster recovery (DR) are critical components in ensuring that your GitLab instance maintains continuous operation and can recover swiftly from catastrophic failures. Ensuring HA and implementing a robust DR strategy involves several techniques and best practices that focus on redundancy, failover mechanisms, data backup, and geographical distribution. This section delves into these aspects, offering detailed guidance on creating a resilient GitLab deployment.

At its core, ensuring high availability involves designing a system architecture where redundancy is key. Redundancy can be achieved by deploying multiple instances of GitLab components across different availability zones or regions of your cloud provider. This fundamentally reduces the risk of a single point of failure affecting your entire system.

Component Redundancy:

1. Application Servers: Deploy multiple GitLab application servers behind a load balancer. This ensures that if one server fails, the load balancer can redistribute requests to remaining healthy instances without interrupting service.

2. Database Layer: Use a cluster of database instances. Most cloud providers offer managed database services that support clustering and automatic failover. For PostgreSQL, which is the database typically used by GitLab, solutions such as Amazon RDS for PostgreSQL with Multi-AZ deployment can be utilized.

```
aws rds create-db-instance \
    --db-instance-identifier mydbinstance \
    --db-instance-class db.m4.large \
    --engine postgres \
    --master-username masteruser \
    --master-user-password masterpassword \
    --allocated-storage 20 \
    --multi-az
```

3. File Storage: Use redundant and highly available file storage solutions. Services like Amazon S3, Google Cloud Storage, or Azure Blob Storage offer high availability and durability, suitable for storing GitLab's assets, artifacts, and registry data.

Load Balancing:

Load balancing distributes incoming network traffic across multiple servers. This component ensures uninterrupted service even when some instances become unavailable. Implement load balancing at various layers of your infrastructure:

1. HTTP/HTTPS Load Balancing: Utilize cloud-native load balancers such as AWS Elastic Load Balancing (ELB), Google Cloud Load Bal-

ancing, or Azure Load Balancer. 2. Application Load Balancer: Set up an application load balancer in your cloud environment to manage and distribute traffic to different application servers.

```
aws elb create-load-balancer \
    --load-balancer-name my-load-balancer \
    --listeners "Protocol=HTTP,LoadBalancerPort=80,InstanceProtocol=HTTP,
        InstancePort=80" \
    --availability-zones us-west-2a us-west-2b
```

Failover Mechanisms:

Designing for failover implies that when a component fails, another component automatically takes over its role to maintain service continuity. This is crucial in minimizing downtime:

1. Database Failover: In a primary-standby DB setup, the standby node takes over automatically if the primary node fails. 2. Distributed Caching: Use distributed caching solutions like Redis with HA capabilities, such as Redis Sentinel or using cloud-native services like Amazon ElastiCache with Redis.

Disaster Recovery:

Disaster recovery planning prepares your GitLab deployment to resume operations smoothly after a catastrophic event. Key considerations include:

1. **Backup Strategies:** Regularly back up GitLab data, including the database, repositories, and configuration. Automate these backups and store them in multiple locations.

```
gitlab-backup create
```

2. **Testing Backups:** Periodically restore from backups to verify their integrity and ensure that the recovery process works as expected.

```
gitlab-backup restore BACKUP=1634758987_2021_10_20_13.0.6
```

3. **Disaster Recovery Sites:** Establish secondary sites in different geographical locations. In the event of a disaster at the primary site, the secondary site can take over.

4. **Documentation and Procedures:** Maintain a comprehensive disaster recovery plan that includes step-by-step restoration procedures, contact information for key personnel, and verification processes.

Geographic Redundancy:

Implementing geographic redundancy involves deploying critical system components in multiple geographical locations. This minimizes the risk of a local disaster impacting the global availability of your GitLab instance. Utilize cloud providers' capabilities to span regions:

1. Use multiple regions for deployment, ensuring that traffic can be dynamically routed to an alternative region during regional outages. 2. Leverage provider-specific tools, such as AWS Route 53 for DNS failover, Google Cloud's Cloud DNS, or Azure Traffic Manager.

```
aws route53 create-health-check \
    --caller-reference 2021-10-10-0152 \
    --health-check-config IPAddress=192.0.2.44,Port=80,Type=HTTP
```

Effective implementation of these HA and DR strategies will significantly enhance the resilience of your GitLab deployment, ensuring continuous service availability and swift recovery from unexpected events.

10.11 Monitoring and Performance Tuning

Effective monitoring and performance tuning are critical for ensuring the reliability and efficiency of your GitLab instances in cloud environments. By continuously observing the system's operational metrics and making necessary adjustments, you can maintain optimal performance and promptly respond to issues that arise.

Starting with monitoring, GitLab provides robust tools and integrations for comprehensive system oversight. GitLab's built-in Prometheus integration is a powerful monitoring and alerting toolkit designed for scalability and deployability. Prometheus collects and stores metrics as time series data, recording information with timestamps.

To enable Prometheus in your GitLab instance, you need to first ensure that it's available and configured correctly. The configuration steps might slightly differ depending on the cloud provider.

```
# To enable and configure Prometheus, add the following in your gitlab.rb file
prometheus['enable'] = true
alertmanager['enable'] = true
gitlab_exporter['enable'] = true
```

Once Prometheus is enabled, it starts collecting metrics automatically. You can access the Prometheus dashboard within GitLab by navigating to the monitoring section under the Admin Area.

Prometheus relies on exporters to gather metrics from other systems and services. GitLab includes several exporters:

- **GitLab Exporter**: Collects metrics from GitLab itself.
- **Node Exporter**: Collects hardware and OS metrics, such as CPU, memory, disk usage, and network statistics.
- **Redis Exporter**: Gathers metrics from Redis.
- **Postgres Exporter**: Collects metrics from PostgreSQL databases.

You can use these exporters to gain insights into various aspects of the GitLab infrastructure.

Prometheus's metric collection is based on time series data, which you can visualize using Grafana. Grafana is a powerful analytics and monitoring platform that integrates seamlessly with Prometheus. To set up Grafana, follow these steps:

```
# Install Grafana using package manager or Docker.
sudo apt-get install -y software-properties-common
wget -q -O - https://packages.grafana.com/gpg.key | sudo apt-key add -
echo "deb https://packages.grafana.com/oss/deb stable main" | sudo tee -a /etc/apt/
    sources.list.d/grafana.list
sudo apt-get update
sudo apt-get install grafana

# Start Grafana service
sudo systemctl start grafana-server
sudo systemctl enable grafana-server.service

# Access Grafana dashboard at http://localhost:3000
```

After setting up Grafana, you can add Prometheus as a data source by providing the Prometheus server URL. Creating dashboards in Grafana allows you to visualize the metrics from Prometheus through various types of graphs and alerts.

Moving on to performance tuning, consider the following key components for optimizing GitLab's performance in cloud environments:

1. **Database Optimization**: PostgreSQL is the recommended database for GitLab. Implementing proper database management practices such as indexing, query optimization, and regular maintenance tasks (vacuum and auto-vacuum) is essential.
2. **Scaling GitLab Runners**: GitLab runners execute jobs and pipelines. Depending on the load, it's important to scale runners appropriately. Use auto-scaling runners in Kubernetes or virtual

machines to dynamically adjust the number of runners based on the demand.

```
[[runners]]
  name = "auto-scaling-runner"
  url = "https://gitlab.example.com"
  token = "your-registration-token"
  executor = "docker+machine"
  limit = 10

  [runners.custom_build_dir]
  [runners.docker]
    image = "ruby:2.7"
    privileged = true
    disable_entrypoint_overwrite = false
    oom_kill_disable = false
    disable_cache = false

  [runners.machine]
    IdleCount = 2
    IdleTime = 1800
    MachineDriver = "amazonec2"
    MachineName = "auto-scaling-runner-%s"
    MachineOptions = [
      "amazonec2-access-key=your-access-key",
      "amazonec2-secret-key=your-secret-key",
      "amazonec2-region=us-west-2",
      "amazonec2-instance-type=t2.medium",
      "amazonec2-vpc-id=vpc-abcdef12",
      "amazonec2-subnet-id=subnet-abcdef12"
    ]
```

3. **Caching**: Utilize caching mechanisms such as Redis for session storage and job artifacts. Redis caching improves performance by reducing the load on the PostgreSQL database and speeding up data retrieval.

4. **Application Server Tuning**: GitLab uses multiple Unicorn or Puma worker processes to handle web traffic. The number of workers should correspond to the available CPU cores. Adjust the unicorn['worker_processes'] or puma['worker_processes'] parameter in the gitlab.rb file.

5. **Load Balancing**: Distribute the load across multiple GitLab instances using load balancers. This improves system responsiveness and ensures high availability.

6. **Resource Management**: Ensure that your cloud environment's resources (CPU, memory, disk I/O) are properly allocated and monitored. Utilize cloud provider tools and services to monitor and manage resource consumption.

By implementing these monitoring tools and performance tuning techniques, you can maintain a high-performing, reliable GitLab environment in the cloud. Continuous monitoring and proactive adjustments are essential to ensure that your GitLab instances can handle the demands of your workflows efficiently.

10.12 Cost Management

Effective cost management in cloud environments is essential for the sustainable operation of GitLab instances. Successfully managing costs involves a sound understanding of pricing models, the application of cost-saving strategies, and the continuous monitoring and adjustment of resource usage. In this section, we will delve into these aspects to ensure an efficient use of financial resources while maintaining optimal performance and scalability.

Understanding Cloud Pricing Models:

Each cloud provider offers a unique pricing structure, which can vary significantly. Typically, cloud services are priced based on usage metrics such as compute hours, storage consumption, data transfer, and additional services like managed databases or machine learning tools. It is crucial to understand these models to make informed decisions about resource allocation.

Amazon Web Services (AWS) provides a pay-as-you-go pricing model, with options for reserved instances that offer significant discounts for long-term commitments. Google Cloud Platform (GCP) uses a similar model but also includes sustained use discounts, which automatically apply discount rates based on the rate of utilization over the month. Azure pricing structures include both pay-as-you-go and reserved instances, similar to AWS.

Cost-Saving Strategies:

To manage costs effectively, employing a range of strategies is recommended. These include:

- **Selecting Appropriate Instance Types:** Choose instance types tailored to the workload requirements. Over-provisioning results in unnecessary costs, whereas under-provisioning can lead to performance degradation.
- **Utilizing Autoscaling:** Implement autoscaling to adjust the num-

ber of instances in response to workload fluctuations. This ensures that you only pay for what you need and use.

- **Taking Advantage of Spot Instances:** Spot instances or preemptible VMs can offer significant savings by utilizing spare capacity, although they may be terminated by the provider with short notice. These are suitable for non-critical, batch processing tasks.

- **Leveraging Cost Monitoring Tools:** Use built-in or third-party tools for cost monitoring and analysis. AWS Cost Explorer, Google Cloud's Billing Reports, and Azure Cost Management can help track spending and identify cost-saving opportunities.

- **Applying Cost Allocation Tags:** Use tags to categorize and allocate costs to different departments, projects, or environments. This practice not only improves cost visibility but also facilitates accountability and budget management.

Continuous Monitoring:

Ongoing monitoring and adjustment of cloud resources are vital to ensure cost efficiency. Implementing automated monitoring scripts and integrating alert systems can be beneficial. Here is an example of a basic AWS Lambda function in Python that monitors unused Elastic IPs and alerts the team.

```
import boto3

def lambda_handler(event, context):
    client = boto3.client('ec2')
    addresses_dict = client.describe_addresses()

    unused_ips = []

    for eip_dict in addresses_dict['Addresses']:
        if 'InstanceId' not in eip_dict:
            unused_ips.append(eip_dict['PublicIp'])

    if unused_ips:
        message = "Unused Elastic IPs detected:\n" + "\n".join(unused_ips)
        sns_client = boto3.client('sns')
        sns_client.publish(
            TopicArn='arn:aws:sns:us-east-1:123456789012:UnusedEIPNotifications',
            Message=message,
            Subject='Unused Elastic IP Addresses'
        )

# Required IAM Roles for the function:
# - AmazonEC2ReadOnlyAccess
# - AmazonSNSFullAccess
```

This function checks for Elastic IPs not associated with any instances and sends a notification. Such automated scripts aid in avoiding unnecessary expenses.

Adjusting Based on Insights:

The insights gathered from cost monitoring tools and scripts should inform decisions about scaling up or down, utilizing reserved instances, and scheduling non-critical workloads for off-peak hours to take advantage of lower rates.

The following is an example of a Terraform script to automate the scaling of a GitLab runner instance group based on average CPU utilization, specifically for GCP:

```
provider "google" {
  project = "my-gitlab-project"
  region = "us-central1"
}

resource "google_compute_instance_group_manager" "gitlab-runner-group" {
  name = "gitlab-runner-group"
  base_instance_name = "gitlab-runner"
  zone = "us-central1-a"
  size = 1
  target_pools = [google_compute_target_pool.gitlab-runner-pool.self_link]

  version {
    instance_template = google_compute_instance_template.gitlab-runner-template.
        self_link
  }

  auto_healing_policies {
    health_check = google_compute_http_health_check.gitlab-runner-health-check.
        self_link
    initial_delay_sec = 300
  }
}

resource "google_compute_autoscaler" "gitlab-runner-autoscaler" {
  name = "gitlab-runner-autoscaler"
  zone = "us-central1-a"
  target = google_compute_instance_group_manager.gitlab-runner-group.self_link
  autoscaling_policy {
    max_replicas = 10
    min_replicas = 1
    cpu_utilization {
      target = 0.6
    }
  }
}
```

The specified script configures an autoscaler to manage GitLab runner instances on GCP. The autoscaler adjusts the number of instances based on CPU usage, ensuring efficient resource allocation.

By consistently applying these practices, it is possible to maintain a balance between cost and performance in the cloud infrastructure supporting GitLab deployments.